絶対『英語の耳』になる！
37のインタビューで鍛える！

ネイティヴ英語リスニング

長尾和夫＋トーマス・マーティン●著

三修社

Preface
はじめに

　本書は、長年ご好評をいただいている『絶対「英語の耳」になる！』シリーズの第11作目となるもので、特に日本人にはなかなかハードルが高い「インタビュー英語の聴き取り」に的を絞って企画されました。

　では、なぜ「インタビュー英語の聴き取り」なのでしょうか？
　あらゆるメディアの中で、インタビューが登場する頻度がわれわれが思っている以上に高い点がその第一の理由です。一般的なニュースの中でもアナウンサーたちはあらゆる人物にインタビューします。事件や災害などを目撃した人に情況を聞いたり、なにかを発明した人にそのきっかけをたずねたりします。花見の見物客に気分をたずねるような気軽なインタビューもあるでしょう。
　ラジオ番組でも、もちろんネット上の放送や YouTube などでも、あらゆる種類の人たちが、その長短にかかわらず、多様なインタビューを受けています。その結果、われわれは、あらゆるメディアを通して、ほぼ毎日、数回ずつはインタビューを目にし、耳にしているのです。

　また、日本語でのインタビューでもそうですが、インタビューにはある種独特の言い回しが登場します。
　「例えば…」「とは言え…」「…ではありますが」「ですから…」
　「…といったものですね」「まず第一に…」「もっとも重要なのは…」
　といった、例示や逆接や順接、あるいは順序の提示や強調の言葉などなど、しゃべっている人の癖や、いつもの口調がとても大きく反映され、とても聴き取りが厄介なのが、本書で紹介している「インタビューの英語」なのです。
　また、話し手の感情の揺れによって、トーンやスピード、抑揚などが変化し、聴き取りをさらに難しくしているのも、もうひとつの特徴と言えるでしょう。このように、英語の聴き取りのハードルを上げる要素が数多く含まれていて、日本人にはなかなか

取り組みが難しいのが「インタビューの英語」なのです。

　本書に用意した37人のプロフェッショナルや一般人への「インタビュー英語を聴き取る訓練」を行えば、メディアに登場するあらゆる番組の理解度が格段にアップすると同時に、いろいろな人たちの会話の癖、言葉の抑揚、発音変化の特徴なども体感・体得することが可能です。そしてこれは、通常の英会話書籍の聴き取り練習程度ではなかなか達成しがたいものなのです。本書が企画・出版される意味はこの点にあると言ってもいいでしょう。(ちなみに、本書に登場する37名の人物や、インタビュアー、あるいは特定の団体名、その他の固有名詞は架空のもので、実際の団体や人物とは一切関係ありません)。

　さあ、みなさんも「インタビューの英語を聴き取る特訓」を本書で行ってください。音声多重放送の英語ニュース、あるいはYouTube動画の英語、TEDのプレゼンテーション英語、ネットのラジオ放送の英語などを聴き取る力が飛躍的に向上するはずです。また、より多くの情報を、多様な人物の語りや会話の中から、これまで以上に引き出すことができるようにもなってくるでしょう。

　本書を通じて、「インタビュー英語の実際」を学んだみなさんの、聴き取り能力や理解力、あるいは情報収集力が飛躍的に向上し、将来のみなさんの針路に大きく貢献することができたとすれば、本書の著者として、これ以上のよろこびはありません。

　最後になりますが、本書の執筆、刊行にご尽力いただいた、三修社のスタッフのみなさんにも、心からの感謝を申し上げます。

A+Café 代表 長尾和夫

2015年1月1日

Contents
もくじ

Preface はじめに ... 2
How to Use 本書の使い方 ... 6
本書に登場する「ルールの用語」と「記号」... 8

Unit 01 INTERVIEW WITH A HEAD CHEF ... 10
料理長のインタビュー

Unit 02 INTERVEIW WITH A FASHION DESIGNER ... 16
ファッション・デザイナーのインタビュー

Unit 03 INTERVIEW WITH A CLASSICAL VIOLINIST ... 22
バイオリニストのインタビュー

Unit 04 INTERVIEW WITH A BILLIONAIRE INVESTOR ... 28
億万長者の投資家のインタビュー

Unit 05 INTERVIEW WITH AN ECONOMIST ... 34
経済学者のインタビュー

Unit 06 INTERVIEW WITH A TRUCK DRIVER ... 40
トラック・ドライバーのインタビュー

Unit 07 INTERVIEW WITH A COMMERCIAL PILOT ... 46
民間航空機パイロットのインタビュー

Unit 08 INTERVIEW WITH A POLICE OFFICER ... 52
警官のインタビュー

Unit 09 INTERVIEW WITH AN ACCIDENT EYEWITNESS ... 58
事故の目撃者のインタビュー

Unit 10 INTERVIEW WITH AN OLYMPIC ATHLETE ... 64
オリンピック選手のインタビュー

Unit 11 INTERVIEW WITH AN INVENTOR ... 70
発明家のインタビュー

Unit 12 INTERVIEW WITH A FAMOUS ARCHITECT ... 76
有名建築家のインタビュー

Unit 13 INTERVIEW WITH A PROFESSIONAL ATHELETE ... 82
プロ・アスリートのインタビュー

Unit 14 INTERVIEW WITH AN ANIMAL RIGHTS ACTIVIST ... 88
動物保護活動家のインタビュー

Unit 15 INTERVIEW WITH PRESIDENTIAL CANDIDATE ... 94
大統領候補のインタビュー

Unit 16 INTERVIEW WITH A BARTENDER ... 100
バーテンダーのインタビュー

Unit 17 INTERVIEW WITH A DOCTOR ... 106
医師のインタビュー

Unit 18 INTERVIEW WITH A FARMER ... 112
農場経営者のインタビュー

Unit 19	INTERVIEW WITH AN ACTRESS ... 118 女優のインタビュー
Unit 20	INTERVEIW WITH A LAWYER ... 124 法律家のインタビュー
Unit 21	INTERVIEW WITH AN ELEMENTARY SCHOOL TEACHER ... 130 小学校教員のインタビュー
Unit 22	INTERVIEW WITH A SOLDIER ... 136 兵士のインタビュー
Unit 23	INTERVIEW WITH A TAXI DRIVER ... 142 タクシー運転手のインタビュー
Unit 24	INTERVIEW WITH AN UNEMPLOYED PERSON ... 148 失業者のインタビュー
Unit 25	INTERVIEW WITH AN MLB BASEBALL PLAYER ... 154 メジャー・リーグ選手のインタビュー
Unit 26	INTERVIEW WITH A FIREFIGHTER ... 160 消防士のインタビュー
Unit 27	INTERVIEW WITH A BEST-SELLING AUTHOR ... 166 ベストセラー作家のインタビュー
Unit 28	INTERVIEW WITH A PASTOR ... 172 牧師のインタビュー
Unit 29	INTERVIEW WITH A FOREIGN CORRESPONDENT ... 178 海外特派員のインタビュー
Unit 30	INTERVIEW WITH AN ASTRONAUT ... 184 宇宙飛行士のインタビュー
Unit 31	INTERVIEW WITH A PROFESSIONAL GAMBLER ... 190 プロ・ギャンブラーのインタビュー
Unit 32	INTERVIEW WITH A BREWERY OWNER ... 196 醸造所の経営者のインタビュー
Unit 33	INTERVIEW WITH A COMPANY CEO ... 202 企業のCEOのインタビュー
Unit 34	INTERVIEW WITH A UN INTERPRETER ... 208 通訳者のインタビュー
Unit 35	INTERVIEW WITH A LEGENDARY MUSICIAN ... 214 伝説のミュージシャンのインタビュー
Unit 36	INTERVIEW WITH A STUNTMAN ... 220 スタントマンのインタビュー
Unit 37	INTERVIEW WITH AN AWARD-WINNING PHOTOGRAPHER ... 226 受賞写真家のインタビュー

もくじ 5

How to Use
本書の使い方

Ⓐ インタビュー番号とインタビューの見出し
　　インタビューの番号と見出しを掲載してあります。見出しを見ればだれがインタビューされているのかがわかるようになっています。

Ⓑ Stage 1: 穴埋めインタビュー・リスニング
　　まず最初のステージでは、CD を聴きながら空欄部分を穴埋めしてみましょう。空欄部分には音声変化を含む英単語や英語のフレーズが入っていますので、注意して聴き取り、空欄に聴き取れたフレーズを記入しましょう。
　　CD には、各ユニットのインタビュー音声が 2 種類収録されています。ユニットの音声を再生すると、最初に聴こえてくるのがナチュラル・スピードのインタビュー音声、さらに次のトラックに収録されているのがスロー・スピードのインタビュー音声です。
　　まず最初は、ナチュラル・スピードの音声で穴埋めを行い、どうしても聴き取れなかった場合は、スロー・スピードの音声で聴き直してみてもいいでしょう。スロー音声はあくまでも参考用とし、最終的にはナチュラル・スピードでインタビューが聴き取れるようになるまでトレーニングを行ってください。

Ⓒ 空欄つきインタビュー原稿
　　① ～ ⑰ の番号の後ろの空欄を穴埋めしてみましょう。

Ⓓ Stage 2: インタビュー解説
　　ここでは、Stage 1 のインタビューで登場した語句と日本語訳をチェック、理解していきましょう。インタビュー頻出の独特な英単語やフレーズ、そして、インタビューの日本語訳を、該当する英文のブロックのすぐ下に、簡潔にまとめておきました。
　　解説や日本語訳で内容をしっかり理解したら、もう一度 Stage 1 に立ち戻って音声を聴き直してみましょ

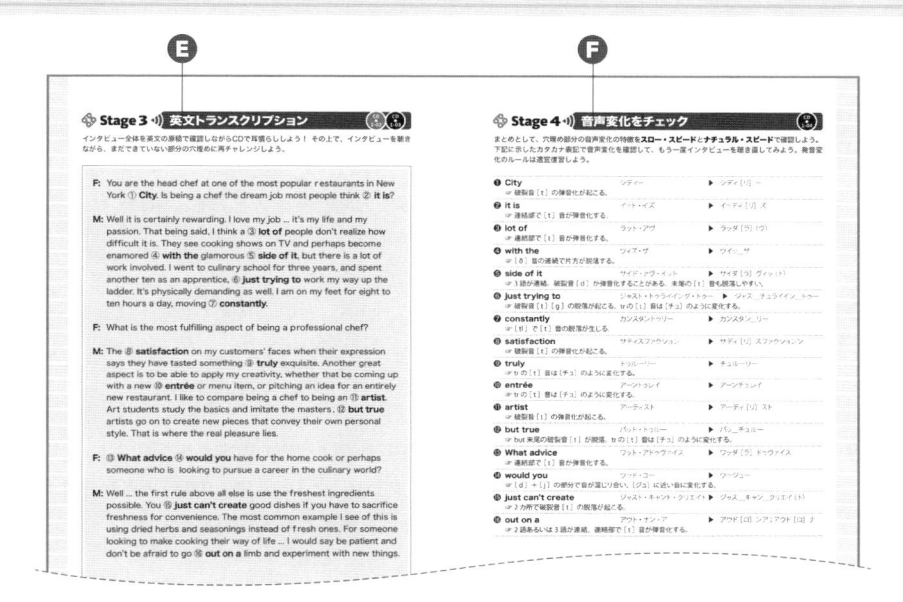

❺ Stage 3: 英文トランスクリプション

Stage 3 はインタビューの英文だけをすべて文字に起こし、読みやすいよう1ページにまとめて書き出してあります。穴埋めできていなかったところを太字部分でチェックしてみてから、もう一度インタビュー音声を聴き取ってみましょう。さらに格段に英文がよく聴き取れるのが実感できるはずです。

❻ Stage 4: 音声変化をチェック

Stage 4 では、インタビュー・リスニングのまとめとして、空欄部分の音声を、変化していないスロー音声と変化後のナチュラル・スピードの音声の両方で掲載、その音声を CD に収録してあります。

テキストでは、左から順に

【英語の語句】ー【変化前のカタカナ音声】ー【変化後のカタカナ音声】

の順で示してあります。また、次の行では ☞ マークのあとに【音声変化のルール】を、わかりやすい平易な表現で解説しておきました。

このステージで、音声変化にさらに耳慣らししてから、最後にもう一度インタビュー英語の聴き取りにチャレンジしてみましょう。

学習の順番はみなさんの考えで変更していただいてもいいでしょう。本書の狙いはあくまでもボキャブラリーと音声変化の法則を身につけながらインタビューに耳慣らししていくことなのです。その点だけをしっかり頭に入れて学習を進めてください。

また、CD 音声は、書籍といっしょに用いる以外にも、音声だけを携帯音楽プレーヤーなどに保存し、日々の空き時間などに聴き取り練習を行ってみてもいいでしょう。インタビュー音声を2種類用意したのは、スロー・スピードとナチュラル・スピードの音声を聴き比べて、ネイティヴの音声変化に、毎日のように親しんでいただきたかったからです。

では、学習をスタートしましょう！

本書に登場する「ルールの用語」と「記号」

　本書では発音のルールを説明するために、次の5つの用語と記号をおもに用いています。本文のCD音声を聴きながら、以下の用語を実地で確認していきましょう。

❶ **脱落**：英語の音の一部が消えてなくなる場合に「脱落」という言葉で説明しています。例えば、good boy の good では [d] の音が脱落してなくなり、「グッ＿ボーイ」のように発話される傾向にあります。

❷ **連結**：英語の音声の中で子音と母音が連続する場面では、音の連結が頻繁に生じます。リエゾンとも呼ばれます。例えば、on it「オン・イット」の [n] の音に it の [i] の音が連なって「オニット」といった発音に変化しますが、これを連結として説明しています。

❸ **弾音化**：英語の破裂音 [t] や [d] などに母音が連なっているところで、よくこの弾音化が起こります。例えば、get away では、get の [t] に away の先頭の母音 [ə] が連なっていますが、この [tə] の部分が［タ］ではなく［ダ］や［ラ］に近い弾くような音に変化してしまいます。「ゲッタウェイ」ではなく「ゲッダ［ラ］ウェイ」のように聴こえるとき、これを弾音化していると言います。

❹ **同化**：同化とは、ふたつの音が混じり合って、元の音とは別の音になってしまうことです。例えば、meet you では、meet 末尾の [t] の音と you の頭の [j] が混じり合って別の「チュ」といった音に変化します。

❺ **声門閉鎖音化**：声門閉鎖音化とは、button のような単語で [tn] が連続する場面などで生じます。この場合、[t] の音が変化して「バトゥン」ではなく、「バんン」のように聴こえる発音になります。このとき、喉の声門が咳払いをする直前のような状態で閉じられているため、この音声変化を声門閉鎖音化と呼んでいます。

❻ **記号**：本書では発音変化をカタカナ表記していますが、その中で次の記号を使用しています。
　　[　] ブラケットは直前の音と入れ換え可能という意味で用いています。
　　(　) 丸括弧は、囲まれている音が脱落する場合があることを示しています。
　　＿　アンダーバーは、その部分の音声が脱落することを示しています。

絶対『英語の耳』になる！
37のインタビューで鍛える！
ネイティヴ英語リスニング

Your New English Ears
Interviews with Professionals

INTERVIEW WITH A HEAD CHEF

Unit 01　料理長のインタビュー

Stage 1　穴埋め インタビュー・リスニング

音声変化に注意してCDでインタビューを聴きながら空欄部分を埋めてみよう。CDのナチュラル音声での聴き取りが難しいときは、次のトラックに収録されたスロー音声で聴いてみよう。

F: You are the head chef at one of the most popular restaurants in New York ① _____. Is being a chef the dream job most people think ② _____ _____?

M: Well it is certainly rewarding. I love my job … it's my life and my passion. That being said, I think a ③ _____ _____ people don't realize how difficult it is. They see cooking shows on TV and perhaps become enamored ④ _____ _____ glamorous ⑤ _____ _____ _____, but there is a lot of work involved. I went to culinary school for three years, and spent another ten as an apprentice, ⑥ _____ _____ _____ work my way up the ladder. It's physically demanding as well. I am on my feet for eight to ten hours a day, moving ⑦ _____.

F: What is the most fulfilling aspect of being a professional chef?

M: The ⑧ _____ on my customers' faces when their expression says they have tasted something ⑨ _____ exquisite. Another great aspect is to be able to apply my creativity, whether that be coming up with a new ⑩ _____ or menu item, or pitching an idea for an entirely new restaurant. I like to compare being a chef to being an ⑪ _____. Art students study the basics and imitate the masters, ⑫ _____ _____ artists go on to create new pieces that convey their own personal style. That is where the real

10

pleasure lies.

F: ⑬ _____ _____ ⑭ _____ _____ have for the home cook or perhaps someone who is looking to pursue a career in the culinary world?

M: Well ... the first rule above all else is use the freshest ingredients possible. You ⑮ _____ _____ _____ good dishes if you have to sacrifice freshness for convenience. The most common example I see of this is using dried herbs and seasonings instead of fresh ones. For someone looking to make cooking their way of life ... I would say be patient and don't be afraid to go ⑯ _____ _____ _____ limb and experiment with new things.

Stage 2 インタビュー解説

日本語訳と、解説を参照しながら、インタビュー内容を確認しよう。そのあとで、Stage1の穴埋めに再チャレンジしてみよう。

F: You are the head chef at one of the most popular restaurants in New York ① **City**. Is being a chef the dream job most people think ② **it is**?

> あなたはニューヨークで大人気のレストランのひとつで料理長を務めていますね。多くの人がそう考えているように、シェフは夢の職業なのでしょうか？

M: Well it is certainly rewarding. I love my job ... it's my life and my passion. That being said, I think a ③ **lot of** people don't realize how difficult it is. They see cooking shows on TV and perhaps become enamored ④ **with the** glamorous ⑤ **side of it**, but there is a lot of work involved. I went to culinary school for three years, and spent another ten as an apprentice, ⑥ **just trying to** work my way up the ladder. It's physically demanding as well. I am on my feet for eight to ten hours a day, moving ⑦ **constantly**.

> そうですね、確かにやりがいのある仕事です。私は自分の仕事を愛しています…私の人生であり、情熱なんですよ。とは言え、多くの人々は、それがどれほど難しいのかわかっていません。みなさんは、テレビで料理番組を観て、おそらくその魅力的な部分に夢中になるんですが、そこには多くの仕事が含まれているのです。私は料理学校に3年通い、さらに10年、上を目指しながら見習いとして過ごしました。肉体的にも骨の折れる仕事です。日に8時間から10時間は、常時動きながらの立ち仕事なんです。
>
> ＊ rewarding「やりがいのある」 passion「情熱」 how difficult it is「それがどれほど難しいか」 become enamored with ...「…に夢中になる」 glamorous side「魅力的な面」 involved「含まれた」 apprentice「見習い」 make one's way up the ladder「出世する」 demanding「骨の折れる」 on one's feet「立っている状態で」

F: What is the most fulfilling aspect of being a professional chef?

> プロのシェフであることで、もっとも満足な部分はなんでしょう？
>
> ＊ fulfilling「満足のいく；満足させる」 aspect「側面」

M: The ⑧ **satisfaction** on my customers' faces when their expression says they have tasted something ⑨ **truly** exquisite. Another great aspect is to be able to apply my creativity, whether that be coming up with a new ⑩ **entrée** or menu item, or pitching an idea for an entirely new restaurant. I like to compare being a chef to being an ⑪ **artist**. Art students study the basics and imitate the masters, ⑫ **but true** artists go on to create new pieces that convey their own personal style. That is where the real pleasure lies.

> お客さまの顔に浮かぶ満足感ですね。その表情が、この上なくすばらしいものを味わったと物語っているときですよ。もうひとつ別の面では、自分の創造性を活用できる場面です。それが、新しいメイン料理やメニューの一品を考え出すときであれ、まったく新しいレストランのためにアイデアを売るときであれですね。私はシェフを芸術家にたとえるのが好きなんです。芸術の学生たちは基本を学び、巨匠のまねをしますが、真の芸術家はさらに進んで、自分の個人的なスタイルを伝える新しい作品を創造するんです。そこにこそ、真のよろこびがあるんです。
>
> ＊ satisfaction「満足」 taste「味わう」 exquisite「この上なくすばらしい；申し分ない」

> creativity「創造性」 whether that be A or B「それがAやBのどちらであっても」
> pitch「(アイデアなどを) 売り出す」 compare A to B「AをBと比較する；たとえる；なぞらえる」
> go on to ...「…に達する」 that's where ... lies「そこにこそ…がある；横たわっている」

F: ⑬ **What advice** ⑭ **would you** have for the home cook or perhaps someone who is looking to pursue a career in the culinary world?

> 家庭で料理する人たちや、おそらく料理の世界で仕事をしようとしている人に、どんなアドバイスがありますか？
>
> ＊ look to ...「…しようとする」 pursue a career「仕事に従事する」
> culinary world「料理の世界」

M: Well ... the first rule above all else is use the freshest ingredients possible. You ⑮ **just can't create** good dishes if you have to sacrifice freshness for convenience. The most common example I see of this is using dried herbs and seasonings instead of fresh ones. For someone looking to make cooking their way of life ... I would say be patient and don't be afraid to go ⑯ **out on a** limb and experiment with new things.

> そうですね…なによりもまず最初に、可能な限り新鮮な素材を使うことが大事です。利便性のために新鮮さを犠牲にしなければならないとすれば、よい料理は作れません。この点でもっとも一般的な例は、新鮮なものの代わりに乾燥ハーブや調味料を使うことです。料理を自分の生きる道にしようとする人には…我慢強くあれ、そして、危険を冒して新たな試みを行うことを恐れるなということでしょうね。
>
> ＊ the freshest ingredients possible「可能な限り新鮮な材料」 sacrifice「犠牲にする」
> go out on a limb「危険を冒す；危ない橋を渡る」

料理長のインタビュー　13

Stage 3 　英文トランスクリプション

インタビュー全体を英文の原稿で確認しながらCDで耳慣らししよう！ その上で、インタビューを聴きながら、まだできていない部分の穴埋めに再チャレンジしよう。

F: You are the head chef at one of the most popular restaurants in New York ① **City**. Is being a chef the dream job most people think ② **it is**?

M: Well it is certainly rewarding. I love my job … it's my life and my passion. That being said, I think a ③ **lot of** people don't realize how difficult it is. They see cooking shows on TV and perhaps become enamored ④ **with the** glamorous ⑤ **side of it**, but there is a lot of work involved. I went to culinary school for three years, and spent another ten as an apprentice, ⑥ **just trying to** work my way up the ladder. It's physically demanding as well. I am on my feet for eight to ten hours a day, moving ⑦ **constantly**.

F: What is the most fulfilling aspect of being a professional chef?

M: The ⑧ **satisfaction** on my customers' faces when their expression says they have tasted something ⑨ **truly** exquisite. Another great aspect is to be able to apply my creativity, whether that be coming up with a new ⑩ **entrée** or menu item, or pitching an idea for an entirely new restaurant. I like to compare being a chef to being an ⑪ **artist**. Art students study the basics and imitate the masters, ⑫ **but true** artists go on to create new pieces that convey their own personal style. That is where the real pleasure lies.

F: ⑬ **What advice** ⑭ **would you** have for the home cook or perhaps someone who is looking to pursue a career in the culinary world?

M: Well … the first rule above all else is use the freshest ingredients possible. You ⑮ **just can't create** good dishes if you have to sacrifice freshness for convenience. The most common example I see of this is using dried herbs and seasonings instead of fresh ones. For someone looking to make cooking their way of life … I would say be patient and don't be afraid to go ⑯ **out on a** limb and experiment with new things.

🎬 Stage 4 🔊 音声変化をチェック

まとめとして、穴埋め部分の音声変化の特徴を**スロー・スピード**と**ナチュラル・スピード**で確認しよう。下記に示したカタカナ表記で音声変化を確認して、もう一度インタビューを聴き直してみよう。発音変化のルールは適宜復習しよう。

❶ City   スィティー   ▶ スィディ［リ］ー
 ☞ 破裂音［t］の弾音化が起こる。

❷ it is   イット・イズ   ▶ イッディ［リ］ズ
 ☞ 連結部で［t］音が弾音化する。

❸ lot of   ラット・アヴ   ▶ ラッダ［ラ］（ヴ）
 ☞ 連結部で［t］音が弾音化する。

❹ with the   ウィズ・ザ   ▶ ウイッ__ザ
 ☞［ð］音の連続で片方が脱落する。

❺ side of it   サイド・アヴ・イット   ▶ サイダ［ラ］ヴィッ（ト）
 ☞ 3語が連結。破裂音［d］が弾音化することがある。末尾の［t］音も脱落しやすい。

❻ just trying to   ジャスト・トゥライイング・トゥー   ▶ ジャス__チュライイン__トゥー
 ☞ 破裂音［t］［g］の脱落が起こる。trの［t］音は［チュ］のように変化する。

❼ constantly   カンスタントゥリー   ▶ カンスタン__リー
 ☞［tl］で［t］音の脱落が生じる。

❽ satisfaction   サティスファクション   ▶ サディ［リ］スファクション
 ☞ 破裂音［t］の弾音化が起こる。

❾ truly   トゥルーリー   ▶ チュルーリー
 ☞ trの［t］音は［チュ］のように変化する。

❿ entrée   アーントゥレイ   ▶ アーンチュレイ
 ☞ trの［t］音は［チュ］のように変化する。

⓫ artist   アーティスト   ▶ アーディ［リ］スト
 ☞ 破裂音［t］の弾音化が起こる。

⓬ but true   バット・トゥルー   ▶ バッ__チュルー
 ☞ but末尾の破裂音［t］が脱落。trの［t］音は［チュ］のように変化する。

⓭ What advice   ワット・アドゥヴァイス   ▶ ワッダ［ラ］ドゥヴァイス
 ☞ 連結部で［t］音が弾音化する。

⓮ would you   ウッド・ユー   ▶ ウッジュー
 ☞［d］+［j］の部分で音が混じり合い、［ジュ］に近い音に変化する。

⓯ just can't create   ジャスト・キャント・クリエイト   ▶ ジャス__キャン__クリエイ（ト）
 ☞ 2カ所で破裂音［t］の脱落が起こる。

⓰ out on a   アウト・オン・ア   ▶ アウド［ロ］ンア；アウド［ロ］ナ
 ☞ 2語あるいは3語が連結。連結部で［t］音が弾音化する。

INTERVEIW WITH A FASHION DESIGNER

Unit 02　ファッション・デザイナーのインタビュー

Stage 1　穴埋め インタビュー・リスニング

音声変化に注意してCDでインタビューを聴きながら空欄部分を埋めてみよう。CDのナチュラル音声での聴き取りが難しいときは、次のトラックに収録されたスロー音声で聴いてみよう。

M: Wondering what's ① _____ _____ _____ the next "in-thing" on the rack this spring? Who ② _____ _____ ask than Marcy Kohl, one of New York's most influential fashion designers? Marcy, what's your take on the new trends for the new year?

F: In a word, pastels are back. I think color is ③ _____ _____ be the biggest fashion statement for the spring and summer this year. Another ④ _____ making a comeback is going to be the cropped shirt for ladies, and the muscle shirts for men. There is a fitness boom going on, and people that "have it" are going to ⑤ _____ _____ flaunt it. By ⑥ _____, I think shoes are going to be the biggest game changer in fashion for this year.

M: With the economy having been rather stagnant the past few years, do you think that has affected how much people are ⑦ _____ for their wardrobe?

F: ⑧ _____ _____ doubt. ⑨ _____ at the middle-class level, people are spending far less on clothes and accessories than in the past. Designers are scrambling to come up with ⑩ _____ ideas that don't cost an arm ⑪ _____ _____ leg, and can ⑫ _____ _____ a variety of ensembles. On the flip side, there is also a ⑬ _____ _____ attention being paid to

16

emerging markets such as China, where new money and interest abounds.

M: You're known as the "dresser of Hollywood," having ⑭ _____ _____ longtime favorite of many of Hollywood's leading superstars. What's it like making clothes for an iconic persona?

F: I love it. I do ⑮ _____ _____ do because I have a passion for it. I think actors and ⑯ _____ are the same way, and when my designs help them look good ⑰ _____ _____ me feel like a million dollars. I'm very proud of the fact that when there's an awards ceremony like the Oscars and whatnot, many of the top stars have my number on speed dial.

Stage 2 インタビュー解説

日本語訳と、解説を参照しながら、インタビュー内容を確認しよう。そのあとで、Stage1の穴埋めに再チャレンジしてみよう。

M: Wondering what's ① **going to be** the next "in-thing" on the rack this spring? Who ② **better to** ask than Marcy Kohl, one of New York's most influential fashion designers? Marcy, what's your take on the new trends for the new year?

> この春の、次の流行の服はなんだろうと思い巡らしているところ？ ニューヨークでもっとも影響力のあるファッション・デザイナーのひとり、マーシー・コールにたずねるのがいちばんでしょう？ マーシー、新しい年の新トレンドに関するあなたのご意見は？
>
> ＊ in-thing「流行」 on the rack「(洋服が) 店頭に並んで」 trend「トレンド」

F: In a word, pastels are back. I think color is ③ **going to** be the biggest fashion statement for the spring and summer this year. Another ④ **item** making a comeback is going to be the cropped shirt for ladies, and the muscle shirts for men. There is a fitness boom going on, and people that "have it" are going to ⑤ **want to** flaunt it. By ⑥ **category**, I think shoes are going to be the biggest game changer in fashion for this year.

> ひとことで言えば、パステルの復活ね。今年の春と夏は、色合いがもっとも大きなファッション的な主張になると思ってるの。ほかにも、戻ってくるアイテムとして、女性用のクロップド・シャツや男性用の筋肉を強調するシャツがあるわ。フィットネス・ブームが続いているので、フィットした肉体をもっている人たちは、見せびらかしたいでしょう。カテゴリーでは、靴が、今年のファッションで最大の驚くべき変化をもたらすことになると思っているのよ。
>
> ＊ fashion statement「ファッション的な主張」 flaunt「これ見よがしに見せびらかす」
>   game changer「予想外に流れを変える物事」

M: With the economy having been rather stagnant the past few years, do you think that has affected how much people are ⑦ **budgeting** for their wardrobe?

> 過去数年は、経済がずいぶん停滞していますが、それは人々が洋服に出費する額に影響を与えていると思いますか？
>
> ＊ budget「お金を割り当てる」 wardrobe「衣服」

F: ⑧ **Without a** doubt. ⑨ **Certainly** at the middle-class level, people are spending far less on clothes and accessories than in the past. Designers are scrambling to come up with ⑩ **creative** ideas that don't cost an arm ⑪ **and a** leg, and can ⑫ **fit into** a variety of ensembles. On the flip side, there is also a ⑬ **lot of** attention being paid to emerging markets such as China, where new money and interest abounds.

> それは間違いありませんね。確かに、中流層では、過去よりも、洋服やアクセサリーに対する出費がはるかに少なくなっていますよ。デザイナーたちは、あたふたと、大枚をはたかずにすみ、たくさんのアンサンブルにフィットさせられるクリエイティヴなアイデアを提案しようとしています。一方で、中国のような新興市場にも多くの注目が集まっています。新たなお金や感心に満ちていますからね。
>
> ＊ spend far less「はるかに少なく出費する」 scramble to ...「あたふたと…する；慌てて…する」

> come up with ... 「…を提案する；考え出す；見つける」　ensemble「調和の取れたそろいの婦人服」
> On the flip side, ... 「一方で…」　emerging market「新興国市場」　abound「満ちている」

M: You're known as the "dresser of Hollywood," having ⑭ **been a** longtime favorite of many of Hollywood's leading superstars. What's it like making clothes for an iconic persona?

> あなたは、「ハリウッドの衣装係」として有名ですよね。ずっと多くのハリウッドの一流スターたちのお気に入りであり続けてきました。有名人に洋服を作るというのは、どういうものなのでしょう？
>
> ＊ leading「一流の」　iconic persona「有名人」

F: I love it. I do ⑮ **what I** do because I have a passion for it. I think actors and ⑯ **actresses** are the same way, and when my designs help them look good ⑰ **it makes** me feel like a million dollars. I'm very proud of the fact that when there's an awards ceremony like the Oscars and whatnot, many of the top stars have my number on speed dial.

> 私は、それが大好きなの。その仕事に強い情熱があるから、それをやるだけなの。俳優も女優も私と同じだと思うわ。そして、私のデザインが彼らをよく見せる手伝いができるのなら、それは最高の気分になるの。オスカーやその他いろいろな授賞式があると、トップ・スターの多くが電話の短縮ダイアルに私の番号を入れてい(てすぐに電話をかけてきてくれ)ることにとても誇りを感じるの。
>
> ＊ passion「情熱；愛着」　feel like a million dollars「最高の気分だ」
> 　... and whatnot「…とかいろいろ；…などもろもろ」　speed dial「短縮ダイアル」

ファッション・デザイナーのインタビュー　19

Stage 3 英文トランスクリプション

インタビュー全体を英文の原稿で確認しながらCDで耳慣らししよう！ その上で、インタビューを聴きながら、まだできていない部分の穴埋めに再チャレンジしよう。

M: Wondering what's ① **going to be** the next "in-thing" on the rack this spring? Who ② **better to** ask than Marcy Kohl, one of New York's most influential fashion designers? Marcy, what's your take on the new trends for the new year?

F: In a word, pastels are back. I think color is ③ **going to** be the biggest fashion statement for the spring and summer this year. Another ④ **item** making a comeback is going to be the cropped shirt for ladies, and the muscle shirts for men. There is a fitness boom going on, and people that "have it" are going to ⑤ **want to** flaunt it. By ⑥ **category**, I think shoes are going to be the biggest game changer in fashion for this year.

M: With the economy having been rather stagnant the past few years, do you think that has affected how much people are ⑦ **budgeting** for their wardrobe?

F: ⑧ **Without a** doubt. ⑨ **Certainly** at the middle-class level, people are spending far less on clothes and accessories than in the past. Designers are scrambling to come up with ⑩ **creative** ideas that don't cost an arm ⑪ **and a** leg, and can ⑫ **fit into** a variety of ensembles. On the flip side, there is also a ⑬ **lot of** attention being paid to emerging markets such as China, where new money and interest abounds.

M: You're known as the "dresser of Hollywood," having ⑭ **been a** longtime favorite of many of Hollywood's leading superstars. What's it like making clothes for an iconic persona?

F: I love it. I do ⑮ **what I** do because I have a passion for it. I think actors and ⑯ **actresses** are the same way, and when my designs help them look good ⑰ **it makes** me feel like a million dollars. I'm very proud of the fact that when there's an awards ceremony like the Oscars and whatnot, many of the top stars have my number on speed dial.

🔗 Stage 4 🔊 音声変化をチェック

まとめとして、穴埋め部分の音声変化の特徴を**スロー・スピード**と**ナチュラル・スピード**で確認しよう。下記に示したカタカナ表記で音声変化を確認して、もう一度インタビューを聴き直してみよう。発音変化のルールは適宜復習しよう。

---

❶ **going to be** ゴウイング・トゥー・ビー ▶ ゴウイヌビ
☞ going から破裂音 [g] が脱落しながら、弱化した to [ə] に連結。be も弱まって [ビ] と発音されることが多い。

❷ **better to** ベター・トゥー ▶ ベダ [ラ] ードゥ [ル] ー
☞ 2 カ所の [t] 音が弾音化する。

❸ **going to** ゴウイング・トゥー ▶ ゴウイン_トゥー
☞ 破裂音 [g] が脱落する。

❹ **item** アイテム ▶ アイデ [レ] ム
☞ 破裂音 [t] の弾音化が起こる。

❺ **want to** ワント・トゥー ▶ ワン_トゥー；ワナ
☞ want の破裂音 [t] が脱落する。さらに変化して [ワナ] という発音になる場合もある。

❻ **category** カテゴリー ▶ カデ [レ] ゴリー
☞ 破裂音 [t] の弾音化が起こる。

❼ **budgeting** バッジェティング ▶ バッジェディ [リ] ン（グ）
☞ 破裂音 [t] の弾音化が起こる。末尾の [g] 音も脱落する場合がある。

❽ **Without a** ウィザウト・ア ▶ ウィザウダ [ラ]
☞ 連結部で破裂音 [t] の弾音化が起こる。

❾ **Certainly** スートゥンリー ▶ スーンンリー
☞ [tn] の [t] 音が声門閉鎖音化する。

❿ **creative** クリエイティヴ ▶ クリエイディ [リ] ヴ
☞ 破裂音 [t] の弾音化が起こる。

⓫ **and a** アンド・ア ▶ アンダ
☞ 2 語が連結する。[d] 音が脱落して連結するときもある。

⓬ **fit into** フィット・イントゥー ▶ フィッディ [リ] ントゥー
☞ 連結部で破裂音 [t] の弾音化が起こる。

⓭ **lot of** ラット・アヴ ▶ ラッダ [ラ] ヴ
☞ 連結部で破裂音 [t] の弾音化が起こる。

⓮ **been a** ビーン・ア ▶ ビナ
☞ 弱化した been [ビン] に a が連結する。

⓯ **what I** ワット・アイ ▶ ワッ_アイ
☞ 破裂音 [t] の脱落が起こる。2 語が連結し、連結部で [t] 音が弾音化する場合もある。

⓰ **actresses** アクトゥレスィズ ▶ アクチュレスィズ
☞ tr の [t] 音は [チュ] のように変化する。

⓱ **it makes** イット・メイクス ▶ イッ_メイクス
☞ it 末尾の破裂音 [t] が脱落する。

INTERVIEW WITH A CLASSICAL VIOLINIST

Unit 03 バイオリニストのインタビュー

Stage 1 穴埋め インタビュー・リスニング

音声変化に注意してCDでインタビューを聴きながら空欄部分を埋めてみよう。CDのナチュラル音声での聴き取りが難しいときは、次のトラックに収録されたスロー音声で聴いてみよう。

M: When were you first introduced to classical music or, more specifically, the violin?

F: My mother took me to a local concert in Louisville, KY ① _____ _____ was four or five years old. Somehow I got my picture in the paper ② _____ ③ _____ _____ a harp! My mother really ④ _____ _____ to play something. ⑤ I _____ _____ remember now why I picked the violin, but I ⑥ _____ taking formal lessons at age seven. My parents were not musicians, but loved classical music so from then on traveling to weekend concerts became a family affair.

M: What ⑦ _____ _____ schooling was involved?

F: I took a series of private lessons, involving the Suzuki method, a method of learning music developed by a Japanese man after the Second World War. ⑧ _____ _____ hugely popular in the US during the 80's, ⑨ _____ _____ still widely taught now. I finished the program by the time I was twelve and then I traveled from Memphis where we lived ⑩ _____ _____ _____ the University of Cincinnati Conservatory, where I studied under Kurt Sassmannshaus. I studied under him all the way through college.

M: ⑪ _____ _____ the most rewarding aspect of being an

orchestra member?

F: Well, the fact of the ⑫ _____ is that there are many different people involved, and each person may have their own idea of how a particular piece ⑬ _____ _____ played, but ⑭ _____ _____ end we all pretty much have to go with how the conductor wants it to be played. This is particularly true with classical music, when we are performing pieces ⑮ _____ _____ been played for centuries. A good example of this is you may like a certain ⑯ _____ _____ _____ song you hear on the radio, but then when you hear the live version it sounds different and you don't ⑰ _____ _____ _____ much.

Stage 2 インタビュー解説

日本語訳と、解説を参照しながら、インタビュー内容を確認しよう。そのあとで、Stage1の穴埋めに再チャレンジしてみよう。

M: When were you first introduced to classical music or, more specifically, the violin?

> はじめてクラシック音楽に、あるいはより具体的にバイオリンに出会ったのはいつですか？
>
> * specifically「とりわけ」

F: My mother took me to a local concert in Louisville, KY ① **when I** was four or five years old. Somehow I got my picture in the paper ② **sitting** ③ **next to** a harp! My mother really ④ **wanted me** to play something. ⑤ I **don't even** remember now why I picked the violin, but I ⑥ **started** taking formal lessons at age seven. My parents were not musicians, but loved classical music so from then on traveling to weekend concerts became a family affair.

> 私が、4つか5つの頃、母がケンタッキー州のルイビルで地元のコンサートに私を連れていってくれたんです。どういうわけか、ハープの隣に座っている私の写真が新聞に載ったんですよ！ 母はほんとうに、私になにかを演奏してほしいと思っていたんです。どうしてバイオリンを選んだかは、いまではもう覚えてもいないんですが、7歳のときには正式なレッスンを受け始めました。両親は音楽家ではありませんでしたが、クラシック音楽が大好きだったんです。で、それ以来、週末にコンサートに出かけていくのが家族の習慣になったんです。
>
> * somehow「どういうわけか」 from then on「それ以来」 family affair「家族の習慣」

M: What ⑦ **kind of** schooling was involved?

> どんな教育を受けたんですか？
>
> * schooling「教育」

F: I took a series of private lessons, involving the Suzuki method, a method of learning music developed by a Japanese man after the Second World War. ⑧ **It became** hugely popular in the US during the 80's, ⑨ **and is** still widely taught now. I finished the program by the time I was twelve and then I traveled from Memphis where we lived ⑩ **and went to** the University of Cincinnati Conservatory, where I studied under Kurt Sassmannshaus. I studied under him all the way through college.

> 鈴木メソッドを含む一連の個人レッスンを受けました。第2次世界大戦後に日本人男性によって開発された音楽の学習メソッドです。これが80年代にアメリカで大ブームになって、いまも広く教えられているんです。12歳になる頃までにはそのプログラムを終え、その後、家族が暮らしていたメンフィスから引っ越して、シンシナチ音楽院に通いました。そこではカート・サスマンシャウスのもとで学びました。彼のもとで大学の終わりまでずっと学んだんですよ。
>
> * a series of ...「一連の…」 developed「開発された」 conservatory「芸術・音楽学校」
>   all the way through ...「…を通してずっと」

M: ⑪ **What is** the most rewarding aspect of being an orchestra member?

> オーケストラのメンバーであることに関して、もっとも大きなやりがいはなんですか？
>
> ✳ rewarding「やりがいのある」

F: Well, the fact of the ⑫ **matter** is that there are many different people involved, and each person may have their own idea of how a particular piece ⑬ **should be** played, but ⑭ **in the** end we all pretty much have to go with how the conductor wants it to be played. This is particularly true with classical music, when we are performing pieces ⑮ **that have** been played for centuries. A good example of this is you may like a certain ⑯ **rock and roll** song you hear on the radio, but then when you hear the live version it sounds different and you don't ⑰ **like it as** much.

> そうですね、実を言うと、オーケストラには多様な人たちが含まれていて、それぞれの人が、特定の楽曲がどう演奏されるべきか、独自の考えをもっているかもしれないんです。しかし、結局は、指揮者がその楽曲をどのように演奏したいかに、かなりの部分、合わせなければならないんです。これはクラシック音楽においては特に顕著なんです。何世紀もの間、演奏されてきた楽曲を演奏しているときにはね。このいい例はですね、あるロックンロールの曲をラジオで聴いて気に入っているとして、しかしそのライブ・バージョンを聴いたとき違った感じがして、同じようには好きになれない場合ですね。
>
> ✳ the fact of the matter is ...「実を言うと…」　in the end「結局は」
>   particularly true「特に顕著な」

Stage 3　英文トランスクリプション

インタビュー全体を英文の原稿で確認しながらCDで耳慣らししよう！ その上で、インタビューを聴きながら、まだできていない部分の穴埋めに再チャレンジしよう。

M: When were you first introduced to classical music or, more specifically, the violin?

F: My mother took me to a local concert in Louisville, KY ① **when I** was four or five years old. Somehow I got my picture in the paper ② **sitting** ③ **next to** a harp! My mother really ④ **wanted me** to play something. ⑤ I **don't even** remember now why I picked the violin, but I ⑥ **started** taking formal lessons at age seven. My parents were not musicians, but loved classical music so from then on traveling to weekend concerts became a family affair.

M: What ⑦ **kind of** schooling was involved?

F: I took a series of private lessons, involving the Suzuki method, a method of learning music developed by a Japanese man after the Second World War. ⑧ **It became** hugely popular in the US during the 80's, ⑨ **and is** still widely taught now. I finished the program by the time I was twelve and then I traveled from Memphis where we lived ⑩ **and went to** the University of Cincinnati Conservatory, where I studied under Kurt Sassmannshaus. I studied under him all the way through college.

M: ⑪ **What is** the most rewarding aspect of being an orchestra member?

F: Well, the fact of the ⑫ **matter** is that there are many different people involved, and each person may have their own idea of how a particular piece ⑬ **should be** played, but ⑭ **in the** end we all pretty much have to go with how the conductor wants it to be played. This is particularly true with classical music, when we are performing pieces ⑮ **that have** been played for centuries. A good example of this is you may like a certain ⑯ **rock and roll** song you hear on the radio, but then when you hear the live version it sounds different and you don't ⑰ **like it as** much.

Stage 4))) 音声変化をチェック

まとめとして、穴埋め部分の音声変化の特徴を**スロー・スピード**と**ナチュラル・スピード**で確認しよう。下記に示したカタカナ表記で音声変化を確認して、もう一度インタビューを聴き直してみよう。発音変化のルールは適宜復習しよう。

❶ **when I**   ウェン・アイ   ▶ ウェナイ
 ☞ 2語の音が連結する。

❷ **sitting**   スィッティング   ▶ スィッディ [リ] ン (グ)
 ☞ [t] 音が弾音化する。末尾の [g] 音が脱落する場合もある。

❸ **next to**   ネクスト・トゥー   ▶ ネクスッ__トゥー
 ☞ 破裂音 [t] 音が脱落する。

❹ **wanted me**   ワンティッド・ミー   ▶ ワニッ__ミー
 ☞ wanted から [t] 音や [d] 音が脱落する。

❺ **don't even**   ドント・イーヴン   ▶ ドニーヴン
 ☞ don't の破裂音 [t] が脱落し、2語が連結。

❻ **started**   スターティードッ   ▶ スターディ [リ] ッ (ド)
 ☞ 破裂音 [t] の弾音化が起こる。末尾の [d] 音も脱落することがある。

❼ **kind of**   カインド・アヴ   ▶ カインダ (ヴ) ; カイナ (ヴ)
 ☞ 2語が連結。kind の [d] 音が脱落して連結することもある。末尾の [v] 音も脱落しやすい。

❽ **It became**   イット・ビケイム   ▶ イッ__ビケイム
 ☞ 破裂音 [t] の脱落が起こる。

❾ **and is**   アンド・イズ   ▶ アンディズ ; アニズ
 ☞ 2語が連結。and の [d] 音が脱落しならが連結する場合もある。

❿ **and went to**   アンド・ウェント・トゥー   ▶ アン__ウェン__トゥー
 ☞ and の [d] 音と went の [t] 音が脱落する。

⓫ **What is**   ワット・イズ   ▶ ワッディ [リ] ズ
 ☞ 連結部で [t] 音が弾音化する。

⓬ **matter**   マター   ▶ マダ [ラ] ー
 ☞ 破裂音 [t] の弾音化が起こる。

⓭ **should be**   シュッド・ビー   ▶ シュッ__ビー
 ☞ 破裂音 [d] が脱落。

⓮ **in the**   イン・ズィ   ▶ イニ
 ☞ [n] + [ð] が [n] 音に変化する。

⓯ **that have**   ザット・ハヴ   ▶ ザッダ [ラ] ヴ
 ☞ 連結部で [t] 音が弾音化する。

⓰ **rock and roll**   ラック・アンド・ロウゥ   ▶ ラッカン__ロウゥ
 ☞ rock and が連結。and の破裂音 [d] の脱落が起こる。

⓱ **like it as**   ライク・イット・アズ   ▶ ライキッダ [ラ] ズ
 ☞ 3語が連結。連結部で [t] 音が弾音化する。

INTERVIEW WITH A BILLIONAIRE INVESTOR

Unit 04 億万長者の投資家のインタビュー

Stage 1 穴埋め インタビュー・リスニング

音声変化に注意してCDでインタビューを聴きながら空欄部分を埋めてみよう。CDのナチュラル音声での聴き取りが難しいときは、次のトラックに収録されたスロー音声で聴いてみよう。

F: Jim Hawthorne, one of the richest men in the world and renowned for his hedge fund management is with us for this evening's financial news cap. Jim, what factors do you look at when deciding whether to invest in a company?

M: There are several that come to mind. First is the ① _____ that the company is embracing. What kind of potential is there? Where are they now and where do they have to grow? Secondly, we look at whether or not their current management team is solid enough to steer them ② _____ _____ right direction. That starts with the CEO and goes ③ _____ _____ the line. Ironically, the last thing we look ④ _____ _____ their balance sheet. Are they ⑤ _____? We examine ⑥ _____ _____ short-term and long-term potential is for expanding their profit margins and growth.

F: Do you have a preference between companies that offer a physical product versus a service, like social media, for example?

M: Well, that's ⑦ _____ _____ _____ catch ⑧ _____. A company that provides a service may represent huge growth potential, ⑨ _____ _____ are much more difficult to forecast and analyze. Users may flock to a particular service en masse, but they may tire of it and move on very quickly ―

⑩ _____ _____ period of weeks. That kind of turnover makes it extremely tough to react to the ⑪ _____ and profit stream. So, from that standpoint, I would say I lean more toward product-based companies for long-term investing.

F: At 68, you've been in the business for a very long time. Have you given any ⑫ _____ _____ retirement?

M: No. ⑬ _____ _____ _____. I love ⑭ _____ _____ do, and I cannot imagine doing anything else. That being said, I have ⑮ _____ _____ a ⑯ _____ _____ my hours to spend more time with my family. To ⑰ _____ _____ I'm trying to delegate more responsibility to others on my management team.

Stage 2 インタビュー解説

日本語訳と、解説を参照しながら、インタビュー内容を確認しよう。そのあとで、Stage1の穴埋めに再チャレンジしてみよう。

F: Jim Hawthorne, one of the richest men in the world and renowned for his hedge fund management is with us for this evening's financial news cap. Jim, what factors do you look at when deciding whether to invest in a company?

> 世界でも指折りのお金持ちであり、ヘッジ・ファンド運用で有名なジム・ホーソーンが、この夕方のファイナンシャル・ニューズの締めくくりに来てくれました。ジム、ある会社への投資を決めるとき、あなたはどんなファクターをチェックするのですか？
>
> * renowned「有名な；名の知れた」 hedge fund management「ヘッジ・ファンドの運用・管理」 cap「締めくくりの話題」 factor「要素」 invest「投資する」

M: There are several that come to mind. First is the ① **opportunity** that the company is embracing. What kind of potential is there? Where are they now and where do they have to grow? Secondly, we look at whether or not their current management team is solid enough to steer them ② **in the** right direction. That starts with the CEO and goes ③ **right down** the line. Ironically, the last thing we look ④ **at is** their balance sheet. Are they ⑤ **profitable**? We examine ⑥ **what their** short-term and long-term potential is for expanding their profit margins and growth.

> 思い浮かぶものがいくつかあります。最初は、その会社が含みもっているチャンスです。どのような潜在力がそこにあるのか？ その会社が、いまどのような状況にあって、どこに成長の要素をもっているのか？ 第二に、現在の経営陣が、会社を正しい方向に操っていくのに十分に健全なのか、あるいはそうではないのかを見ます。CEOから始めて、次から次へと（取締役を）見ていきます。皮肉にも、われわれが最後にチェックするのが会社のバランス・シートなんです。収益性は高いか？ 利益率の拡大や成長性の短期・長期の可能性はどうかを検討します。
>
> * embrace「包含する；範囲に含む」　potential「潜在力；可能性」
> 　solid「健全な；強固な；信頼できる」　steer「操縦する」
> 　... right down the line「…次から次へとどんどん」　profitable「もうけになる；利益をもたらす」

F: Do you have a preference between companies that offer a physical product versus a service, like social media, for example?

> 実際の製品を提供している企業と、例えばソーシャル・メディアのようなサービス企業の間では好みはありますか？
>
> * physical「実際の；現実の」　A versus B「Aに対してB；A対B」

M: Well, that's ⑦ **kind of** a catch ⑧ **22**. A company that provides a service may represent huge growth potential, ⑨ **but they** are much more difficult to forecast and analyze. Users may flock to a particular service en masse, but they may tire of it and move on very quickly — ⑩ **in a** period of weeks. That kind of turnover makes it extremely tough to react to the ⑪ **data** and profit stream. So, from that standpoint, I would say I lean more toward product-based companies for long-term investing.

そうですね、それはある種のジレンマなんです。サービスを提供しているある企業はものすごい潜在力をもっているかもしれませんが、そういった企業は予測や分析がはるかに難しいのです。ユーザーたちは特定のサービスに集団になって群がるかもしれませんが、すぐに飽きてしまって、数週間といった単位で離れていってしまうかもしれません。そういった人の移動が、データや収益源への対応をとても難しくしているんです。なので、その点から、私としては、長期投資では、より製品ベースの企業に傾いていると言えるでしょう。

∗ catch 22「ジレンマ（のある状態）」 flock「群がる」 en masse「集団で」
move on「移る；移動する」 turnover「（人員；人材など）回転」
react to ...「…に対応・反応する」 profit stream「収益源」 lean「傾く」

F: At 68, you've been in the business for a very long time. Have you given any ⑫ **thought to** retirement?

68歳になられ、とても長くビジネスの世界にいらっしゃいますね。引退について考えたことはありますか？

∗ retirement「引退」

M: No. ⑬ **Not at all**. I love ⑭ **what I** do, and I cannot imagine doing anything else. That being said, I have ⑮ **cut back** a ⑯ **bit on** my hours to spend more time with my family. To ⑰ **that end** I'm trying to delegate more responsibility to others on my management team.

いいえ、まったくありませんよ。自分の仕事が大好きだし、なにかほかのことをやっているのは想像できません。とは言え、家族ともっと過ごすために、少し仕事の時間を削ってはいますけどね。そのためにも、私の経営チームのほかの人材に、もっと責任を委譲しようとしているんです。

∗ To that end ...「そのためにも…」 delegate「委任する」

Stage 3　英文トランスクリプション

インタビュー全体を英文の原稿で確認しながらCDで耳慣らししよう！ その上で、インタビューを聴きながら、まだできていない部分の穴埋めに再チャレンジしよう。

F: Jim Hawthorne, one of the richest men in the world and renowned for his hedge fund management is with us for this evening's financial news cap. Jim, what factors do you look at when deciding whether to invest in a company?

M: There are several that come to mind. First is the ① **opportunity** that the company is embracing. What kind of potential is there? Where are they now and where do they have to grow? Secondly, we look at whether or not their current management team is solid enough to steer them ② **in the** right direction. That starts with the CEO and goes ③ **right down** the line. Ironically, the last thing we look ④ **at is** their balance sheet. Are they ⑤ **profitable**? We examine ⑥ **what their** short-term and long-term potential is for expanding their profit margins and growth.

F: Do you have a preference between companies that offer a physical product versus a service, like social media, for example?

M: Well, that's ⑦ **kind of a** catch ⑧ **22**. A company that provides a service may represent huge growth potential, ⑨ **but they** are much more difficult to forecast and analyze. Users may flock to a particular service en masse, but they may tire of it and move on very quickly — ⑩ **in a** period of weeks. That kind of turnover makes it extremely tough to react to the ⑪ **data** and profit stream. So, from that standpoint, I would say I lean more toward product-based companies for long-term investing.

F: At 68, you've been in the business for a very long time. Have you given any ⑫ **thought to** retirement?

M: No. ⑬ **Not at all**. I love ⑭ **what I** do, and I cannot imagine doing anything else. That being said, I have ⑮ **cut back** a ⑯ **bit on** my hours to spend more time with my family. To ⑰ **that end** I'm trying to delegate more responsibility to others on my management team.

🎧 Stage 4 🔊 音声変化をチェック

まとめとして、穴埋め部分の音声変化の特徴を**スロー・スピード**と**ナチュラル・スピード**で確認しよう。下記に示したカタカナ表記で音声変化を確認して、もう一度インタビューを聴き直してみよう。発音変化のルールは適宜復習しよう。

---

❶ **opportunity**　　　　アーパチューナティー　　▶ アーパチューナディ［リ］ー
☞ 破裂音［t］の弾音化が起こる。

❷ **in the**　　　　　　イン・ザ　　　　　　　　▶ イナ
☞ ［n］+［ð］が［n］音に変化する。

❸ **right down**　　　　ライト・ダウン　　　　　▶ ライッ＿ダウン
☞ 破裂音［t］が脱落する。

❹ **at is**　　　　　　　アット・イズ　　　　　　▶ アッディ［リ］ズ
☞ 連結部で［t］音が弾音化する。

❺ **profitable**　　　　プラーファタブゥ　　　　▶ プラーファダ［ラ］ブゥ
☞ 破裂音［t］の弾音化が起こる。

❻ **what their**　　　　ワット・ゼア　　　　　　▶ ワッ＿ゼア
☞ 破裂音［t］の脱落が起こる。

❼ **kind of a**　　　　　カインド・アヴ・ア　　　▶ カインダヴァ；カイナヴァ
☞ 3語が連結する。［d］音が脱落して連結する場合もある。

❽ **22**　　　　　　　　トゥエンティートゥー　　▶ トゥエニートゥー
☞ ［nt］で［t］音の脱落が生じる。

❾ **but they**　　　　　バット・ゼイ　　　　　　▶ バッ＿ゼイ
☞ 破裂音［t］の脱落が起こる。

❿ **in a**　　　　　　　イン・ア　　　　　　　　▶ イナ
☞ 2語が連結する。

⓫ **data**　　　　　　　データ　　　　　　　　　▶ データ［ラ］
☞ 破裂音［t］の弾音化が起こる。

⓬ **thought to**　　　　ソート・トゥー　　　　　▶ ソーッ＿トゥー
☞ 破裂音［t］の脱落が起こる。

⓭ **Not at all**　　　　ナット・アット・オーゥ　▶ ナッダ［ラ］ッド［ロ］ーゥ
☞ 2カ所の連結部で破裂音［t］の弾音化が起こる。

⓮ **what I**　　　　　　ワット・アイ　　　　　　▶ ワッダ［ラ］イ
☞ 連結部で［t］音が弾音化する。

⓯ **cut back**　　　　　カット・バック　　　　　▶ カッ＿バック
☞ 破裂音［t］の脱落が起こる。

⓰ **bit on**　　　　　　ビット・オン　　　　　　▶ ビッド［ロ］ン
☞ 連結部で［t］音が弾音化する。

⓱ **that end**　　　　　ザット・エンド　　　　　▶ ザッデ［レ］ン（ド）
☞ 連結部で［t］音が弾音化する。末尾の［d］音が脱落する場合もある。

🎤 億万長者の投資家のインタビュー

INTERVIEW WITH AN ECONOMIST

Unit 05 経済学者のインタビュー

Stage 1 　穴埋め インタビュー・リスニング

音声変化に注意してCDでインタビューを聴きながら空欄部分を埋めてみよう。CDのナチュラル音声での聴き取りが難しいときは、次のトラックに収録されたスロー音声で聴いてみよう。

M: From your ① _____, ② _____ _____ the state of the U.S. economy? Are we over the hump from the 2008 recession and ③ _____ recovering?

F: Well, I certainly believe so based on the recent data, but it's often a ④ _____ of perspective. Employers are hiring. Home prices, sales and construction are on the rise. Corporate profits and stocks have hit records, and consumers have ⑤ _____ picked up their spending. By the middle of this year, after years of steady but sluggish improvement, the United States is ⑥ _____ _____ have finally regained all the 8.7 million jobs lost during the recession. Many economic forecasters say the economy should grow 3 percent or more this year. ⑦ _____ _____ _____ its best performance since 2005.

M: Let's talk a ⑧ _____ more about the job market. While there is a ⑨ _____ _____ positive market and industry data, there are still a lot of disgruntled voices to be heard.

F: That's certainly ⑩ _____. Much of the U.S. labor force has gone without pay increases. Millions have ⑪ _____ for more than six months to find work and others have ⑫ _____ _____ accept lower-paying jobs and diminished career prospects. According to recent surveys, ⑬ _____ percent of Americans

⑭ _____ themselves as lower or lower-middle class, whereas similar polls showed that only ⑮ _____-five percent of the country felt that way in 2008.

M: Where do you see the US and the global economy heading in the near future?

F: Well, to be frank with you, I believe that the world economy still remains very fragile. That was driven home ⑯ _____ by the turmoil in emerging economies that sent the U.S. stock market falling after a surprising 2013 rally that rewrote the record books. The unrest abroad represents a real ⑰ _____ _____ the progress we have been making. Another potentially huge factor domestically is the terrible drought in California that is threatening unforeseen price increases in produce and other agricultural products.

Stage 2 インタビュー解説

日本語訳と、解説を参照しながら、インタビュー内容を確認しよう。そのあとで、Stage1の穴埋めに再チャレンジしてみよう。

M: From your ① **standpoint**, ② **what is** the state of the U.S. economy? Are we over the hump from the 2008 recession and ③ **actually** recovering?

> あなたの見立てでは、アメリカ経済の現状はいかがですか？ 2008年の不景気からの危機を乗り越えて、実際に回復しているのでしょうか？
>
> ＊ hump「危機」 recover「回復する」

F: Well, I certainly believe so based on the recent data, but it's often a ④ **matter** of perspective. Employers are hiring. Home prices, sales and construction are on the rise. Corporate profits and stocks have hit records, and consumers have ⑤ **finally** picked up their spending. By the middle of this year, after years of steady but sluggish improvement, the United States is ⑥ **expected to** have finally regained all the 8.7 million jobs lost during the recession. Many economic forecasters say the economy should grow 3 percent or more this year. ⑦ **That would be** its best performance since 2005.

> えー、最近のデータに基づいて、私はそう考えていますが、おおかたは観点の問題なのです。雇用主は雇用を行いつつあります。家の価格や販売、建築は上がっています。企業収益や株価は記録をたたき出していますし、消費者もとうとう支出を増やし始めています。着実だがのろのろとした改善の数年を経て、今年の中旬までには、アメリカは、不景気の間に失われた870万の雇用をついに取り戻すと予測されています。経済予測をする多くの人たちは、今年は3%以上の経済成長になると言っています。これは2005年以来、最高の結果となるでしょう。
>
> ＊ perspective「相対的な見方；観点」　be on the rise「上がっている；上昇傾向にある」
>   profit「収益」　hit records「記録を出す」　steady「着実な；安定して」
>   sluggish「緩やかな；鈍い」　performance「業績；成果」

M: Let's talk a ⑧ **little** more about the job market. While there is a ⑨ **lot of** positive market and industry data, there are still a lot of disgruntled voices to be heard.

> 雇用市場についてもう少しお話ししましょう。市場や産業のポジティヴなデータが数多くある一方で、いまだに多くの不満の声が聞かれます。
>
> ＊ disgruntled「不満な」

F: That's certainly ⑩ **true**. Much of the U.S. labor force has gone without pay increases. Millions have ⑪ **struggled** for more than six months to find work and others have ⑫ **had to** accept lower-paying jobs and diminished career prospects. According to recent surveys, ⑬ **forty** percent of Americans ⑭ **identify** themselves as lower or lower-middle class, whereas similar polls showed that only ⑮ **twenty**-five percent of the country felt that way in 2008.

それは、確かにそのとおりです。ほとんどのアメリカの労働者たちは昇給をもらっていません。何百万もの人が仕事を見つけるのに 6 カ月以上も、もがき続けています。また、給与の少ない仕事や落ち込んだキャリアの見通しを受け入れざるを得ない状況です。最近の調査によると、40%のアメリカ人が、自らを下流あるいは中流の下のクラスであると考えています。一方、同様の世論調査で、2008 年にはこのように感じていたのは 25%に過ぎなかったのです。

---

* pay increase「昇給」　struggle「奮闘する；もがく；あがく」
　diminished「減少された；下落した」　prospect「見通し；将来性」
　identify oneself ...「自分が…であると確認する；認める」

M: Where do you see the US and the global economy heading in the near future?

近い将来、アメリカや世界の経済は、どの方向へ進んでいくと見ていますか？

F: Well, to be frank with you, I believe that the world economy still remains very fragile. That was driven home ⑯ **recently** by the turmoil in emerging economies that sent the U.S. stock market falling after a surprising 2013 rally that rewrote the record books. The unrest abroad represents a real ⑰ **threat to** the progress we have been making. Another potentially huge factor domestically is the terrible drought in California that is threatening unforeseen price increases in produce and other agricultural products.

えー、率直に話しますと、世界経済は、まだ脆弱であり続けると思っています。これは最近、新興国市場の混乱によって痛感されました。これが、記録を更新した驚異的な 2013 年の回復のあとで、アメリカの株式市場を下落させたのです。不安定な海外情勢が、われわれの前進に対する、ほんとうの脅威となるのです。そのほかの、国内の大きな潜在要因は、カリフォルニアのひどい干ばつです。これは農産物やその他の農業製品の不意の価格上昇への脅威となっています。

---

* fragile「脆弱な；もろい」
　be driven home by ...「…によって痛感される；強く理解される；核心を突かれる」
　turmoil「混乱」　emerging economies「新興国の経済」　rally「持ち直し；反発」
　unrest「不安な状態」　represent a real threat = be a real threat
　potentially「潜在的に」　threaten ...「…への脅威となる」

Stage 3 英文トランスクリプション

インタビュー全体を英文の原稿で確認しながらCDで耳慣らししよう！ その上で、インタビューを聴きながら、まだできていない部分の穴埋めに再チャレンジしよう。

M: From your ① **standpoint**, ② **what is** the state of the U.S. economy? Are we over the hump from the 2008 recession and ③ **actually** recovering?

F: Well, I certainly believe so based on the recent data, but it's often a ④ **matter** of perspective. Employers are hiring. Home prices, sales and construction are on the rise. Corporate profits and stocks have hit records, and consumers have ⑤ **finally** picked up their spending. By the middle of this year, after years of steady but sluggish improvement, the United States is ⑥ **expected to** have finally regained all the 8.7 million jobs lost during the recession. Many economic forecasters say the economy should grow 3 percent or more this year. ⑦ **That would be** its best performance since 2005.

M: Let's talk a ⑧ **little** more about the job market. While there is a ⑨ **lot of** positive market and industry data, there are still a lot of disgruntled voices to be heard.

F: That's certainly ⑩ **true**. Much of the U.S. labor force has gone without pay increases. Millions have ⑪ **struggled** for more than six months to find work and others have ⑫ **had to** accept lower-paying jobs and diminished career prospects. According to recent surveys, ⑬ **forty** percent of Americans ⑭ **identify** themselves as lower or lower-middle class, whereas similar polls showed that only ⑮ **twenty**-five percent of the country felt that way in 2008.

M: Where do you see the US and the global economy heading in the near future?

F: Well, to be frank with you, I believe that the world economy still remains very fragile. That was driven home ⑯ **recently** by the turmoil in emerging economies that sent the U.S. stock market falling after a surprising 2013 rally that rewrote the record books. The unrest abroad represents a real ⑰ **threat to** the progress we have been making. Another potentially huge factor domestically is the terrible drought in California that is threatening unforeseen price increases in produce and other agricultural products.

Stage 4))) 音声変化をチェック

まとめとして、穴埋め部分の音声変化の特徴を**スロー・スピード**と**ナチュラル・スピード**で確認しよう。下記に示したカタカナ表記で音声変化を確認して、もう一度インタビューを聴き直してみよう。発音変化のルールは適宜復習しよう。

❶ **standpoint** スタンドポイント ▶ スタン__ポイン（ト）
☞ 破裂音 [d] の脱落が起こる。

❷ **what is** ワット・イズ ▶ ワッディ [リ] ズ
☞ 連結部で [t] 音が弾音化する。

❸ **actually** アクチュアリー ▶ アクシュアリー
☞ 破裂音 [t] の脱落が起こる。

❹ **matter** マター ▶ マダ [ラ] ー
☞ [t] 音の弾音化が起こる。

❺ **finally** ファイナリー ▶ ファインリー
☞ [ə] 音が脱落する。

❻ **expected to** イクスペクティッド・トゥー ▶ イクスペクティッ__トゥー
☞ 破裂音 [d] の脱落が起こる。

❼ **That would be** ザット・ウッド・ビー ▶ ザッ__ウッ__ビー
☞ 破裂音 [t] と [d] の脱落が生じる。

❽ **little** リトゥー ▶ リドゥ [ル] ゥ
☞ 破裂音 [t] の弾音化が起こる。

❾ **lot of** ラット・アヴ ▶ ラッダ [ラ] ヴ
☞ 連結部で破裂音 [t] の弾音化が起こる。

❿ **true** トゥルー ▶ チュルー
☞ tr の [t] 音は [チュ] のように変化する。

⓫ **struggled** ストゥラッグッド ▶ スチュラッグッド
☞ tr の [t] 音は [チュ] のように変化する。

⓬ **had to** ハッド・トゥー ▶ ハッ__トゥー
☞ 破裂音 [d] の脱落が起こる。

⓭ **forty** フォーティー ▶ フォーディ [リ] ー
☞ 破裂音 [t] の弾音化が起こる。

⓮ **identify** アイデンティファイ ▶ アイデニファイ
☞ [nt] で [t] 音の脱落が生じる。

⓯ **twenty** トゥエンティー ▶ トゥエニー
☞ [nt] で [t] 音の脱落が生じる。

⓰ **recently** リースントゥリー ▶ リースン__リー
☞ [tl] で [t] 音の脱落が生じる。

⓱ **threat to** スレット・トゥー ▶ スレッ__トゥー
☞ 破裂音の連続で片方が脱落する。

経済学者のインタビュー

INTERVIEW WITH A TRUCK DRIVER

Unit 06　トラック・ドライバーのインタビュー

🎵 Stage 1 🔊 穴埋め インタビュー・リスニング

音声変化に注意してCDでインタビューを聴きながら空欄部分を埋めてみよう。CDのナチュラル音声での聴き取りが難しいときは、次のトラックに収録されたスロー音声で聴いてみよう。

F: We often take it for granted that when we go to a store or supermarket, ① _____ _____ are looking for will be there. For tonight's lifestyle clip we talk to big-rig driver Ted Simmons, whose job ② _____ _____ to make sure that product gets to the shelves. Ted, ③ _____ _____ _____ driving a truck for a living?

M: Well, I've been doin' it now for over ④ _____ years. It can be tough, ⑤ _____ _____ tell ya. Long hours on the road … living in your cab or in cheap motels. Not knowing where you're going to be from week to week or when you can get home to see your family are all aspects of the job that ⑥ _____ _____ really difficult.

F: How many miles ⑦ _____ _____ say you drive in a typical month?

M: That depends on the route and the product I am ⑧ _____. I'm a freelancer, so it changes from week to week. Off the top of my head though, I'd say I average ⑨ _____ _____ _____ ten thousand miles a month. It's a lot tougher now, because new safety regulations say we can only drive twelve hours during any ⑩ _____-four hour period. The idea behind that is to ensure drivers get enough rest and make the roads safer. Sometimes our

⑪ _____ and deadlines don't take ⑫ _____ _____ consideration though.

F: Have you ever thought about giving up driving a truck for a living?

M: Hell no! Number one it's all I know ⑬ _____ _____ do. Number two ... after working for myself for all ⑭ _____ _____ I can't imagine wearing a suit and ⑮ _____ _____ _____ desk, answering to someone else. This job is feast or famine though ... so you have to plan for that. Make hay when the sun shines, ⑯ _____ _____ speak. I'm sure I'll be ⑰ _____ _____ big-rig until I retire.

F: Thanks for your time and be safe out there.

M: 10-4 good buddy.

Stage 2 インタビュー解説

日本語訳と、解説を参照しながら、インタビュー内容を確認しよう。そのあとで、Stage1の穴埋めに再チャレンジしてみよう。

F: We often take it for granted that when we go to a store or supermarket, ① **what we** are looking for will be there. For tonight's lifestyle clip we talk to big-rig driver Ted Simmons, whose job ② **it is** to make sure that product gets to the shelves. Ted, ③ **what's it like** driving a truck for a living?

しばしば私たちは、お店やスーパーに行ったとき、探しているものがそこにあることを当然のことと思っています。今夜のライフスタイル・クリップでは、大型トラック運転手のテッド・シモンズに話を聞きます。彼は商品がお店の棚に並ぶのを確保する仕事をしています。テッド、職業運転手としてトラックを運転するのはいかがですか？

* big-rig driver「大型トラック運転手」　whose job it is = whose job is
  for a living「暮らしのために；生計を立てるために」

トラック・ドライバーのインタビュー　41

M: Well, I've been doin' it now for over ④ **thirty** years. It can be tough, ⑤ **let me** tell ya. Long hours on the road ... living in your cab or in cheap motels. Not knowing where you're going to be from week to week or when you can get home to see your family are all aspects of the job that ⑥ **make it** really difficult.

> ああ、俺はもう30年以上この仕事をしてるんだよ。確かに大変なこともあるよ。運転席（のベッド）や安いモーテルで生活して、長時間を道路上で過ごすこととか。毎週毎週、自分がどこに行くことになるのかとか、いつ家族に会いに家に戻れるのかわからない。そういういろんなことが、この仕事を大変なものにしているんだよ。
>
> ＊ let me tell ya「確かに」強調のフレーズ。　cab「運転席の後部にある睡眠のスペース；運転席」all aspects of ...「…のあらゆる側面」

F: How many miles ⑦ **would you** say you drive in a typical month?

> ふつうは1カ月にどのくらいの距離を走るんでしょう？
>
> ＊ typical「典型的な」

M: That depends on the route and the product I am ⑧ **transporting**. I'm a freelancer, so it changes from week to week. Off the top of my head though, I'd say I average ⑨ **about eight to** ten thousand miles a month. It's a lot tougher now, because new safety regulations say we can only drive twelve hours during any ⑩ **twenty**-four hour period. The idea behind that is to ensure drivers get enough rest and make the roads safer. Sometimes our ⑪ **quotas** and deadlines don't take ⑫ **that into** consideration though.

> それは、ルートと、運んでいる商品によるんだ。俺はフリーだから、毎週変化するんだよね。でもざっくりと言えば、月に平均で8千から1万マイルだろうね。いまは、以前より大変になっているよ。なぜかって、新しい安全規則ができて、24時間の間には12時間しか運転できないんだ。ドライバーがきちんと休憩を取るようにして、道路をより安全にしたいって考えだよね。でも、ときには、俺たちのノルマや納期はこの規則を無視して考えられることもあるわけさ。
>
> ＊ Off the top of my head ...「ざっと言うと…」　safety regulations「安全規則・条例」

quota「仕事のノルマ；割り当て」 take ... into consideration「…を考慮に入れる」

F: Have you ever thought about giving up driving a truck for a living?

トラック運転手の仕事をやめようと思ったことはありますか？

* give up「あきらめる；やめる」

M: Hell no! Number one it's all I know ⑬ **how to** do. Number two ... after working for myself for all ⑭ **these years** I can't imagine wearing a suit and ⑮ **sitting at a** desk, answering to someone else. This job is feast or famine though ... so you have to plan for that. Make hay when the sun shines, ⑯ **so to** speak. I'm sure I'll be ⑰ **driving a** big-rig until I retire.

絶対にないよ！　まず、これしかできることがないからさ。次に、ずっと自営で働いてきたあとで、スーツを着て、机に腰掛けて、だれかほかのやつの下で働くなんて想像できないよ。でも、この仕事は儲かるときと儲けのないときが極端なんだ…だから、備えておかなければダメなんだよ。言わば、「日差しのあるうちに干し草を作れ」ってことだよ。俺はきっと引退までずっと大型トラックを運転してると思うよ。

* work for myself「自営で働く」 answer to ...「…の下で働く」
feast or famine「大宴会と欠乏の両極端」
Make hay when the sun shines.「チャンスを逃すな」 so to speak「言わば」

F: Thanks for your time and be safe out there.

お時間をいただきありがとうございました。安全運転でいってください。

* safe「安全な」

M: 10-4 good buddy.

了解、相棒。

* 10-4「了解」　good buddy「相棒」トラック運転手が無線などの交信でよく使うあいさつ表現。

トラック・ドライバーのインタビュー

Stage 3 英文トランスクリプション

インタビュー全体を英文の原稿で確認しながらCDで耳慣らししよう！ その上で、インタビューを聴きながら、まだできていない部分の穴埋めに再チャレンジしよう。

F: We often take it for granted that when we go to a store or supermarket, ① **what we** are looking for will be there. For tonight's lifestyle clip we talk to big-rig driver Ted Simmons, whose job ② **it is** to make sure that product gets to the shelves. Ted, ③ **what's it like** driving a truck for a living?

M: Well, I've been doin' it now for over ④ **thirty** years. It can be tough, ⑤ **let me** tell ya. Long hours on the road ... living in your cab or in cheap motels. Not knowing where you're going to be from week to week or when you can get home to see your family are all aspects of the job that ⑥ **make it** really difficult.

F: How many miles ⑦ **would you** say you drive in a typical month?

M: That depends on the route and the product I am ⑧ **transporting**. I'm a freelancer, so it changes from week to week. Off the top of my head though, I'd say I average ⑨ **about eight to** ten thousand miles a month. It's a lot tougher now, because new safety regulations say we can only drive twelve hours during any ⑩ **twenty**-four hour period. The idea behind that is to ensure drivers get enough rest and make the roads safer. Sometimes our ⑪ **quotas** and deadlines don't take ⑫ **that into** consideration though.

F: Have you ever thought about giving up driving a truck for a living?

M: Hell no! Number one it's all I know ⑬ **how to** do. Number two ... after working for myself for all ⑭ **these years** I can't imagine wearing a suit and ⑮ **sitting at a** desk, answering to someone else. This job is feast or famine though ... so you have to plan for that. Make hay when the sun shines, ⑯ **so to** speak. I'm sure I'll be ⑰ **driving a** big-rig until I retire.

F: Thanks for your time and be safe out there.

M: 10-4 good buddy.

Stage 4 音声変化をチェック

まとめとして、穴埋め部分の音声変化の特徴を**スロー・スピード**と**ナチュラル・スピード**で確認しよう。下記に示したカタカナ表記で音声変化を確認して、もう一度インタビューを聴き直してみよう。発音変化のルールは適宜復習しよう。

❶ **what we**　　　　　　　　　　　ワット・ウィ　　　　　　　▶ ワッ＿ウィ
　☞ 破裂音 [t] の脱落が起こる。

❷ **it is**　　　　　　　　　　　　　イット・イズ　　　　　　　▶ イッディ [リ] ーズ
　☞ 連結部で [t] 音が弾音化する。

❸ **what's it like**　　　　　　　　　ワッツ・イット・ライク　　▶ ワッツィッ＿ライク
　☞ what's it は連結する。it の破裂音 [t] が脱落する。

❹ **thirty**　　　　　　　　　　　　サーティー　　　　　　　　▶ サーディ [リ] ー
　☞ 破裂音 [t] の弾音化が起こる。

❺ **let me**　　　　　　　　　　　　レット・ミー　　　　　　　▶ レッ＿ミ
　☞ 破裂音 [t] の脱落が起こる。me は弱化。

❻ **make it**　　　　　　　　　　　メイク・イット　　　　　　▶ メイキッ（ト）
　☞ 2語が連結する。末尾の破裂音 [t] も脱落しやすい。

❼ **would you**　　　　　　　　　　ウッド・ユー　　　　　　　▶ ウッジュー
　☞ [d] ＋ [j] の部分で音が混じり合い、[ジュ] に近い音に変化する。

❽ **transporting**　　　　　　　　　トゥランスポーティング　　▶ トゥランスポーディ [リ] ン（グ）
　☞ 破裂音 [t] の弾音化が起こる。末尾の [g] 音が脱落する場合もある。

❾ **about eight to**　　　　　　　　アバウト・エイト・トゥー　▶ アバウデ [レ] イ＿ドゥ [ル] ー；
　　　　　　　　　　　　　　　　　　　　　　　　　　　　　　　　アバウッ＿エイ＿ドゥ [ル] ー
　☞ about eight の連結部や to で破裂音 [t] が弾音化する。eight 末尾の [t] 音に加え、about の [t] 音が脱落する場合もある。

❿ **twenty**　　　　　　　　　　　　トゥエンティー　　　　　　▶ トゥエニー
　☞ [nt] で [t] 音の脱落が生じる。

⓫ **quotas**　　　　　　　　　　　　クゥオウタズ　　　　　　　▶ クゥオウダ [ラ] ズ
　☞ 破裂音 [t] の弾音化が起こる。

⓬ **that into**　　　　　　　　　　　ザット・イントゥー　　　　▶ ザッディ [リ] ンドゥ [ル] ー
　☞ 2語の連結部や into で破裂音 [t] の弾音化が起こる。

⓭ **how to**　　　　　　　　　　　　ハウ・トゥー　　　　　　　▶ ハウドゥ [ル] ー
　☞ to で破裂音 [t] の弾音化が起こる。

⓮ **these years**　　　　　　　　　ズィーズ・イヤーズ　　　　▶ ズィージャーズ
　☞ [z] ＋ [j] の部分で音が混じり合い、[ジュ] に近い音に変化する。

⓯ **sitting at a**　　　　　　　　　スィッティング・アット・ア　▶ スィッディ [リ] ン（グ）アッダ [ラ]
　☞ sitting の [t] 音や、at a の連結部の [t] 音で弾音化が起こる。sitting の [g] 音が脱落することもある。

⓰ **so to**　　　　　　　　　　　　　ソウ・トゥー　　　　　　　▶ ソウドゥ [ル] ー
　☞ to で破裂音 [t] の弾音化が起こる。

⓱ **driving a**　　　　　　　　　　　ドゥライヴィング・ア　　　▶ ドゥライヴィナ
　☞ driving から [g] 音が脱落しつつ、2語が連結する。

INTERVIEW WITH A COMMERCIAL PILOT

Unit 07　民間航空機パイロットのインタビュー

Stage 1　穴埋め インタビュー・リスニング

音声変化に注意してCDでインタビューを聴きながら空欄部分を埋めてみよう。CDのナチュラル音声での聴き取りが難しいときは、次のトラックに収録されたスロー音声で聴いてみよう。

F: We're talking today with Captain Davis of Freedom Airlines, to ① _____ _____ _____ insight on ② _____ _____ like in the pilot seat of a commercial airliner. Captain, what's the ③ _____ _____ about your job as a pilot?

M: Well the answer may surprise you, because it is the same thing that plagues the passengers—jet lag. ④ _____ _____ adapt to so many ⑤ _____ _____ zones is difficult, and it's not something that gets any easier with practice. After a long overseas flight, it can be difficult to ⑥ _____ _____ sleep during a layover before we have to get right back up ⑦ _____ fly again. Unlike most of our customers, we are only there for a day or so before we have to do ⑧ _____ _____ over again, often flying right back where we came from. ⑨ _____ really takes a toll on you. ⑩ _____ _____ _____ food of course. Even as pilots we still have to choose between chicken and beef too!

F: Superman is often ⑪ _____ as saying "statistically speaking flying is the safest way to travel." Do you agree? Have you ever had any near misses?

M: You have to keep in mind that there are roughly 50,000 flights per day world-wide. That's a ⑫ _____ _____ take offs and landings. I've had my share of scary moments up there—sudden

46

turbulence, landing with wind shear, ⑬ _____ we are trained for those situations and when they do occur, ⑭ _____ kicks in immediately. While it is ⑮ _____ that modern, newer aircraft have a lot more computer-aided instruments and indeed there is ⑯ _____ "_____-pilot" it's still the job of the pilot to command the plane. Those things make it safer and easier, but ⑰ _____ and mechanical equipment can fail too, so we have to train to fly with them or without them, as the case may warrant.

F: Well folks, that wraps up today's "Day in the Life" segment. Captain, thank you for your time.

M: My pleasure. Thank you for having me.

Stage 2 インタビュー解説

日本語訳と、解説を参照しながら、インタビュー内容を確認しよう。そのあとで、Stage1の穴埋めに再チャレンジしてみよう。

F: We're talking today with Captain Davis of Freedom Airlines, to ① **get a little** insight on ② **what it's** like in the pilot seat of a commercial airliner. Captain, what's the ③ **hardest part** about your job as a pilot?

> 本日は、民間航空機の操縦席に座るのがどんなものなのか、少々の理解を得るために、フリーダム・エアラインのデイヴィス機長とお話ししています。機長、パイロットとしての仕事でもっとも大変な部分とはなんでしょうか?
>
> ＊ insight「理解」　commercial「民間の；商業用の」

M: Well the answer may surprise you, because it is the same thing that plagues the passengers—jet lag. ④ **Having to** adapt to so many ⑤ **different time** zones is difficult, and it's not something that gets any easier with practice. After a long overseas flight, it can be difficult to ⑥ **get enough** sleep during a layover before we have to get right back up ⑦ **and** fly again. Unlike most of our customers, we are only there for a day or so before we have to do ⑧ **it all** over again, often flying right back where we came from. ⑨ **That** really takes a toll on you. ⑩ **That and the** food of course. Even as pilots we still have to choose between chicken and beef too!

> えー、あなたを驚かせる答えかもしれませんね、なぜならそれは搭乗客も悩ませているものだからです―つまり、時差ぼけですよ。非常に多くの異なる時間帯に適応しなければならないのは、難しいことなんです。さらに、時差ぼけは訓練で軽くなったりするものではないのです。長距離の海外フライトのあと、職務に戻って再びフライトを行う前、乗り継ぎ待ちの宿泊の間に、十分な睡眠を取ることは難しいときもあるんです。ほとんどのお客さまと違って、われわれは１日かそこいらしかその場所に滞在しません。それから、また同じことを最初から丸ごとやらねばならないのです。たいていはやってきた場所にそのまま飛行機で戻りながらですが。それが大きな負担になるのです。それと、もちろんですが食事もです。パイロットであっても、鶏肉と牛肉のどちらかを選ばねばならないんですよ！
>
> ＊ plague「悩ませる」 jet lag「時差ぼけ；時差による疲れ」 practice「訓練；練習」
>   get right back up and ...「すぐにまた…する」 take a toll on ...「…の負担になる」

F: Superman is often ⑪ **quoted** as saying "statistically speaking flying is the safest way to travel." Do you agree? Have you ever had any near misses?

> 「統計上は飛行機を使うのがもっとも安全な旅行の方法だ」というスーパーマンの言葉がしばしば引用されます。あなたも同意見ですか？ これまでにニアミスに遭遇したことはありますか？
>
> ＊ statistically speaking「統計上は；統計的には」 near miss「（航空機同士の）異常接近」

M: You have to keep in mind that there are roughly 50,000 flights per day world-wide. That's a ⑫ **lot of** take offs and landings. I've had my share of scary moments up there—sudden turbulence, landing with wind shear, ⑬ **but** we are trained for those situations and when they do occur, ⑭ **training** kicks in immediately. While it is ⑮ **true** that modern, newer aircraft have a lot more computer-aided instruments and indeed there is ⑯ **an "auto**-pilot" it's still the job of the pilot to command the plane. Those things make it safer and easier, but ⑰ **electronics** and mechanical equipment can fail too, so we have to train to fly with them or without them, as the case may warrant.

> 世界中で、大まかに言って1日につき5万件のフライトがあることを頭に入れておく必要があります。すごくたくさんの離陸と着陸の数ですよ。私も空の上で恐ろしい瞬間を味わったことはあります―突然の乱気流やウインド・シアでの着陸などです。しかし、私たちはこのような状況の訓練を受けていますから、そういった事態が発生したときには、即座にトレーニングの効果が現れます。現代の新しい航空機にはより多くのコンピューターに支援された機器が搭載されているし、確かにオートパイロットのシステムもあるのですが、それでも、いまだに飛行機を操るのはパイロットの仕事なのです。そういったものは航行や操縦をより安全で楽なものにするのですが、エレクトロニクスや機械的な装備は故障することもあるのです。だからわれわれは、機器があってもなくても、どのような状況であっても、航行できるよう訓練をしなければならないのです。
>
> * roughly「おおよそ」 have one's share of ...「…を経験したことがある」 turbulence「乱気流」 wind shear「晴天乱流」 kick in「効果が現れる」 command「操る；命令する」 fail「故障する」 as the case may warrant = as the case may be「どのような状況であっても；場合に応じて」

F: Well folks, that wraps up today's "Day in the Life" segment. Captain, thank you for your time.

> さて、みなさん、これで、本日の「デイ・イン・ザ・ライフ」のコーナーは終わりです。機長、お時間をいただきありがとうございます。
>
> * wrap up「終わりにする」

M: My pleasure. Thank you for having me.

> こちらこそ。ご招待いただきありがとうございました。

Stage 3 　英文トランスクリプション

インタビュー全体を英文の原稿で確認しながらCDで耳慣らししよう！　その上で、インタビューを聴きながら、まだできていない部分の穴埋めに再チャレンジしよう。

F: We're talking today with Captain Davis of Freedom Airlines, to ① **get a little** insight on ② **what it's** like in the pilot seat of a commercial airliner. Captain, what's the ③ **hardest part** about your job as a pilot?

M: Well the answer may surprise you, because it is the same thing that plagues the passengers—jet lag. ④ **Having to** adapt to so many ⑤ **different time** zones is difficult, and it's not something that gets any easier with practice. After a long overseas flight, it can be difficult to ⑥ **get enough** sleep during a layover before we have to get right back up ⑦ **and** fly again. Unlike most of our customers, we are only there for a day or so before we have to do ⑧ **it all** over again, often flying right back where we came from. ⑨ **That** really takes a toll on you. ⑩ **That and the** food of course. Even as pilots we still have to choose between chicken and beef too!

F: Superman is often ⑪ **quoted** as saying "statistically speaking flying is the safest way to travel." Do you agree? Have you ever had any near misses?

M: You have to keep in mind that there are roughly 50,000 flights per day world-wide. That's a ⑫ **lot of** take offs and landings. I've had my share of scary moments up there—sudden turbulence, landing with wind shear, ⑬ **but** we are trained for those situations and when they do occur, ⑭ **training** kicks in immediately. While it is ⑮ **true** that modern, newer aircraft have a lot more computer-aided instruments and indeed there is ⑯ **an "auto**-pilot" it's still the job of the pilot to command the plane. Those things make it safer and easier, but ⑰ **electronics** and mechanical equipment can fail too, so we have to train to fly with them or without them, as the case may warrant.

F: Well folks, that wraps up today's "Day in the Life" segment. Captain, thank you for your time.

M: My pleasure. Thank you for having me.

🎧 Stage 4 🔊 音声変化をチェック

まとめとして、穴埋め部分の音声変化の特徴を**スロー・スピード**と**ナチュラル・スピード**で確認しよう。下記に示したカタカナ表記で音声変化を確認して、もう一度インタビューを聴き直してみよう。発音変化のルールは適宜復習しよう。

❶ **get a little**   ゲット・ア・リトゥ   ▶ ゲッダ［ラ］リドゥ［ル］ゥ
☞ get a の連結部で破裂音［t］の弾音化が起こる。little の［t］音も弾音化する。

❷ **what it's**   ワット・イッツ   ▶ ワッディ［リ］ッツ
☞ 連結部で［t］音が弾音化する。

❸ **hardest part**   ハーデスト・パート   ▶ ハーデ［レ］ス__パート
☞ 破裂音の連続で［t］音が脱落する。hardest の［d］音は弾音化することもある。

❹ **Having to**   ハヴィング・トゥー   ▶ ハヴィン__トゥー
☞ 破裂音の連続で［g］音が脱落する。

❺ **different time**   ディファラント・タイム   ▶ ディファラン__タイム
☞ 破裂音の連続で［t］音が脱落する。

❻ **get enough**   ゲット・イナフ   ▶ ゲッディ［リ］ナフ
☞ 連結部で破裂音［t］の弾音化が起こる。

❼ **and**   アンド   ▶ アン__
☞ 末尾の破裂音［d］の脱落が生じる。

❽ **it all**   イット・オーウ   ▶ イッド［ロ］ーウ
☞ 連結部で破裂音［t］の弾音化が起こる。

❾ **That**   ザット   ▶ ザッ__
☞ 末尾の破裂音［t］の脱落が生じる。

❿ **That and the**   ザット・アンド・ザ   ▶ ザッ__アン__ザ
☞ That と and 末尾の破裂音［t］と［d］が脱落する。

⓫ **quoted**   クゥオウティッド   ▶ クゥオウディ［リ］ッ（ド）
☞ 破裂音［t］の弾音化が起こる。

⓬ **lot of**   ラット・アヴ   ▶ ラッダ［ラ］ヴ
☞ 連結部で破裂音［t］の弾音化が起こる。

⓭ **but**   バット   ▶ バッ__
☞ but 末尾の破裂音［t］が脱落。

⓮ **training**   トゥレイニング   ▶ チュレイニン（グ）
☞ ［tr］部分の［t］音が［チュ］に近い音に変化する。

⓯ **true**   トゥルー   ▶ チュルー
☞ ［tr］部分の［t］音が［チュ］に近い音に変化する。

⓰ **an "auto**   アン・オートウ   ▶ アノード［ロ］ウ
☞ 2語が連結。auto の［t］音が弾音化する。

⓱ **electronics**   イレクトゥラーニックス   ▶ イレクチュラーニックス
☞ ［tr］部分の［t］音が［チュ］に近い音に変化する。

🎤 民間航空機パイロットのインタビュー   51

INTERVIEW WITH A POLICE OFFICER

Unit 08　警官のインタビュー

Stage 1　穴埋め インタビュー・リスニング

音声変化に注意してCDでインタビューを聴きながら空欄部分を埋めてみよう。CDのナチュラル音声での聴き取りが難しいときは、次のトラックに収録されたスロー音声で聴いてみよう。

M: WKCY news has just learned that two men just robbed the Manhattan ① _____ Bank at East 15th and Broadway. On the phone with us is Sgt. Bradley, ② _____ _____ the first officers on the scene. Sgt. Marie Bradley, what can you tell us?

F: ③ _____ _____ _____ fifteen PM two men wearing baseball caps and sunglasses entered the bank and demanded money from the tellers. Following bank protocol, the tellers did not resist and gave the two men an undisclosed ④ _____ _____ money. The men then exited the bank and escaped in a late model, blue Ford Explorer. The license plates were removed, but we have confirmed the truck ⑤ _____ _____ crack in the windshield. Anyone who sees a vehicle matching this description should dial 911 immediately.

M: Were the men armed?

F: That's not clear ⑥ _____ _____ time. We are still interviewing witnesses on the scene, as well as reviewing the bank's security videos, so we haven't been able to confirm ⑦ _____ _____. Regardless, we're asking the public to be on the lookout for the two suspects, and we are considering them to be armed and dangerous.

M: We're hearing some reports that someone was ⑧ _____. Is that ⑨ _____?

F: ⑩ _____ _____ _____ customers at the bank during the

52

incident suffered a ⑪ _____ _____. The man was ⑫ _____ _____ a local hospital for treatment. I don't have any updates on his condition.

M: There was a similar robbery last week ⑬ _____ _____ branch of the same bank. Do you think these cases are connected?

F: Right now we can't be sure of anything, as the investigation is ongoing. I have spoken with detectives ⑭ _____ the other case and the MO is very similar. For now we are ⑮ _____ this as a separate incident, but that may change as time goes on. We hope to release sketches or pictures of the suspects ⑯ _____, and ask anyone with information relevant to the case to contact their local police department.

M: Thank you for your time Sergeant. We will follow up this report as any new details emerge.

Stage 2 インタビュー解説

日本語訳と、解説を参照しながら、インタビュー内容を確認しよう。そのあとで、Stage1の穴埋めに再チャレンジしてみよう。

M: WKCY news has just learned that two men just robbed the Manhattan ① **Central** Bank at East 15th and Broadway. On the phone with us is Sgt. Bradley, ② **one of** the first officers on the scene. Sgt. Marie Bradley, what can you tell us?

> WKCYニュースにいま入った情報では、東15通りとブロードウェーの交差点にあるマンハッタン・セントラル・バンクにふたりの男が強盗に入ったということです。電話口には、現場にいち早く駆けつけた警官のひとり、ブラッドリー巡査部長にいらしてもらっています。マリー・ブラッドリー巡査部長、状況を教えてください。
>
> * rob「強盗する」 Sgt. = Sergeant「巡査部長」

F: ③ **At about two** fifteen PM two men wearing baseball caps and sunglasses entered the bank and demanded money from the tellers. Following bank protocol, the tellers did not resist and gave the two men an undisclosed ④ **amount of** money. The men then exited the bank and escaped in a late model, blue Ford Explorer. The license plates were removed, but we have confirmed the truck ⑤ **had a** crack in the windshield. Anyone who sees a vehicle matching this description should dial 911 immediately.

> だいたい、午後2時15分頃に、野球帽をかぶり、サングラスをつけたふたりの男が銀行に入り、窓口の行員に金銭を要求しました。銀行の規則に従って行員は抵抗せず、ふたりの男に、金を渡しましたが、金額は公開されていません。ふたりは、それから銀行を出て新型の青のフォード・エクスプローラーに乗って逃走しました。ナンバー・プレートは取り外されていましたが、トラックのフロント・グラスにひび割れがあったことを警察で確認しています。この特徴に一致する車を目撃した人は、すぐに911に通報を願います。
>
> ＊ protocol「規約」　undisclosed「公開されていない；未公開の」　late model「（比較的）新型の」　license plate「ナンバー・プレート」　crack「ひび；割れ目」

M: Were the men armed?

> ふたりは武装していたのですか？
>
> ＊ armed「武器を携行して；武装して」

F: That's not clear ⑥ **at this** time. We are still interviewing witnesses on the scene, as well as reviewing the bank's security videos, so we haven't been able to confirm ⑦ **that yet**. Regardless, we're asking the public to be on the lookout for the two suspects, and we are considering them to be armed and dangerous.

> いまのところ、それは判明していません。まだ現場の目撃者を調査し、銀行のセキュリティー・ビデオを確認しているところですから、まだ確認が取れていません。それでも、警察は市民のみなさんにふたりの容疑者への用心を呼びかけています。また、われわれは、ふたりが武装していて危険であると考えています。
>
> ＊ confirm「確認する」　Regardless, ...「それでも…」　lookout「用心」

M: We're hearing some reports that someone was ⑧ **hospitalized**. Is that ⑨ **true**?

> 病院に運ばれた人がいるという報告を聞いているのですが、それはほんとうですか？
>
> ＊ hospitalize「入院させる；病院に送る」

F: ⑩ **One of the** customers at the bank during the incident suffered a ⑪ **heart attack**. The man was ⑫ **admitted to** a local hospital for treatment. I don't have any updates on his condition.

> 銀行の客のひとりが、事件当時、心臓発作を起こしました。その男性が、治療のため地元の病院に入院しました。彼の状態に関する新たな情報は得ておりません。
>
> * be admitted to a hospital「入院する」 updates「更新情報」

M: There was a similar robbery last week ⑬ **at another** branch of the same bank. Do you think these cases are connected?

> 先週、同じ銀行の別の支店で同様の強盗がありましたね。これらの事件は関連があると思いますか？
>
> * connected「関連した」

F: Right now we can't be sure of anything, as the investigation is ongoing. I have spoken with detectives ⑭ **handling** the other case and the MO is very similar. For now we are ⑮ **treating** this as a separate incident, but that may change as time goes on. We hope to release sketches or pictures of the suspects ⑯ **shortly**, and ask anyone with information relevant to the case to contact their local police department.

> いまのところはなにもはっきりしていません。捜査が継続中ですので。もう一方の事件を担当している刑事と話をしましたが、手口はとても似ています。いまのところ別の事件として扱っていますが、今後、変化するかもしれません。すぐにも、容疑者の似顔絵か写真を発表したいと考えていて、事件に関連する情報をもっている人に、地元の警察への連絡を呼びかけています。
>
> * investigation「捜査」 MO = modus operandi「手口」 relevant to ...「…に関連した」

M: Thank you for your time Sergeant. We will follow up this report as any new details emerge.

> 巡査部長、お時間をいただきありがとうございました。なんらかの新しい情報が出次第、続報をお伝えしていきます。
>
> * follow up「追跡する」 emerge「現れる」

Stage 3 英文トランスクリプション

インタビュー全体を英文の原稿で確認しながらCDで耳慣らししよう！ その上で、インタビューを聴きながら、まだできていない部分の穴埋めに再チャレンジしよう。

M: WKCY news has just learned that two men just robbed the Manhattan ① **Central** Bank at East 15th and Broadway. On the phone with us is Sgt. Bradley, ② **one of** the first officers on the scene. Sgt. Marie Bradley, what can you tell us?

F: ③ **At about two** fifteen PM two men wearing baseball caps and sunglasses entered the bank and demanded money from the tellers. Following bank protocol, the tellers did not resist and gave the two men an undisclosed ④ **amount of** money. The men then exited the bank and escaped in a late model, blue Ford Explorer. The license plates were removed, but we have confirmed the truck ⑤ **had a** crack in the windshield. Anyone who sees a vehicle matching this description should dial 911 immediately.

M: Were the men armed?

F: That's not clear ⑥ **at this** time. We are still interviewing witnesses on the scene, as well as reviewing the bank's security videos, so we haven't been able to confirm ⑦ **that yet**. Regardless, we're asking the public to be on the lookout for the two suspects, and we are considering them to be armed and dangerous.

M: We're hearing some reports that someone was ⑧ **hospitalized**. Is that ⑨ **true**?

F: ⑩ **One of the** customers at the bank during the incident suffered a ⑪ **heart attack**. The man was ⑫ **admitted to** a local hospital for treatment. I don't have any updates on his condition.

M: There was a similar robbery last week ⑬ **at another** branch of the same bank. Do you think these cases are connected?

F: Right now we can't be sure of anything, as the investigation is ongoing. I have spoken with detectives ⑭ **handling** the other case and the MO is very similar. For now we are ⑮ **treating** this as a separate incident, but that may change as time goes on. We hope to release sketches or pictures of the suspects ⑯ **shortly**, and ask anyone with information relevant to the case to contact their local police department.

M: Thank you for your time Sergeant. We will follow up this report as any new details emerge.

🎯 Stage 4 🔊 音声変化をチェック

まとめとして、穴埋め部分の音声変化の特徴を**スロー・スピード**と**ナチュラル・スピード**で確認しよう。下記に示したカタカナ表記で音声変化を確認して、もう一度インタビューを聴き直してみよう。発音変化のルールは適宜復習しよう。

---

❶ Central　　　　セントゥラウ　　　　▶ センチュラウ
☞ [tr] 部分の [t] 音が [チュ] に近い音に変化する。

❷ one of　　　　ワン・アヴ　　　　▶ ワナ (ヴ)
☞ 2語が連結する。末尾の [v] 音が脱落することもある。

❸ At about two　　　　アット・アバウト・トゥー　　　　▶ アッダ [ラ] バウッ_トゥー
☞ At about の連結部で [t] 音が弾音化する。about 末尾の [t] 音が脱落する。

❹ amount of　　　　アマウント・アヴ　　　　▶ アマウンダ [ラ] ヴ
☞ 連結部で [t] 音が弾音化する。

❺ had a　　　　ハッド・ア　　　　▶ ハッダ [ラ]
☞ 連結部で [d] 音が弾音化する。

❻ at this　　　　アット・ズィス　　　　▶ アッ_ズィス
☞ 破裂音 [t] の脱落が生じる。

❼ that yet　　　　ザット・イェット　　　　▶ ザッ_イェッ (ト) ; ザッチェッ (ト)
☞ that の破裂音 [t] の脱落が起こる。that yet の連結、[t] + [j] の部分で音が混じり合い、[チュ] に近い音に変化することもある。また、yet 末尾の [t] 音が脱落することもある。

❽ hospitalized　　　　ハスピトゥライズド　　　　▶ ハスピドゥ [ル] ライズド
☞ 破裂音 [t] の弾音化が生じる。

❾ true　　　　トゥルー　　　　▶ チュルー
☞ [tr] 部分の [t] 音が [チュ] に近い音に変化する。

❿ One of the　　　　ワン・アヴ・ザ　　　　▶ ワナ (ヴ) ザ
☞ One of の音が連結する。of の [v] 音が脱落することもある。

⓫ heart attack　　　　ハート・アタック　　　　▶ ハーダ [ラ] ダ [ラ] ック
☞ 2語の連結部で [t] 音の弾音化が起こる。attack の [t] 音が弾音化することもある。

⓬ admitted to　　　　アドゥミティッド・トゥー　　　　▶ アドゥミディ [リ] ッ_トゥー
☞ admitted 中程の [t] 音が弾音化し、末尾の [d] 音が脱落する。

⓭ at another　　　　アット・アナザー　　　　▶ アッダ [ラ] ナザー
☞ 連結部で [t] 音が弾音化する。

⓮ handling　　　　ハンドゥリング　　　　▶ ハン_リン (グ)
☞ [dl] で [d] 音の脱落が生じる。末尾の [g] 音が脱落することもある。

⓯ treating　　　　トゥリーティング　　　　▶ トゥリーディ [リ] ン (グ)
☞ 破裂音 [t] が弾音化する。末尾の [g] 音が脱落することもある。

⓰ shortly　　　　ショートリー　　　　▶ ショーッ_リー
☞ [tl] で [t] 音の脱落が生じる。

INTERVIEW WITH AN ACCIDENT EYEWITNESS

Unit 09 事故の目撃者のインタビュー

Stage 1 穴埋め インタビュー・リスニング

音声変化に注意してCDでインタビューを聴きながら空欄部分を埋めてみよう。CDのナチュラル音声での聴き取りが難しいときは、次のトラックに収録されたスロー音声で聴いてみよう。

M: Tom Sawyer here with WKYT news. I'm standing here with Linda Carter, an eyewitness to the horrific ten car pileup ① _____ _____ earlier this morning on I- ② _____. Ma'am can you tell us ③ _____ _____ saw?

F: Yeah, um … sure. I was in my car on the on ramp to the ④ _____ when a semi-truck in the far lane seemed to lose control. It came straight across two other lanes, plowing into cars along the way, before ⑤ _____ the cement divider and coming to a stop ⑥ _____ _____ _____ _____ me. Other cars were crashing into each other as they tried to ⑦ _____ _____ _____ the way. I was terrified. My adrenaline is still pumping. If I had ⑧ _____ _____ the highway a few seconds earlier I would have been right ⑨ _____ _____ middle of everything. I still can't believe … I can't believe I came through it without getting hit myself.

M: I'm sure that must have been terrifying, indeed. Were you still on the scene when the first responders arrived?

F: Of course. I couldn't ⑩ _____ _____ the wreckage of the other vehicles. I saw the paramedics save a pregnant woman by ⑪ _____ her ⑫ _____ _____ her burning car. It was just horrible. I heard that the driver of the truck that caused the accident ⑬ _____ _____ _____ _____ behind the wheel and that's why he lost control, ⑭ _____ _____ not really sure. Judging by the way the truck careened out of control that would make sense. Either ⑮ _____ _____ he fell asleep behind the wheel. Either way, it was a horrible horrible scene. I'm sure I'll be having nightmares ⑯ _____ _____ for a long time.

M: There you ⑰ _____ _____. Ms. Carter, thank you for sharing what you saw with us. We'll have an update on the cause of the accident and the rest of the story on our 11 o'clock broadcast.

Stage 2 インタビュー解説

日本語訳と、解説を参照しながら、インタビュー内容を確認しよう。そのあとで、Stage 1 の穴埋めに再チャレンジしてみよう。

M: Tom Sawyer here with WKYT news. I'm standing here with Linda Carter, an eyewitness to the horrific ten car pileup ① **that occurred** earlier this morning on I- ② **87**. Ma'am can you tell us ③ **what you** saw?

> こちら WKYT ニュースのトム・ソーヤーです。私はここにリンダ・カーターといっしょに立っていますが、彼女は今朝早く、高速 87 号線で起こった恐ろしい車 10 台の衝突事故の目撃者です。失礼ですが、あなたが見たことをお話しいただけますか？
>
> ＊ eyewitness to ... 「…の目撃者」 pileup 「玉突き衝突事故」
>   ma'am 「お嬢さま；奥さま」女性へのていねいな呼びかけ。

F: Yeah, um ... sure. I was in my car on the on ramp to the ④ **interstate** when a semi-truck in the far lane seemed to lose control. It came straight across two other lanes, plowing into cars along the way, before ⑤ **hitting** the cement divider and coming to a stop ⑥ **right in front of** me. Other cars were crashing into each other as they tried to ⑦ **get out of** the way. I was terrified. My adrenaline is still pumping. If I had ⑧ **gotten onto** the highway a few seconds earlier I would have been right ⑨ **in the** middle of everything. I still can't believe … I can't believe I came through it without getting hit myself.

> ええ、わかりました。遠くのレーンにいた大型トラックがコントロールを失ったように見えたとき、私は高速の入り口で自分の車の中にいました。トラックは、道路沿いにいた車に衝突しながら、まっすぐにほかのふたつのレーンを横切ってきました。そして、セメントの仕切りにぶつかって、まさに私の目の前で止まったんです。避けようとしたほかの自動車は互いにぶつかり合っていました。恐怖でした。まだ（アドレナリンがカラダにあふれて）どきどきしてます。あと数秒早く高速に乗っていたら、私はまさにこの事故に巻き込まれていたでしょう。いまだに信じられません…自分がぶつかられずに切り抜けられたことが信じられないんです。
>
> * ramp「高速道路の出入り口」 interstate「州間幹線道路」
> plow into ...「(車などが) …に衝突する」 divider「仕切り」
> get out of the way「避ける；道を空ける」 terrified「ぞっとした；おびえた」
> pump「あふれ出る；上下に早く動く」 be in the middle of ...「…の真っただ中にいる」
> come through ...「…を切り抜ける」

M: I'm sure that must have been terrifying, indeed. Were you still on the scene when the first responders arrived?

> 確かに恐ろしいことだったに違いありませんね。最初の救援が駆けつけたとき、まだ現場にいたのですか？
>
> * first responder「最初の応答者」ここでは、救助や事故処理の隊などを指す。

F: Of course. I couldn't ⑩ **get around** the wreckage of the other vehicles. I saw the paramedics save a pregnant woman by ⑪ **getting** her ⑫ **out of** her burning car. It was just horrible. I heard that the driver of the truck that caused the accident ⑬ **had a heart attack** behind the wheel and that's why he lost control, ⑭ **but I'm** not really sure. Judging by the way the truck careened out of control that would make sense. Either ⑮ **that or** he fell asleep behind the wheel. Either way, it was a horrible horrible scene. I'm sure I'll be having nightmares ⑯ **about it** for a long time.

> もちろんです。ほかの車の残骸を避けて通ることはできませんでした。救急救命隊が燃えさかる車の中から妊婦さんを助け出すのを見ました。ただただ恐ろしい光景でした。事故を起こしたトラック運転手は、運転席で心臓発作を起こし、それで彼はコントロールを失ったのだと聞きましたが、はっきりとはわかりません。トラックが不安定に疾走してコントロールを失った様子から判断すれば、つじつまは合うのでしょう。それかあるいは、運転中に眠ってしまったか。いずれにせよ、恐ろしい恐ろしい光景でした。きっと長い間事故の悪夢を見続けるでしょう。
>
> ＊ get around「避けて通る；ぐるっと回っていく」 wreckage「壊れたものの残骸」
>   paramedics「救急救命隊」 behind the wheel「運転席で」
>   careen「(衝突などで) 不安定に方向を変えながら疾走する」
>   Either that or ...「それか、あるいは…」 Either way ...「いずれにせよ…」

M: There you ⑰ **have it**. Ms. Carter, thank you for sharing what you saw with us. We'll have an update on the cause of the accident and the rest of the story on our 11 o'clock broadcast.

> ということです。カーターさん、ご覧になったことを私たちにお伝えいただきありがとうございました。事故原因に関しての最新情報と事故の詳細は11時の放送で更新いたします。
>
> ＊ There you have it.「そういうことです；ということです」

事故の目撃者のインタビュー

Stage 3 英文トランスクリプション

インタビュー全体を英文の原稿で確認しながらCDで耳慣らししよう！ その上で、インタビューを聴きながら、まだできていない部分の穴埋めに再チャレンジしよう。

M: Tom Sawyer here with WKYT news. I'm standing here with Linda Carter, an eyewitness to the horrific ten car pileup ① **that occurred** earlier this morning on I- ② **87**. Ma'am can you tell us ③ **what you** saw?

F: Yeah, um ... sure. I was in my car on the on ramp to the ④ **interstate** when a semi-truck in the far lane seemed to lose control. It came straight across two other lanes, plowing into cars along the way, before ⑤ **hitting** the cement divider and coming to a stop ⑥ **right in front of** me. Other cars were crashing into each other as they tried to ⑦ **get out of** the way. I was terrified. My adrenaline is still pumping. If I had ⑧ **gotten onto** the highway a few seconds earlier I would have been right ⑨ **in the** middle of everything. I still can't believe ... I can't believe I came through it without getting hit myself.

M: I'm sure that must have been terrifying, indeed. Were you still on the scene when the first responders arrived?

F: Of course. I couldn't ⑩ **get around** the wreckage of the other vehicles. I saw the paramedics save a pregnant woman by ⑪ **getting** her ⑫ **out of** her burning car. It was just horrible. I heard that the driver of the truck that caused the accident ⑬ **had a heart attack** behind the wheel and that's why he lost control, ⑭ **but I'm** not really sure. Judging by the way the truck careened out of control that would make sense. Either ⑮ **that or** he fell asleep behind the wheel. Either way, it was a horrible horrible scene. I'm sure I'll be having nightmares ⑯ **about it** for a long time.

M: There you ⑰ **have it**. Ms. Carter, thank you for sharing what you saw with us. We'll have an update on the cause of the accident and the rest of the story on our 11 o'clock broadcast.

🎧 Stage 4 🔊 音声変化をチェック

まとめとして、穴埋め部分の音声変化の特徴を**スロー・スピード**と**ナチュラル・スピード**で確認しよう。下記に示したカタカナ表記で音声変化を確認して、もう一度インタビューを聴き直してみよう。発音変化のルールは適宜復習しよう。

---

❶ that occurred   ザット・オクゥード   ▶ ザッド [ロ] クゥード
☞ 連結部で破裂音 [t] の弾音化が起こる。

❷ 87   エイティーセヴン   ▶ エイディ [リ] ーセヴン
☞ eighty の破裂音 [t] が弾音化する。

❸ what you   ワット・ユー   ▶ ワッチュー
☞ [t] + [j] の部分で音が混じり合い、[チュ] に近い音に変化する。

❹ interstate   インターステイト   ▶ イナーステイト
☞ [nt] で [t] 音の脱落が生じる。

❺ hitting   ヒッティング   ▶ ヒッディ [リ] ン (グ)
☞ 破裂音 [t] が弾音化する。末尾の [g] 音も脱落しやすい。

❻ right in front of   ライト・イン・フラント・アヴ   ▶ ライディ [リ] ンフラナ (ヴ)
☞ right in の連結部で破裂音 [t] の弾音化が起こる。front of では [t] が脱落して連結。末尾の [v] 音が脱落することも多い。

❼ get out of   ゲット・アウト・アヴ   ▶ ゲッダ [ラ] ウダ [ラ] (ヴ)
☞ 3語が連結。2カ所の連結部で破裂音 [t] の弾音化が起こる。末尾の [v] 音が脱落することも多い。

❽ gotten onto   ガットゥン・オントゥー   ▶ ガッンンオンドゥ [ル] ー
☞ gotten の [tn] の [t] 音が声門閉鎖音化する。onto の [t] 音が弾音化する。

❾ in the   イン・ザ   ▶ イナ
☞ [n] + [ð] が [n] 音に変化する。

❿ get around   ゲット・アラウンド   ▶ ゲッダ [ラ] ラウン (ド)
☞ 連結部で [t] 音が弾音化する。末尾の [d] 音が脱落することもある。

⓫ getting   ゲッティング   ▶ ゲッディ [リ] ン (グ)
☞ [t] 音が弾音化する。末尾の [g] 音が脱落することもある。

⓬ out of   アウト・アヴ   ▶ アウダ [ラ] (ヴ)
☞ 連結部で [t] 音が弾音化する。末尾の [v] 音が脱落することもある。

⓭ had a heart attack   ハッド・ア・ハート・アタック   ▶ ハッダ [ラ] ハーダ [ラ] タック
☞ had a と heart attack の連結部のそれぞれで、破裂音 [d] [t] が弾音化する。

⓮ but I'm   バット・アイム   ▶ バッダ [ラ] イム
☞ 連結部で [t] 音が弾音化する。

⓯ that or   ザット・オー   ▶ ザッド [ロ] ー
☞ 連結部で [t] 音が弾音化する。

⓰ about it   アバウト・イット   ▶ アバウディ [リ] ッ (ト)
☞ 連結部で破裂音 [t] の弾音化が起こる。末尾の [t] 音も脱落しやすい。

⓱ have it   ハヴ・イット   ▶ ハヴィッ (ト)
☞ 2語が連結。末尾の [t] 音も脱落しやすい。

INTERVIEW WITH AN OLYMPIC ATHLETE

Unit 10　オリンピック選手のインタビュー

🎧 Stage 1 🔊 穴埋め インタビュー・リスニング

音声変化に注意してCDでインタビューを聴きながら空欄部分を埋めてみよう。CDのナチュラル音声での聴き取りが難しいときは、次のトラックに収録されたスロー音声で聴いてみよう。

F: ① _____ _____ clock ticking towards the summer Olympics of 2016, we ② _____ _____ with two-time Olympic gold medalist and swimmer Marc Shultz to ③ _____ _____ _____ of what being an Olympian means. Take a look.
Marc, give us an idea of a day in the life of a training athlete.

M: My days start at four a.m. I have a light breakfast and then a two-hour cardio workout. After ④ _____ _____ time for my regular breakfast which is usually a five-egg omelet with sausage, two ham sandwiches, a salad and two twelve ounce protein shakes. My regimen continues with four hours in the pool ⑤ _____ _____ afternoon, and my coach ⑥ _____ _____ study films of previous events and other swimmers. I ⑦ _____ _____ college from five to eight during the week. Sunday is my only day off. Even I ⑧ _____ take a break once in a while!

F: What is your take on some athletes boycotting the Olympics to make a ⑨ _____ statement?

M: To be honest with you, I think that's sad. It's their prerogative, of course, but we train so hard to first make the team, and ⑩ _____ _____ realize our dream of medaling. I wouldn't give ⑪ _____ _____ for anything. I feel the Olympics should be regarded as the one time ⑫ _____ around the world can come together for something other than politics. To me that's the true spirit of ⑬ _____ _____ Olympics represents.

F: Having already been in two previous Olympics this is your twelfth year of competition. You are one of the older ⑭ _____ in the competition. Do you think this will be your last appearance?

M: Down the road ... maybe. ⑮ _____ _____ I feel that I'm ⑯ _____ _____ best shape I've ever been. I'm focused solely on the next event. After that, depending on my performance and conditioning, I will certainly have that conversation with myself, ⑰ _____ _____ _____ _____.

Stage 2 インタビュー解説

日本語訳と、解説を参照しながら、インタビュー内容を確認しよう。そのあとで、Stage1の穴埋めに再チャレンジしてみよう。

F: ① **With the** clock ticking towards the summer Olympics of 2016, we ② **sat down** with two-time Olympic gold medalist and swimmer Marc Shultz to ③ **get an idea** of what being an Olympian means. Take a look.
Marc, give us an idea of a day in the life of a training athlete.

> 2016年の夏のオリンピックを目前に控え、私たちは二度のオリンピックの金メダリスト水泳選手であるマーク・シュルツと席をともにして、オリンピック選手になるとはどういうことなのかを考えました。ご覧ください。
> マーク、トレーニング選手の生活の一日がどんなものか教えてもらえますか。
>
> ＊ with the clock ticking towards ...「…が差し迫って；目前に控えて」
>   a day in the life of ...「…の生活の中の一日」

M: My days start at four a.m. I have a light breakfast and then a two-hour cardio workout. After ④ **that it's** time for my regular breakfast which is usually a five-egg omelet with sausage, two ham sandwiches, a salad and two twelve ounce protein shakes. My regimen continues with four hours in the pool ⑤ **in the** afternoon, and my coach ⑥ **and I** study films of previous events and other swimmers. I ⑦ **go to** college from five to eight during the week. Sunday is my only day off. Even I ⑧ **gotta** take a break once in a while!

> 僕の一日は、午前 4 時にスタートします。軽い朝食を取り、2 時間の有酸素運動トレーニングをします。そのあとは、通常の朝食の時間です。たいてい、卵 5 つとソーセージを入れたオムレツ、ハムサンドふたつ、サラダと 12 オンスのプロテイン・シェイクを 2 本取ります。私の規則的なトレーニング・プランは、午後の 4 時間のプールへと続きます。さらに、コーチと私は過去の試合やほかの水泳選手の映像の研究も行います。平日の 5 時から 8 時までは大学へ通います。日曜だけはオフです。私だってたまには休息が必要なんですよ！
>
> * cardio workout「有酸素運動」　ounce「オンス」1 オンスは約 29.57 ml。
>   regimen「決められたプラン」

F: What is your take on some athletes boycotting the Olympics to make a ⑨ **political** statement?

> 政治的な主張のために、オリンピックのボイコットを行っているアスリートについてはどう思われますか？
>
> * boycott「ボイコットする」

M: To be honest with you, I think that's sad. It's their prerogative, of course, but we train so hard to first make the team, and ⑩ **then to** realize our dream of medaling. I wouldn't give ⑪ **that up** for anything. I feel the Olympics should be regarded as the one time ⑫ **countries** around the world can come together for something other than politics. To me that's the true spirit of ⑬ **what the** Olympics represents.

> 正直なところ、悲しいことだと思います。もちろん、それは彼らの特権ではありますが、私たちは、まずはチームに入るため、そしてメダル獲得の夢を実現するために非常に懸命にト

レーニングしているんです。僕には、それをなにと引き替えにもあきらめることはできません。オリンピックは、政治以外のことで世界中の国々がひとつに集まることができるひとときとして考えられるべきだと感じています。私にとっては、それこそがオリンピックが象徴するほんとうの精神なのです。

---

* prerogative「特権」 make the team「チームに入る」 realize「実現する」
 be regarded as ...「…と考えられる；…と評価される」 represent「象徴する」

F: Having already been in two previous Olympics this is your twelfth year of competition. You are one of the older ⑭ **competitors** in the competition. Do you think this will be your last appearance?

すでに前回、前々回とオリンピックに出場されていますから、今回があなたの 12 年目の競技に当たりますね。大会でも年齢が高い選手のおひとりです。これがあなたの最後のオリンピックになると思いますか？

---

* competitor「競技者；出場選手」 appearance「登場；姿を現すこと」

M: Down the road ... maybe. ⑮ **Right now** I feel that I'm ⑯ **in the best shape** I've ever been. I'm focused solely on the next event. After that, depending on my performance and conditioning, I will certainly have that conversation with myself, ⑰ **but not right now**.

そのうち、そうなるかもしれません。いまは、自分がこれまでになく最高の仕上がりだと感じています。今度の大会にだけ集中しているんです。そのあとは、パフォーマンスやコンディションにもよりますが、必ず自分自身と対話するつもりです。しかし、いまはそのときではないんです。

---

* down the road「そのうち」 solely「もっぱら」

オリンピック選手のインタビュー

Stage 3 英文トランスクリプション

インタビュー全体を英文の原稿で確認しながらCDで耳慣らししよう！ その上で、インタビューを聴きながら、まだできていない部分の穴埋めに再チャレンジしよう。

F: ① **With the** clock ticking towards the summer Olympics of 2016, we ② **sat down** with two-time Olympic gold medalist and swimmer Marc Shultz to ③ **get an idea** of what being an Olympian means. Take a look.
Marc, give us an idea of a day in the life of a training athlete.

M: My days start at four a.m. I have a light breakfast and then a two-hour cardio workout. After ④ **that it's** time for my regular breakfast which is usually a five-egg omelet with sausage, two ham sandwiches, a salad and two twelve ounce protein shakes. My regimen continues with four hours in the pool ⑤ **in the** afternoon, and my coach ⑥ **and I** study films of previous events and other swimmers. I ⑦ **go to** college from five to eight during the week. Sunday is my only day off. Even I ⑧ **gotta** take a break once in a while!

F: What is your take on some athletes boycotting the Olympics to make a ⑨ **political** statement?

M: To be honest with you, I think that's sad. It's their prerogative, of course, but we train so hard to first make the team, and ⑩ **then to** realize our dream of medaling. I wouldn't give ⑪ **that up** for anything. I feel the Olympics should be regarded as the one time ⑫ **countries** around the world can come together for something other than politics. To me that's the true spirit of ⑬ **what the** Olympics represents.

F: Having already been in two previous Olympics this is your twelfth year of competition. You are one of the older ⑭ **competitors** in the competition. Do you think this will be your last appearance?

M: Down the road ... maybe. ⑮ **Right now** I feel that I'm ⑯ **in the** best shape I've ever been. I'm focused solely on the next event. After that, depending on my performance and conditioning, I will certainly have that conversation with myself, ⑰ **but not right now.**

Stage 4 ◀)) 音声変化をチェック

まとめとして、穴埋め部分の音声変化の特徴を**スロー・スピード**と**ナチュラル・スピード**で確認しよう。下記に示したカタカナ表記で音声変化を確認して、もう一度インタビューを聴き直してみよう。発音変化のルールは適宜復習しよう。

❶ **With the**　　　　　　　ウィズ・ザ　　　　　　　▶ ウィッ＿ザ
　☞ 同じ子音の連続で片方が脱落する。

❷ **sat down**　　　　　　　サット・ダウン　　　　　　▶ サッ＿ダウン
　☞ 破裂音の連続で片方が脱落する。

❸ **get an idea**　　　　　　ゲット・アン・アイディア　　▶ ゲッダ［ラ］ナイディア
　☞ get an の連結部で［t］音が弾音化する。an idea も連結。

❹ **that it's**　　　　　　　ザット・イッツ　　　　　　▶ ザッディ［リ］ッツ
　☞ 連結部で破裂音［t］の弾音化が生じる。

❺ **in the**　　　　　　　　イン・ズィ　　　　　　　　▶ イニ
　☞ ［n］＋［ð］が［n］音に変化する。

❻ **and I**　　　　　　　　アンド・アイ　　　　　　　▶ アナイ
　☞ 破裂音［d］が脱落しつつ 2 語が連結する。

❼ **go to**　　　　　　　　ゴウ・トゥー　　　　　　　▶ ゴウドゥ［ル］ー
　☞ to の破裂音［t］が弾音化する。

❽ **gotta**　　　　　　　　ガッタ　　　　　　　　　　▶ ガッダ［ラ］
　☞ 破裂音［t］が弾音化する。

❾ **political**　　　　　　　パリティカゥ　　　　　　　▶ パリディ［リ］カゥ
　☞ 破裂音［t］が弾音化する。

❿ **then to**　　　　　　　ゼン・トゥー　　　　　　　▶ ゼヌー
　☞ then が弱化した to［u］に連結する。

⓫ **that up**　　　　　　　ザット・アップ　　　　　　▶ ザッダ［ラ］ップ
　☞ 連結部で破裂音［t］の弾音化が生じる。

⓬ **countries**　　　　　　カントゥリーズ　　　　　　▶ カンチュリーズ
　☞ ［tr］部分の［t］音が［チュ］に近い音に変化する。

⓭ **what the**　　　　　　ワット・ザ　　　　　　　　▶ ワッ＿ザ
　☞ 破裂音［t］が脱落する。

⓮ **competitors**　　　　　カムペティターズ　　　　　▶ カムペディ［リ］ダ［ラ］ーズ
　☞ 2 カ所の破裂音［t］が弾音化する。

⓯ **Right now**　　　　　　ライト・ナウ　　　　　　　▶ ライッ＿ナウ
　☞ 破裂音［t］が脱落する。

⓰ **in the**　　　　　　　　イン・ザ　　　　　　　　　▶ イナ
　☞ ［n］＋［ð］が［n］音に変化する。

⓱ **but not right now**　　バット・ナット・ライト・ナウ　▶ バッ＿ナッ＿ライッ＿ナウ
　☞ but not right 3 語の末尾で、それぞれ破裂音［t］が脱落する。

INTERVIEW WITH AN INVENTOR

Unit 11 発明家のインタビュー

Stage 1 穴埋め インタビュー・リスニング

音声変化に注意してCDでインタビューを聴きながら空欄部分を埋めてみよう。CDのナチュラル音声での聴き取りが難しいときは、次のトラックに収録されたスロー音声で聴いてみよう。

F: Tonight we have Mr. Tom Welling with us in the studio. Mr. Welling is the CEO of GRILLMATES LLC and inventor of the GRILLMATE MAT. Mr. Welling ... welcome. Tell us how you came up ① _____ _____ idea for the GRILLMATE MAT.

M: Thanks for having me Betty. Well ... ah ... ② _____ _____ started about two years ago. I always liked grilling and my friends and I would often ③ _____ _____ and cookout either at home or at the park. And ... as I'm sure you know ... cleaning up was always a pain. Or, when using a grill in the park ④ _____ _____ often covered with the burnt remains of ⑤ _____ the last person using it cooked. That's when it hit me ⑥ _____ _____ we had something we could put over the grill plate to cook on it would make everything easier. I ⑦ _____ _____ with another friend of mine — who is now my business partner — and we spent about six months trying out different materials until we hit on the right one.

F: ⑧ _____ _____ some of the other benefits of the GRILLMATE MAT?

M: For ⑨ _____ it is a non-stick material. So ⑩ _____ you're grilling won't stick to it, which makes cooking ⑪ _____ _____ a breeze. It's also dishwasher-safe, so when you're done grilling you just ⑫ _____ _____ _____, ⑬ _____ _____ _____ the dishwasher and presto — it's clean.

Another great aspect of its design is even though it is a mat, you still get perfect grill marks on the food, so you still ⑭ _____ _____ grilled flavor and appearance. Of course, when you use the GRILLMATE MAT food never falls into the grill, no ⑮ _____ how small or what shape the food is.

F: How many have you sold worldwide?

M: We've sold over two million units ⑯ _____ _____ last six months. Right now we are only selling domestically, but we expect to be shipping ⑰ _____ within the next month or two. For more information, your viewers can visit our website at www.grillmatemat.com.

F: That's incredible. Thank you for being here and all the best of success to you.

M: Thanks, Betty.

Stage 2 インタビュー解説

日本語訳と、解説を参照しながら、インタビュー内容を確認しよう。そのあとで、Stage1の穴埋めに再チャレンジしてみよう。

F: Tonight we have Mr. Tom Welling with us in the studio. Mr. Welling is the CEO of GRILLMATES LLC and inventor of the GRILLMATE MAT. Mr. Welling … welcome. Tell us how you came up ① **with the** idea for the GRILLMATE MAT.

> 今夜はトム・ウェリング氏をスタジオにお招きしています。ウェリング氏はグリルメイツ有限責任会社のCEOでグリルメイト・マットの発明者でもあります。ウェリングさん、ようこそ。どのようにグリルメイト・マットのアイデアを思いついたのか、私たちに教えてもらえますか？
>
> ＊ CEO = chief executive officer「最高経営責任者」　LLC「有限責任会社」　inventor「発明家」
>   come up with …「…を思いつく；考えつく」

M: Thanks for having me Betty. Well … ah … ② **it all** started about two years ago. I always liked grilling and my friends and I would often

③ **get together** and cookout either at home or at the park. And … as I'm sure you know … cleaning up was always a pain. Or, when using a grill in the park ④ **it was** often covered with the burnt remains of ⑤ **whatever** the last person using it cooked. That's when it hit me ⑥ **that if** we had something we could put over the grill plate to cook on it would make everything easier. I ⑦ **got together** with another friend of mine — who is now my business partner — and we spent about six months trying out different materials until we hit on the right one.

> ご招待いただき感謝します、ベティー。ええ…ああ…すべては約 2 年前に始まりました。私はグリル料理がずっと大好きでして、友人たちとよく集まっては、家や公園でバーベキューをしていたんです。で、みなさんも、きっとおわかりだと思いますが、後片付けがいつもひと苦労だったんです。あるいは、公園でグリルを使うときは、前の人の料理の焼け焦げで覆われていることがよくあったんです。そのとき、グリル・プレートの上に載せて、上で料理できるものがあれば、すべてがもっと便利になると思いついたんですよ。いまはビジネスパートナーである別の友人といっしょになって、約 6 カ月をかけ、ぴったりなものにたどり着くまで、さまざまな素材を試したのです。
>
> * pain「苦労；苦痛」 burnt remains「焼け残り；燃えかす」
>   using it「それを使いながら」挿入的に用いられたフレーズ。
>   hit someone「（考え・アイデアなどが）…に思い浮かぶ」 get together「いっしょになる」
>   try out「試す；試験的に使ってみる」 material「素材」 hit on ...「…に出くわす」

F: ⑧ **What are** some of the other benefits of the GRILLMATE MAT?

> グリルメイト・マットはほかにはどんな利点がありますか？
>
> * benefit「利点；恩恵」

M: For ⑨ **starters** it is a non-stick material. So ⑩ **whatever** you're grilling won't stick to it, which makes cooking ⑪ **on it** a breeze. It's also dishwasher-safe, so when you're done grilling you just ⑫ **rinse it off**, ⑬ **put it in** the dishwasher and presto — it's clean. Another great aspect of its design is even though it is a mat, you still get perfect grill marks on the food, so you still ⑭ **get that** grilled flavor and appearance. Of course, when you use the GRILLMATE MAT food never falls into the grill, no ⑮ **matter** how small or what shape the food is.

まず、マットはくっつかない素材です。ですから、焼いているものがなんであってもくっつきません。なので、マットの上での料理が容易になるんです。また、食器洗い器に入れても安全ですから、グリルを終えたら洗い流して食洗機に入れるだけ—さっときれいになっちゃうんです。設計上もうひとつのすばらしい点は、マットであるにもかかわらず、食材に完璧な焼き目が入れられることです。なので、あの網焼きの香りと外見が手に入るんです。もちろん、グリルメイト・マットを使えば、食材がグリルの中に落ちることもありません。食材がどんなに小さくても、どんな形をしていてもです。

＊ breeze「容易なこと；楽なこと」 rinse「すすぐ」 presto「さっと；パッと；瞬時に」
design「設計；デザイン」 grill marks「焼き目」

F: How many have you sold worldwide?

世界中でどのくらいの数を販売してきたのでしょう？

M: We've sold over two million units ⑯ **in the** last six months. Right now we are only selling domestically, but we expect to be shipping ⑰ **internationally** within the next month or two. For more information, your viewers can visit our website at www.grillmatemat.com.

この6カ月で、2百万本以上を販売しました。現在、弊社では国内での販売しかしていませんが、1、2カ月以内には、国際的に出荷する予定です。さらに情報が必要なら、視聴者のみなさんには、弊社のウェブサイト www.grillmatemat.com を訪問してもらえますよ。

＊ domestically「国内で」 internationally「国際的に」

F: That's incredible. Thank you for being here and all the best of success to you.

それは、すばらしいですね。お越しいただきありがとうございます。御社の大成功を祈っています。

M: Thanks, Betty.

ありがとう、ベティー。

発明家のインタビュー

Stage 3 英文トランスクリプション

インタビュー全体を英文の原稿で確認しながらCDで耳慣らししよう！ その上で、インタビューを聴きながら、まだできていない部分の穴埋めに再チャレンジしよう。

F: Tonight we have Mr. Tom Welling with us in the studio. Mr. Welling is the CEO of GRILLMATES LLC and inventor of the GRILLMATE MAT. Mr. Welling ... welcome. Tell us how you came up ① **with the** idea for the GRILLMATE MAT.

M: Thanks for having me Betty. Well ... ah ... ② **it all** started about two years ago. I always liked grilling and my friends and I would often ③ **get together** and cookout either at home or at the park. And ... as I'm sure you know ... cleaning up was always a pain. Or, when using a grill in the park ④ **it was** often covered with the burnt remains of ⑤ **whatever** the last person using it cooked. That's when it hit me ⑥ **that if** we had something we could put over the grill plate to cook on it would make everything easier. I ⑦ **got together** with another friend of mine — who is now my business partner — and we spent about six months trying out different materials until we hit on the right one.

F: ⑧ **What are** some of the other benefits of the GRILLMATE MAT?

M: For ⑨ **starters** it is a non-stick material. So ⑩ **whatever** you're grilling won't stick to it, which makes cooking ⑪ **on it** a breeze. It's also dishwasher-safe, so when you're done grilling you just ⑫ **rinse it off**, ⑬ **put it in** the dishwasher and presto — it's clean. Another great aspect of its design is even though it is a mat, you still get perfect grill marks on the food, so you still ⑭ **get that** grilled flavor and appearance. Of course, when you use the GRILLMATE MAT food never falls into the grill, no ⑮ **matter** how small or what shape the food is.

F: How many have you sold worldwide?

M: We've sold over two million units ⑯ **in the** last six months. Right now we are only selling domestically, but we expect to be shipping ⑰ **internationally** within the next month or two. For more information, your viewers can visit our website at www.grillmatemat.com.

F: That's incredible. Thank you for being here and all the best of success to you.

M: Thanks, Betty.

🎲 Stage 4 🔊 音声変化をチェック

まとめとして、穴埋め部分の音声変化の特徴を**スロー・スピード**と**ナチュラル・スピード**で確認しよう。下記に示したカタカナ表記で音声変化を確認して、もう一度インタビューを聴き直してみよう。発音変化のルールは適宜復習しよう。

---

❶ with the   ウィズ・ズィ   ▶ ウィッ__ズィ
☞ [ð] 音の連続で片方が脱落する。

❷ it all   イット・オーゥ   ▶ イッド [ロ] ーゥ
☞ 連結部で [t] 音が弾音化する。

❸ get together   ゲット・トゥギャザー   ▶ ゲッ__トゥギャザー
☞ 破裂音 [t] の連続で片方が脱落する。

❹ it was   イット・ワズ   ▶ イッ__ワズ
☞ it の破裂音 [t] が脱落する。

❺ whatever   ワッテヴァー   ▶ ワッデ [レ] ヴァー
☞ 破裂音 [t] が弾音化する。

❻ that if   ザット・イフ   ▶ ザッディ [リ] フ
☞ 連結部で破裂音 [t] の弾音化が起こる。

❼ got together   ガット・トゥギャザー   ▶ ガッ__トゥギャザー
☞ 破裂音 [t] の連続で片方が脱落する。

❽ What are   ワット・アー   ▶ ワッダ [ラ] ー
☞ 連結部で破裂音 [t] の弾音化が起こる。

❾ starters   スターターズ   ▶ スターダ [ラ] ーズ
☞ 破裂音 [t] の弾音化が起こる。

❿ whatever   ワッテヴァー   ▶ ワッデ [レ] ヴァー
☞ 破裂音 [t] が弾音化する。

⓫ on it   オン・イット   ▶ オニッ (ト)
☞ 2 語が連結。末尾の [t] 音も脱落しやすい。

⓬ rinse it off   リンス・イット・オフ   ▶ リンスィッド [ロ] フ
☞ 3 語が連結。it の破裂音 [t] の弾音化が起こる。

⓭ put it in   プット・イット・イン   ▶ プッディ [リ] ッディ [リ] ン
☞ 3 語が連結。2 カ所の連結部で破裂音 [t] の弾音化が起こる。

⓮ get that   ゲット・ザット   ▶ ゲッ__ザッ (ト)
☞ get の破裂音 [t] が脱落する。that 末尾の [t] 音も脱落しやすい。

⓯ matter   マター   ▶ マダ [ラ] ー
☞ 破裂音 [t] の弾音化が起こる。

⓰ in the   イン・ザ   ▶ イナ
☞ [n] + [ð] が [n] 音に変化する。

⓱ internationally   インターナショナリー   ▶ イナナショナリー
☞ [nt] で [t] 音の脱落が生じる。

🎤 発明家のインタビュー

INTERVIEW WITH A FAMOUS ARCHITECT

Unit 12 有名建築家のインタビュー

Stage 1 穴埋めインタビュー・リスニング

音声変化に注意してCDでインタビューを聴きながら空欄部分を埋めてみよう。CDのナチュラル音声での聴き取りが難しいときは、次のトラックに収録されたスロー音声で聴いてみよう。

F: With the recent completion of the new One World Trade Center in NYC, our feature tonight focuses on skyscrapers ① _____ under construction that will eclipse this newest modern marvel. With us is Steve Ryder, architect and designer of the Chicago Spire. Steve what is the ② _____ of your current project?

M: The Chicago Spire has been on the drawing board for more than a decade. Construction ③ _____ _____ 2008 but was stalled until just recently due to the economic downturn and need for more investment. The proposed height of the building is two thousand feet, which would surpass the OWTC which stands at one thousand seven hundred and ④ _____-six feet. The unique thing ⑤ _____ _____ project is that the finished tower will have one hundred and fifty floors, far more than any other skyscraper ever built.

F: As chief designer for the Spire, ⑥ _____ _____ your biggest challenge?

M: Chicago is known as the "Windy ⑦ _____," and when you're taking about buildings this tall, wind shear is a huge challenge. We accommodated for that by changing the shape of the corners of the building and orienting the building to "flow" ⑧ _____ _____ wind. Another hurdle for buildings like this is the placement of the elevators. I studied some of the largest buildings

⑨ _____ _____ world, and came up with an innovative design that spaces the elevator banks out to provide more ⑩ _____ for the ⑪ _____.

F: Your design firm just ⑫ _____ work in a completely new direction. Tell us about ⑬ _____ _____ you would.

M: After watching the aftermath of hurricane Katrina, I decided that after the Spire was completed, I ⑭ _____ _____ see if I could design better fabricated temporary shelters for victims of natural disasters like hurricanes, floods ⑮ _____ _____ you. The basic element of these will be semi-truck trailers, which can be quickly ⑯ _____ by rail and then trucked to wherever they are needed. We are working closely with FEMA, and expect to have several models ready for demonstration by the end of ⑰ _____ _____.

Stage 2 インタビュー解説

日本語訳と、解説を参照しながら、インタビュー内容を確認しよう。そのあとで、Stage1の穴埋めに再チャレンジしてみよう。

F: With the recent completion of the new One World Trade Center in NYC, our feature tonight focuses on skyscrapers ① **currently** under construction that will eclipse this newest modern marvel. With us is Steve Ryder, architect and designer of the Chicago Spire. Steve what is the ② **status** of your current project?

> ニューヨークの新しいワン・ワールド・トレード・センターが完成したところですが、今夜、私たちの特集では、この最新の現代の驚異をしのぐ現在建設中の高層ビルにフォーカスを当てます。お招きしたのは、建築家でシカゴ・スパイアーの設計者でもあるスティーヴ・ライダーです。
> スティーヴ、あなたの現在のプロジェクトの状況はどうですか？
>
> ＊ eclipse「しのぐ」 marvel「驚異」 spire「尖塔」

M: The Chicago Spire has been on the drawing board for more than a decade. Construction ③ **started in** 2008 but was stalled until just recently due to the economic downturn and need for more investment. The proposed height of the building is two thousand feet, which would surpass the OWTC which stands at one thousand seven hundred and ④ **seventy**-six feet. The unique thing ⑤ **about our** project is that the finished tower will have one hundred and fifty floors, far more than any other skyscraper ever built.

> シカゴ・スパイアーは、十年以上の間、計画が進められてきました。建設は2008年にスタートしましたが、つい最近まで、不景気と資金不足の問題で中断されていました。提案されたビルの高さは2,000フィートで、これは1,776フィートの高さのOWTCをしのぐことになります。われわれのプロジェクトのユニークさは、完成された塔が150階のフロアをもつことで、これはこれまでのどの高層ビルをも、はるかにしのぐものです。
>
> ＊ on the drawing board「設計中の；計画中の」 be stalled「引き延ばされる；停止される」
>   economic downturn「不景気」 investment「投資」

F: As chief designer for the Spire, ⑥ **what was** your biggest challenge?

> 尖塔のチーフ・デザイナーとして、もっとも困難だったことはなんでしょう？
>
> ＊ challenge「難問；課題」

M: Chicago is known as the "Windy ⑦ **City**," and when you're taking about buildings this tall, wind shear is a huge challenge. We accommodated for that by changing the shape of the corners of the building and orienting the building to "flow" ⑧ **with the** wind. Another hurdle for buildings like this is the placement of the elevators. I studied some of the largest buildings ⑨ **in the** world, and came up with an innovative design that spaces the elevator banks out to provide more ⑩ **stability** for the ⑪ **structure**.

> シカゴは「風の街」として知られていて、この高さのビルの話をする場合、晴天乱流が大きな問題になるのです。われわれは、ビルの角の形を変えて、さらにビルが風を受け流すよ

うに方角を変え晴天乱流に適応させました。こういったビルのもうひとつの障害となるのは、エレベーターの設置です。世界中のもっとも高いビルのいくつかを研究し、構造にさらなる安定をもたらすため、エレベーター群を間隔を置いて配置する革新的な設計を考えました。

* windy「風の強い」 wind shear「晴天乱流」 accommodate for ...「...に合わせる；適応する」
  orient「方角を変える」 space out「広く間隔を置いて設置する」
  elevator bank「エレベーターの列；エレベーター群」 stability「安定」 structure「構造」

F: Your design firm just ⑫ **started** work in a completely new direction. Tell us about ⑬ **that if** you would.

あなたの設計事務所はまったく新しい方向性の仕事を始めたところですよね。よろしければ、お話を聞かせてください。

* design firm「設計事務所」

M: After watching the aftermath of hurricane Katrina, I decided that after the Spire was completed, I ⑭ **wanted to** see if I could design better fabricated temporary shelters for victims of natural disasters like hurricanes, floods ⑮ **what have** you. The basic element of these will be semi-truck trailers, which can be quickly ⑯ **transported** by rail and then trucked to wherever they are needed. We are working closely with FEMA, and expect to have several models ready for demonstration by the end of ⑰ **this year**.

ハリケーン・カトリーナのあとの状態を見てから、決めたんですよ。スパイアーが完成したら、ハリケーンや洪水など自然災害の犠牲者のための組み立て式の仮設シェルターをもっとうまく設計できないものか試してみたいと。シェルターの基本となる構成要素は、大型トレーラーになるでしょう。必要な場所ならどこにでも鉄道とそれからトラックでかんたんに輸送できますから。FEMAと密接に関連して作業を行っていて、今年の終わりまでには、いくつかの試用モデルを用意する予定です。

* aftermath「余波；結果；その後の状態」 fabricated「組み立て式の」
  ... (or) what have you「...など」 element「構成要素」 semi-truck trailer「大型トレーラー」

Stage 3))) 英文トランスクリプション

インタビュー全体を英文の原稿で確認しながらCDで耳慣らししよう！ その上で、インタビューを聴きながら、まだできていない部分の穴埋めに再チャレンジしよう。

F: With the recent completion of the new One World Trade Center in NYC, our feature tonight focuses on skyscrapers ① **currently** under construction that will eclipse this newest modern marvel. With us is Steve Ryder, architect and designer of the Chicago Spire.
Steve what is the ② **status** of your current project?

M: The Chicago Spire has been on the drawing board for more than a decade. Construction ③ **started in** 2008 but was stalled until just recently due to the economic downturn and need for more investment. The proposed height of the building is two thousand feet, which would surpass the OWTC which stands at one thousand seven hundred and ④ **seventy**-six feet. The unique thing ⑤ **about our** project is that the finished tower will have one hundred and fifty floors, far more than any other skyscraper ever built.

F: As chief designer for the Spire, ⑥ **what was** your biggest challenge?

M: Chicago is known as the "Windy ⑦ **City**," and when you're taking about buildings this tall, wind shear is a huge challenge. We accommodated for that by changing the shape of the corners of the building and orienting the building to "flow" ⑧ **with the** wind. Another hurdle for buildings like this is the placement of the elevators. I studied some of the largest buildings ⑨ **in the** world, and came up with an innovative design that spaces the elevator banks out to provide more ⑩ **stability** for the ⑪ **structure**.

F: Your design firm just ⑫ **started** work in a completely new direction. Tell us about ⑬ **that if** you would.

M: After watching the aftermath of hurricane Katrina, I decided that after the Spire was completed, I ⑭ **wanted to** see if I could design better fabricated temporary shelters for victims of natural disasters like hurricanes, floods ⑮ **what have** you. The basic element of these will be semi-truck trailers, which can be quickly ⑯ **transported** by rail and then trucked to wherever they are needed. We are working closely with FEMA, and expect to have several models ready for demonstration by the end of ⑰ **this year**.

Stage 4 音声変化をチェック

まとめとして、穴埋め部分の音声変化の特徴を**スロー・スピード**と**ナチュラル・スピード**で確認しよう。下記に示したカタカナ表記で音声変化を確認して、もう一度インタビューを聴き直してみよう。発音変化のルールは適宜復習しよう。

❶ currently カレントゥリー ▶ カレン_リー
☞ [tl] で [t] 音の脱落が生じる。

❷ status スタータス ▶ スターダ [ラ] ス
☞ 破裂音 [t] が弾音化する。

❸ started in スターティッド・イン ▶ スターディ [リ] ッディ [リ] ン
☞ started の破裂音 [t] が弾音化する。連結部で [d] 音が弾音化することもある。

❹ seventy セヴンティー ▶ セヴニー
☞ [nt] で [t] 音の脱落が生じる。

❺ about our アバウト・アウア ▶ アバウダ [ラ] ウア
☞ 連結部で破裂音 [t] が弾音化する。

❻ what was ワット・ワズ ▶ ワッ_ワズ
☞ 破裂音 [t] の脱落が起こる。

❼ City スィティー ▶ スィディ [リ] ー
☞ 破裂音 [t] の弾音化が起こる。

❽ with the ウィズ・ザ ▶ ウィッ_ザ
☞ [ð] 音の連続で片方が脱落する。

❾ in the イン・ザ ▶ イナ
☞ [n] + [ð] が [n] 音に変化する。

❿ stability スタビリティー ▶ スタビラディ [リ] ー
☞ 破裂音 [t] が弾音化する。

⓫ structure ストゥラクチャー ▶ ストゥラクシャー
☞ 破裂音 [t] の脱落が起こる。

⓬ started スターティッド ▶ スターディ [リ] ッ (ド)
☞ 破裂音 [t] の弾音化が起こる。末尾の [d] 音が脱落することもある。

⓭ that if ザット・イフ ▶ ザッディ [リ] フ
☞ 連結部で破裂音 [t] が弾音化する。

⓮ wanted to ワンティッド・トゥー ▶ ワニッ_トゥー
☞ wanted から破裂音 [t] や [d] が脱落する。

⓯ what have ワット・ハヴ ▶ ワッダ [ラ] ヴ
☞ 連結部で破裂音 [t] が弾音化する。

⓰ transported トゥランスポーティッド ▶ トゥランスポーディ [リ] ッ (ド)
☞ 破裂音 [t] の弾音化が起こる。末尾の [d] 音が脱落することもある。

⓱ this year ズィス・イヤー ▶ ズィシャー
☞ [s] + [j] の部分で音が混じり合い、[シュ] に近い音に変化する。

有名建築家のインタビュー

INTERVIEW WITH A PROFESSIONAL ATHLETE

Unit 13　プロ・アスリートのインタビュー

🎧 Stage 1))) 穴埋め インタビュー・リスニング

音声変化に注意してCDでインタビューを聴きながら空欄部分を埋めてみよう。CDのナチュラル音声での聴き取りが難しいときは、次のトラックに収録されたスロー音声で聴いてみよう。

M: Steve McMahon here with the world number one golfer Stephanie Nichols, who is leading the field here at the LPGA championship, just finishing with a third-round score of 65. Stephie, what were the keys to your success ① _____ _____ today?

F: Well Steve, you know ... this is a course that demands precision. If you ② _____ _____ the ball in the fairway ③ _____ _____ _____ _____ score well. That's the biggest thing. Playing the smart shots and ④ _____ _____ course management is the key. Of course, you have to be aggressive, ⑤ _____ you also have to know when to be patient and play safe shots when necessary. I also came here a few days early and played a few practice rounds ... that really helped.

M: What did you think of the course conditions out there today?

F: The course is in fantastic shape. ⑥ _____ _____ rain we had last night the greens were a ⑦ _____ _____ softer, so depending on the pin placement, you could really shoot ⑧ _____ for the flagstick on some holes. You ⑨ _____ watch out though, because some of these greens are really difficult and if you aren't accurate, they will punish you. You can ⑩ _____ _____ trouble ⑪ _____ _____ _____ with bogey or worse really quick if you're not careful.

82

M: You lead the field by six shots. What is your game plan for tomorrow?

F: I ⑫ _____ a ⑬ _____ _____ with the putter today, ⑭ _____ _____ _____ _____ I feel really confident about my game. I'll probably hit the range or the practice green a little bit before dinner. Then I'll ⑮ _____ _____ _____ _____ good night's sleep and get ready to do ⑯ _____ _____ over again tomorrow. We're forecasted to get some more rain tonight so that may affect the course conditions tomorrow. We'll just have to ⑰ _____ _____ _____.

M: Great playing out there today Stephanie. Thanks for your time.

F: Thank you Steve.

Stage 2 🔊 インタビュー解説

日本語訳と、解説を参照しながら、インタビュー内容を確認しよう。そのあとで、Stage1の穴埋めに再チャレンジしてみよう。

M: Steve McMahon here with the world number one golfer Stephanie Nichols, who is leading the field here at the LPGA championship, just finishing with a third-round score of 65. Stephie, what were the keys to your success ① **out there** today?

> 私、スティーヴ・マクマホンはここで、世界一のゴルファー、ステファニー・ニコラスとごいっしょしています。彼女はここLPGA選手権でトップを走っており、3日目を65のスコアで終えたところです。ステフィー、今日のあなたの成功のカギはなんだったのでしょう?
>
> * LPGA = Ladies Professional Golfers' Association
>   be just finishing = has just finished   key to one's success「成功のカギ」

F: Well Steve, you know ... this is a course that demands precision. If you ② **don't keep** the ball in the fairway ③ **you're not going to**

プロ・アスリートのインタビュー 83

score well. That's the biggest thing. Playing the smart shots and ④ **having good** course management is the key. Of course, you have to be aggressive, ⑤ **but** you also have to know when to be patient and play safe shots when necessary. I also came here a few days early and played a few practice rounds … that really helped.

> はい、スティーヴ、あのですね、ここは正確さを要求されるコースなんです。ボールをフェアウェーにキープしなければ、いいスコアが出せません。それがいちばん大事なことです。スマートなショットを打って、いいコース戦略を立てることがカギになります。もちろん、攻めの姿勢は必要ですが、いつ我慢をして、必要なときに安全なショットを打つかを知っていなければなりません。私は、また、数日前にこちらに来て、数回、練習ラウンドを回りました…それがずいぶんと、助けになりました。
>
> ＊ precision「正確さ」　course management「コース戦略」　aggressive「攻撃的な」
>   patient「我慢強い」　help「役に立つ」

M: What did you think of the course conditions out there today?

> 今日のコースの状態についてはどう思いましたか？
>
> ＊ condition「状態」

F: The course is in fantastic shape. ⑥ **With the** rain we had last night the greens were a ⑦ **little bit** softer, so depending on the pin placement, you could really shoot ⑧ **right** for the flagstick on some holes. You ⑨ **gotta** watch out though, because some of these greens are really difficult and if you aren't accurate, they will punish you. You can ⑩ **get into** trouble ⑪ **and end up** with bogey or worse really quick if you're not careful.

> コースはすばらしい状態です。昨夜降った雨のせいで、グリーンがちょっと柔らかめでしたので、ピンの配置によっては、いくつかのホールでは、ホントにちょうどピン（の旗）をめがけて打つことができたでしょう。ただし、注意が必要です。いくつかのグリーンはとても難しくて、正確さがないと、苦しめられるからです。注意深くしなければ、即、トラブルになって、ボギーやさらに悪いスコアで終わってしまいます。
>
> ＊ shape「状態；様子；調子」　pin placement「ピンの配置；切り方」　flagstick「（ゴルフの）ピン」

> punish「懲らしめる」　end up with ...「結局…で終わる」　bogey「(ゴルフ・スコアの) ボギー」
> really quick「すぐに；即座に」

M: You lead the field by six shots. What is your game plan for tomorrow?

> あなたは、6打差でトップを走っています。明日のゲーム・プランは？

F: I ⑫ **struggled** a ⑬ **little bit** with the putter today, ⑭ **but other than that** I feel really confident about my game. I'll probably hit the range or the practice green a little bit before dinner. Then I'll ⑮ **try to get a** good night's sleep and get ready to do ⑯ **it all** over again tomorrow. We're forecasted to get some more rain tonight so that may affect the course conditions tomorrow. We'll just have to ⑰ **wait and see**.

> 今日は、パターで少し苦しみましたが、それ以外は、自分のゲームにとても自信をもっています。おそらく夕食のちょっと前に、打ちっ放しの練習場かパッティング・グリーンに出るつもりです。それからしっかり睡眠を取って、明日のゲーム再開に備えようと思います。今夜はもうちょっと雨が降る予報ですから、明日のコース状態に影響するかもしれません。様子を見るしかありませんね。
>
> ---
> * struggle「もがく」　other than ...「…以外は」　confident「自信に満ちた」
>   hit the range「打ちっ放しで練習する」
>   do it all over again「もう一度それ (同じこと) をやり直す」　forecast「予報する」
>   affect「影響する」　wait and see「待って様子を見る」

M: Great playing out there today Stephanie. Thanks for your time.

> ステファニー、今日はすばらしいプレーでした。お時間をいただきありがとうございます。

F: Thank you Steve.

> ありがとう、スティーヴ。

Stage 3　英文トランスクリプション

インタビュー全体を英文の原稿で確認しながらCDで耳慣らししよう！　その上で、インタビューを聴きながら、まだできていない部分の穴埋めに再チャレンジしよう。

M: Steve McMahon here with the world number one golfer Stephanie Nichols, who is leading the field here at the LPGA championship, just finishing with a third-round score of 65. Stephie, what were the keys to your success ① **out there** today?

F: Well Steve, you know ... this is a course that demands precision. If you ② **don't keep** the ball in the fairway ③ **you're not going to** score well. That's the biggest thing. Playing the smart shots and ④ **having good** course management is the key. Of course, you have to be aggressive, ⑤ **but** you also have to know when to be patient and play safe shots when necessary. I also came here a few days early and played a few practice rounds ... that really helped.

M: What did you think of the course conditions out there today?

F: The course is in fantastic shape. ⑥ **With the** rain we had last night the greens were a ⑦ **little bit** softer, so depending on the pin placement, you could really shoot ⑧ **right** for the flagstick on some holes. You ⑨ **gotta** watch out though, because some of these greens are really difficult and if you aren't accurate, they will punish you. You can ⑩ **get into** trouble ⑪ **and end up** with bogey or worse really quick if you're not careful.

M: You lead the field by six shots. What is your game plan for tomorrow?

F: I ⑫ **struggled** a ⑬ **little bit** with the putter today, ⑭ **but other than that** I feel really confident about my game. I'll probably hit the range or the practice green a little bit before dinner. Then I'll ⑮ **try to get a** good night's sleep and get ready to do ⑯ **it all** over again tomorrow. We're forecasted to get some more rain tonight so that may affect the course conditions tomorrow. We'll just have to ⑰ **wait and see**.

M: Great playing out there today Stephanie. Thanks for your time.

F: Thank you Steve.

Stage 4))) 音声変化をチェック

まとめとして、穴埋め部分の音声変化の特徴を**スロー・スピード**と**ナチュラル・スピード**で確認しよう。下記に示したカタカナ表記で音声変化を確認して、もう一度インタビューを聴き直してみよう。発音変化のルールは適宜復習しよう。

❶ **out there** アウト・ゼア ▶ アウッ__ゼア
☞ 破裂音 [t] の脱落が起こる。

❷ **don't keep** ドント・キープ ▶ ドン__キープ
☞ 破裂音 [t] が脱落する。

❸ **you're not going to** ユア・ナット・ゴウイング・トゥー ▶ ユアナッ__ゴウイン__トゥー
☞ not の [t] 音、going の [g] 音が脱落する。going to は [ゴウイヌー] という発音になることもある。

❹ **having good** ハヴィング・グッド ▶ ハヴィン__グッ (ド)
☞ 破裂音 [g] の連続で片方が脱落する。末尾の [d] が脱落することもある。

❺ **but** バット ▶ バッ__
☞ 末尾の破裂音 [t] が脱落する。

❻ **With the** ウィズ・ザ ▶ ウィッ__ザ
☞ [ð] 音の連続で片方が脱落する。

❼ **little bit** リトゥゥ・ビット ▶ リドゥ [ル] ゥビッ (ト)
☞ little の [t] 音の弾音化が起こる。bit 末尾の [t] 音の脱落が生じることもある。

❽ **right** ライト ▶ ライッ__
☞ 末尾の破裂音 [t] の脱落が起こる。

❾ **gotta** ガッタ ▶ ガッダ [ラ]
☞ 破裂音 [t] の弾音化が起こる。

❿ **get into** ゲット・イントゥー ▶ ゲッディ [リ] ントゥー
☞ 連結部で [t] 音が弾音化する。

⓫ **and end up** アンド・エンド・アップ ▶ アネンダップ
☞ and の [d] 音が脱落しながら、3 語が連結する。

⓬ **struggled** ストゥラッグゥド ▶ スチュラッグゥド
☞ [tr] 部分の [t] 音が [チュ] に近い音に変化する。

⓭ **little bit** リトゥゥ・ビット ▶ リドゥ [ル] ゥビッ (ト)
☞ little の [t] 音の弾音化が起こる。bit 末尾の [t] 音の脱落が生じることもある。

⓮ **but other than that** バット・アザー・ザン・ザット ▶ バッダ [ラ] ザーザナッ (ト)
☞ but other の連結部で [t] 音が弾音化する。than that の連結部では、[n] + [ð] が [n] 音に変化する。

⓯ **try to get a** トゥライ・トゥー・ゲット・ア ▶ トゥライドゥ [ル] ーゲッダ [ラ]
☞ to の [t] 音が弾音化する。get a の連結部でも [t] 音の弾音化が起こる。

⓰ **it all** イット・オーゥ ▶ イッド [ロ] ーゥ
☞ 連結部で [t] 音の弾音化が起こる。

⓱ **wait and see** ウェイト・アンド・スィー ▶ ウェイッ__アン__スィー
☞ wait と and の末尾で、破裂音 [t] [d] が、それぞれ脱落する。

プロ・アスリートのインタビュー 87

INTERVIEW WITH AN ANIMAL RIGHTS ACTIVIST

Unit 14 動物保護活動家のインタビュー

🎧 Stage 1 🔊 穴埋め インタビュー・リスニング

音声変化に注意してCDでインタビューを聴きながら空欄部分を埋めてみよう。CDのナチュラル音声での聴き取りが難しいときは、次のトラックに収録されたスロー音声で聴いてみよう。

M: This weekend marked the largest Vegan rally in history, with more than ten thousand gathered in Washington DC. We've asked for some input from a keynote speaker ① _____ _____ rally, Jeniffer Holmes. Jeniffer, ② _____ _____ the primary goal of this rally?

F: We're here to raise awareness for and educate people ③ _____ _____ atrocities occurring daily against animals around the world. Our ④ _____ has been brainwashed into ignoring the abuse suffered by animals and inflicted by big business.

M: Tell us a ⑤ _____ about Veganism.

F: People become vegan for a ⑥ _____ of reasons. Some change their lifestyle to improve their health through ⑦ _____ diet, others like me are moved to be vegan to protest the mass killing that ⑧ _____ animal products represents. These are living creatures, they did not ask to be your breakfast, lunch, dinner or clothing.

M: I must say I saw many people at the rally wearing leather shoes. Isn't ⑨ _____ _____ double standard?

F: First off I would say ⑩ _____ _____ _____ more likely you saw vinyl or some other synthetic imitation. However, people aren't born vegan, they convert to that lifestyle ⑪ _____

_____ times ⑫ _____ _____ lives. They may already have leather shoes, for example. I often tell them ⑬ _____ _____ foolish to throw away a pair of shoes, because the damage has already been done. The animal is dead. They can simply wear them out and not buy another pair.

M: How ⑭ _____ _____ rate the success of this rally?

F: Look ... there's no doubt we are facing a huge uphill ⑮ _____. Societies around the world have been indoctrinated to use animal products and not even think ⑯ _____ _____ source. The whole invention of words like leather, bacon, steak etc., is intended to take attention away from the fact that these are living creatures. ⑰ _____ _____ movement is growing, and the more people who take up the cause the more our voices will be heard.

Stage 2 インタビュー解説

日本語訳と、解説を参照しながら、インタビュー内容を確認しよう。そのあとで、Stage1の穴埋めに再チャレンジしてみよう。

M: This weekend marked the largest Vegan rally in history, with more than ten thousand gathered in Washington DC. We've asked for some input from a keynote speaker ① **at the** rally, Jeniffer Holmes. Jeniffer, ② **what is** the primary goal of this rally?

> この週末は史上最大の菜食主義者の集会が行われ、1万人以上の人々がワシントンDCに結集しました。私たちは、集会で基調演説を行ったジェニファー・ホームズに情報の提供をお願いしました。ジェニファー、この集会の主目的はなんでしょうか？
>
> * mark「(記念すべき事柄などが) …となる；…を記録する；…がある」 rally「集会」
>   input「情報提供」 keynote「基調方針」 primary goal「主要目標」

F: We're here to raise awareness for and educate people ③ **about the** atrocities occurring daily against animals around the world. Our ④ **society** has been brainwashed into ignoring the abuse suffered by animals and inflicted by big business.

> 世界中で日々動物に対して行われている残虐な行為についての認知度を高め、人々を教育するために、われわれはここに集まっています。私たちの社会は、動物に対して大企業によって加えられている虐待を見過ごすように洗脳されてきたのです。
>
> ＊ raise awareness for ...「…に対する認知度を高める」 atrocity「残虐な行為」
>   brainwash「洗脳する」 ignore「無視する；見ないふりをする」 abuse「虐待」 suffer「被る」
>   inflict「苦痛などを加える」 big business「大企業」

M: Tell us a ⑤ **little** about Veganism.

> 菜食主義に関して、もうちょっと教えてください。
>
> ＊ veganism「極端な菜食主義」肉・魚類に加え、卵・乳製品なども食べない菜食主義。

F: People become vegan for a ⑥ **variety** of reasons. Some change their lifestyle to improve their health through ⑦ **better** diet, others like me are moved to be vegan to protest the mass killing that ⑧ **eating** animal products represents. These are living creatures, they did not ask to be your breakfast, lunch, dinner or clothing.

> 人は多くの理由から菜食主義者になります。より優れた食餌を通して健康を向上させるためにライフスタイルを変える人もいますし、私のように心を動かされて、動物由来の製品を食べることに代表される大量虐殺に抗議するために菜食主義者になる者もいます。動物たちは生き物なんです。彼らはみなさんの朝食やランチ、ディナーや洋服になりたいと頼んだりはしていません。
>
> ＊ be moved to be ...「心が動かされ…になる」 mass killing「大量虐殺」
>   represent「代表する；象徴する」 living creature「生き物」

M: I must say I saw many people at the rally wearing leather shoes. Isn't ⑨ **that a** double standard?

> 集会でたくさんの人が革靴を履いていたのを見たと申し上げないといけないのですが。これはご都合主義なのでしょうか？
>
> ＊ double standard「二重基準；場合によって基準を変えること；ご都合主義」

F: First off I would say ⑩ **that it was** more likely you saw vinyl or some other synthetic imitation. However, people aren't born vegan, they convert to that lifestyle ⑪ **at different** times ⑫ **in their** lives. They may already have leather shoes, for example. I often tell them ⑬ **it is** foolish to throw away a pair of shoes, because the damage has already been done. The animal is dead. They can simply wear them out and not buy another pair.

> まず、おそらくビニールなど合成の模造品をご覧になったのだろうと申し上げておきます。しかしながら、人は生まれながらに菜食主義者なのではなく、人生のいろいろな時期に菜食主義にライフスタイルを転換するのです。例えば、すでに革靴をもっていたかもしれません。私はよく、靴を捨てるのはバカげたことだと言っています。すでに損害は出てしまっているのですからね。その動物は死んでしまっています。単純に靴をはきつぶし、新しいものを買わないという選択は可能です。
>
> ＊ synthetic「作り物の；合成の」 imitation「模造品」 throw away「捨てる」

M: How ⑭ **would you** rate the success of this rally?

> この集会の成功をどの程度だと評価しますか？
>
> ＊ rate「評価する」

F: Look ... there's no doubt we are facing a huge uphill ⑮ **battle**. Societies around the world have been indoctrinated to use animal products and not even think ⑯ **about the** source. The whole invention of words like leather, bacon, steak etc., is intended to take attention away from the fact that these are living creatures. ⑰ **But our** movement is growing, and the more people who take up the cause the more our voices will be heard.

> あのですね…われわれがものすごく苦しい闘いに直面していることは間違いありません。世界中の社会は、動物由来の製品を使い、その出所を考えもしないように教え込まれているのです。レザーやベーコン、ステーキなどのすべての言葉のでっち上げには、これらが生き物であるという事実から注意をそらす意図があるのです。しかし、私たちの運動は成長しています。多くの人が主張を受け入れるほどに、私たちの声もより多くの人に届くのです。
>
> ＊ uphill battle「苦しい闘い」 indoctrinate to ...「…するように吹き込む；教え込む」
>   source「由来；出所」 invention「考案；でっち上げ」 attention「注意；注目」
>   take up「受け入れる」 cause「主張；運動」

🎯 Stage 3 🔊 英文トランスクリプション

インタビュー全体を英文の原稿で確認しながらCDで耳慣らししよう！ その上で、インタビューを聴きながら、まだできていない部分の穴埋めに再チャレンジしよう。

M: This weekend marked the largest Vegan rally in history, with more than ten thousand gathered in Washington DC. We've asked for some input from a keynote speaker ① **at the** rally, Jeniffer Holmes. Jeniffer, ② **what is** the primary goal of this rally?

F: We're here to raise awareness for and educate people ③ **about the** atrocities occurring daily against animals around the world. Our ④ **society** has been brainwashed into ignoring the abuse suffered by animals and inflicted by big business.

M: Tell us a ⑤ **little** about Veganism.

F: People become vegan for a ⑥ **variety** of reasons. Some change their lifestyle to improve their health through ⑦ **better** diet, others like me are moved to be vegan to protest the mass killing that ⑧ **eating** animal products represents. These are living creatures, they did not ask to be your breakfast, lunch, dinner or clothing.

M: I must say I saw many people at the rally wearing leather shoes. Isn't ⑨ **that a** double standard?

F: First off I would say ⑩ **that it was** more likely you saw vinyl or some other synthetic imitation. However, people aren't born vegan, they convert to that lifestyle ⑪ **at different** times ⑫ **in their** lives. They may already have leather shoes, for example. I often tell them ⑬ **it is** foolish to throw away a pair of shoes, because the damage has already been done. The animal is dead. They can simply wear them out and not buy another pair.

M: How ⑭ **would you** rate the success of this rally?

F: Look ... there's no doubt we are facing a huge uphill ⑮ **battle**. Societies around the world have been indoctrinated to use animal products and not even think ⑯ **about the** source. The whole invention of words like leather, bacon, steak etc., is intended to take attention away from the fact that these are living creatures. ⑰ **But our** movement is growing, and the more people who take up the cause the more our voices will be heard.

🌸 Stage 4 🔊 音声変化をチェック

まとめとして、穴埋め部分の音声変化の特徴を**スロー・スピード**と**ナチュラル・スピード**で確認しよう。下記に示したカタカナ表記で音声変化を確認して、もう一度インタビューを聴き直してみよう。発音変化のルールは適宜復習しよう。

---

❶ at the　　　　　　　　　　　　　アット・ザ　　　　　　　▶ アッ＿ザ
☞ 破裂音 [t] の脱落が起こる。

❷ what is　　　　　　　　　　　　ワット・イズ　　　　　　▶ ワッディ [リ] ズ
☞ 連結部で [t] 音が弾音化する。

❸ about the　　　　　　　　　　アバウト・ズィ　　　　　　▶ アバウッ＿ズィ
☞ 破裂音 [t] の脱落が起こる。

❹ society　　　　　　　　　　　ササイアティー　　　　　　▶ ササイアディ [リ] ー
☞ 破裂音 [t] の弾音化が起こる。

❺ little　　　　　　　　　　　　リトゥ　　　　　　　　　　▶ リドゥ [ル] ゥ
☞ 破裂音 [t] の弾音化が起こる。

❻ variety　　　　　　　　　　　ヴァライアティー　　　　　▶ ヴァライアディ [リ] ー
☞ 破裂音 [t] の弾音化が起こる。

❼ better　　　　　　　　　　　ベター　　　　　　　　　　▶ ベダ [ラ] ー
☞ 破裂音 [t] の弾音化が起こる。

❽ eating　　　　　　　　　　　イーティング　　　　　　　▶ イーディ [リ] ン（グ）
☞ 破裂音 [t] の弾音化が起こる。末尾の破裂音 [g] が脱落する場合もある。

❾ that a　　　　　　　　　　　ザット・ア　　　　　　　　▶ ザッダ [ラ]
☞ 連結部で破裂音 [t] の弾音化が起こる。

❿ that it was　　　　　　　　ザット・イット・ワズ　　　　▶ ザッディ [リ] ッ＿ワズ
☞ that it の連結部で [t] 音が弾音化する。it の [t] 音は脱落する。

⓫ at different　　　　　　　　アット・ディファラント　　　▶ アッ＿ディファラン（ト）
☞ at の [t] 音は脱落。different 末尾の [t] 音も脱落することがある。

⓬ in their　　　　　　　　　　イン・ゼァ　　　　　　　　▶ イネア
☞ [n] + [ð] が [n] 音に変化する。

⓭ it is　　　　　　　　　　　イット・イズ　　　　　　　▶ イッディ [リ] ズ
☞ 連結部で破裂音 [t] の弾音化が起こる。

⓮ would you　　　　　　　　ウッド・ユー　　　　　　　▶ ウッジュー
☞ [d] + [j] の部分で音が混じり合い、[ジュ] に近い音に変化する。

⓯ battle　　　　　　　　　　バトゥ　　　　　　　　　　▶ バドゥ [ル] ゥ
☞ 破裂音 [t] の弾音化が起こる。

⓰ about the　　　　　　　　アバウト・ザ　　　　　　　▶ アバウッ＿ザ
☞ 破裂音 [t] の脱落が起こる。

⓱ But our　　　　　　　　　バット・アウア　　　　　　▶ バッダ [ラ] ウア
☞ 連結部で破裂音 [t] の弾音化が起こる。

INTERVIEW WITH PRESIDENTIAL CANDIDATE

Unit 15　大統領候補のインタビュー

🌸 Stage 1 🔊 穴埋め インタビュー・リスニング 〔CD 2-04〕 〔CD 2-05〕

音声変化に注意してCDでインタビューを聴きながら空欄部分を埋めてみよう。CDのナチュラル音声での聴き取りが難しいときは、次のトラックに収録されたスロー音声で聴いてみよう。

F: Senator Simmons, welcome to the show. Please tell our listeners what you plan on doing if you're elected President of the United States.

M: Look Julie, it's simple. The current administration has had four years to make things ① _____ for the citizens of this country, and instead, they've made things worse. They ② _____ _____ provide more jobs, to balance the budget and to lower the deficit. These are all promises that they have failed to keep. All of the polls show that the President's popularity is ③ _____ _____ _____-_____ low, and it ④ _____ _____ because he ⑤ _____ _____ doing his job. We need a change, and my platform can be summed up ⑥ _____ _____ single word ... change.

F: Speaking of "change," what is your position on immigration reform?

M: That's a good question. I'm glad you ⑦ _____. For ⑧ _____, we need to change our policies on immigration across the board. The first ⑨ _____ is to ⑩ _____ secure our borders, and crack down on illegal immigration. The flood of people coming into this country illegally has been a financial drain on our economy, and it has to be stopped. We are losing billions of dollars annually on social services and lost tax revenue. I realize that there are considerable legal and logistical hurdles that make immigration reform difficult, ⑪ _____ _____ bottom line is ⑫ _____

_____ problem can no longer be ignored.

F: And healthcare? What is your take ⑬ _____ _____?

M: The American healthcare system is broken. Past administrations have simply been trying to ⑭ _____ _____ Band-Aid on it, instead of tackling the issue as a whole. Insurance premiums have risen to the point where the average American family can hardly afford health-care. That is absolutely inexcusable. We are the most powerful country in the world and we ⑮ _____ _____ provide our citizens with medical care? I have long ⑯ _____ _____ _____ of a single-payer system and if elected, I will push for our healthcare system to be completely overhauled. ⑰ _____ _____ _____ _____ American people want ... and what they deserve.

Stage 2 インタビュー解説

日本語訳と、解説を参照しながら、インタビュー内容を確認しよう。そのあとで、Stage1の穴埋めに再チャレンジしてみよう。

F: Senator Simmons, welcome to the show. Please tell our listeners what you plan on doing if you're elected President of the United States.

> シモンズ上院議員、番組へようこそ。リスナーに向かって、あなたがアメリカの大統領に当選した暁に、なにをなさるつもりかお話しください。
>
> ＊ senator「上院議員」 be elected ...「…に選出される」
> (the) President of the United States「アメリカ合衆国大統領」

M: Look Julie, it's simple. The current administration has had four years to make things ① **better** for the citizens of this country, and instead, they've made things worse. They ② **promised to** provide more jobs, to balance the budget and to lower the deficit. These are all promises that they have failed to keep. All of the polls show that the President's popularity is ③ **at an all-time** low, and it ④ **should be** because he ⑤ **hasn't been** doing his job. We need a change, and my platform can be summed up ⑥ **in that** single word … change.

あのですね、ジュリー、それはシンプルなことですよ。現在の政府はこの国の市民生活の改善のために4年もかけてきましたが、そうではなくて、改悪してしまった。より多くの仕事を供給し、財政のバランスを取り、赤字を減らすと約束したんです。これらすべての約束を、彼らは守ることに失敗したのです。すべての世論調査が、大統領の人気が史上最低であることを示していて、それは彼が自分の仕事をやっていないからでしょう。われわれには変化が必要なんです。そして、私の公約は、その「変化」というひとことに尽きるのです。

* administration「政府」 make things better「事態を好転させる」 provide「供給する」
 budget「予算」 deficit「赤字」 fail to ...「…することに失敗する」 poll「世論調査」
 popularity「人気」 all-time low「史上最低」 platform「公約」 sum up「要約する」

F: Speaking of "change," what is your position on immigration reform?

「変化」と言えば、移民に関する制度改革におけるあなたの立場は？

* position「立場」 immigration「移民」 reform「改革」

M: That's a good question. I'm glad you ⑦ **asked**. For ⑧ **starters**, we need to change our policies on immigration across the board. The first ⑨ **priority** is to ⑩ **better** secure our borders, and crack down on illegal immigration. The flood of people coming into this country illegally has been a financial drain on our economy, and it has to be stopped. We are losing billions of dollars annually on social services and lost tax revenue. I realize that there are considerable legal and logistical hurdles that make immigration reform difficult, ⑪ **but the** bottom line is ⑫ **that the** problem can no longer be ignored.

それはいい質問ですね。たずねていただいてうれしいですよ。まず、移民政策全般に関して、方針を変更する必要があります。第一優先は、国境をさらに安全に守ることです、そして、不法入国を厳しく取り締まるのです。この国に不法に入国する大量の人たちは、ずっとわが国の経済における財政的な無駄遣いのもととなっていて、これを止めなければなりません。例年、社会保障と脱税によって、何十億ドルも損害を被っているのです。移民政策の制度改革を難しくしている、法律上あるいは遂行上の大きなハードルがあることはわかっていま

すが、この問題はもはや無視できないものだというのが結論なのです。

---

* across the board「全般に；全面的に」　better secure「さらなる安全を確保する」
  crack down on ...「…を厳しく取り締まる」　flood of people「大量の人々」　illegally「不法に」
  drain「流出（のもと）」　social services「社会保障；政府が行う各種の社会事業サービス」
  legal「法的な」　logistical「遂行上の」　the bottom line is ...「結論としては…だ；要するに…だ」
  ignore「無視する」

F: And healthcare? What is your take ⑬ **on that**?

それと、医療制度は？ どのようなご見解ですか？

---

* healthcare (system)「医療制度」　take「意見；見解」

M: The American healthcare system is broken. Past administrations have simply been trying to ⑭ **put a** Band-Aid on it, instead of tackling the issue as a whole. Insurance premiums have risen to the point where the average American family can hardly afford healthcare. That is absolutely inexcusable. We are the most powerful country in the world and we ⑮ **can't even** provide our citizens with medical care? I have long ⑯ **been an advocate** of a single-payer system and if elected, I will push for our healthcare system to be completely overhauled. ⑰ **That is what the** American people want ... and what they deserve.

アメリカの健康医療システムは崩壊しています。過去の政権は、単にシステムにバンドエイドを貼ろうとしてきたのです。問題全体にきちんと取り組む代わりにね。保険料は、平均的なアメリカの家庭が到底、医療サービスを受けられないようなレベルにまで上昇しています。これは絶対に許しがたいことなのです。アメリカは世界でもっともパワフルな国なのに、国民に医療さえ提供できないのでしょうか？　私はずっと国民皆保険制度を支持してきましたから、もし当選すれば、保険システムの完全見直しを推し進めます。それこそアメリカの国民が望み、当然与えられるべきものなのです。

---

* put a Band-Aid on ...「…にバンドエイドを貼る」　tackle「(真剣に) 取り組む」　issue「問題」
  insurance premium「保険料」　afford「(経済的に) …する余裕がある」
  inexcusable「許しがたい」　advocate「支持者」　single-payer system「国民皆保険制度」
  push for A to B「AがBするよう推し進める」　deserve ...「…を受けるに値する」

Stage 3 　英文トランスクリプション

インタビュー全体を英文の原稿で確認しながらCDで耳慣ししよう！　その上で、インタビューを聴きながら、まだできていない部分の穴埋めに再チャレンジしよう。

F: Senator Simmons, welcome to the show. Please tell our listeners what you plan on doing if you're elected President of the United States.

M: Look Julie, it's simple. The current administration has had four years to make things ① **better** for the citizens of this country, and instead, they've made things worse. They ② **promised to** provide more jobs, to balance the budget and to lower the deficit. These are all promises that they have failed to keep. All of the polls show that the President's popularity is ③ **at an all-time** low, and it ④ **should be** because he ⑤ **hasn't been** doing his job. We need a change, and my platform can be summed up ⑥ **in that** single word ... change.

F: Speaking of "change," what is your position on immigration reform?

M: That's a good question. I'm glad you ⑦ **asked**. For ⑧ **starters**, we need to change our policies on immigration across the board. The first ⑨ **priority** is to ⑩ **better** secure our borders, and crack down on illegal immigration. The flood of people coming into this country illegally has been a financial drain on our economy, and it has to be stopped. We are losing billions of dollars annually on social services and lost tax revenue. I realize that there are considerable legal and logistical hurdles that make immigration reform difficult, ⑪ **but the** bottom line is ⑫ **that the** problem can no longer be ignored.

F: And healthcare? What is your take ⑬ **on that**?

M: The American healthcare system is broken. Past administrations have simply been trying to ⑭ **put a** Band-Aid on it, instead of tackling the issue as a whole. Insurance premiums have risen to the point where the average American family can hardly afford health-care. That is absolutely inexcusable. We are the most powerful country in the world and we ⑮ **can't even** provide our citizens with medical care? I have long ⑯ **been an advocate** of a single-payer system and if elected, I will push for our healthcare system to be completely overhauled. ⑰ **That is what the** American people want ... and what they deserve.

🎧 Stage 4 🔊 音声変化をチェック

まとめとして、穴埋め部分の音声変化の特徴を**スロー・スピード**と**ナチュラル・スピード**で確認しよう。下記に示したカタカナ表記で音声変化を確認して、もう一度インタビューを聴き直してみよう。発音変化のルールは適宜復習しよう。

❶ **better** ベター ▶ ベダ[ラ]ー
☞ 破裂音[t]の弾音化が起こる。

❷ **promised to** プラミスト・トゥー ▶ プラミスッ＿トゥー
☞ 破裂音[t]の連続で片方が脱落する。

❸ **at an all-time** アット・アン・オーゥタイム ▶ アッダ[ラ]ノーゥタイム
☞ 3語が連結。at an の連結部で[t]音が弾音化する。

❹ **should be** シュッド・ビー ▶ シュッ＿ビー
☞ 破裂音の連続で[d]音が脱落する。

❺ **hasn't been** ハズント・ビーン ▶ ハズン＿ビン
☞ hasn't から[t]音が脱落する。been は弱化して[ビン]と発音される。

❻ **in that** イン・ザット ▶ イナッ(ト)
☞ [n]+[ð]が[n]音に変化する。末尾の[t]音も脱落しやすい。

❼ **asked** アスクト ▶ アスッ＿ト
☞ 破裂音[k]の脱落が生じる。

❽ **starters** スターターズ ▶ スターダ[ラ]ーズ
☞ 破裂音[t]の弾音化が起こる。

❾ **priority** プライオーラティー ▶ プライオーラディ[リ]ー
☞ 破裂音[t]の弾音化が起こる。

❿ **better** ベター ▶ ベダ[ラ]ー
☞ 破裂音[t]の弾音化が起こる。

⓫ **but the** バット・ザ ▶ バッ＿ザ
☞ 破裂音[t]の脱落が起こる。

⓬ **that the** ザット・ザ ▶ ザッ＿ザ
☞ 破裂音[t]の脱落が起こる。

⓭ **on that** オン・ザット ▶ オナッ(ト)
☞ [n]+[ð]が[n]音に変化する。末尾の[t]音も脱落しやすい。

⓮ **put a** プット・ア ▶ プッダ[ラ]
☞ 連結部で[t]音が弾音化する。

⓯ **can't even** キャント・イーヴン ▶ キャニーヴン
☞ 破裂音[t]が脱落しながら、2語が連結する。

⓰ **been an advocate** ビーン・アン・アドヴォキット ▶ ビナナドヴォキット
☞ been は弱化して[ビン]と発音。3語が連結。

⓱ **That is what the** ザット・イズ・ワット・ズィ ▶ ザッディ[リ]ズワッ＿ズィ
☞ That is の連結部で[t]音が弾音化する。what the では[t]音が脱落する。

🎤 大統領候補のインタビュー

INTERVIEW WITH A BARTENDER

Unit 16 バーテンダーのインタビュー

Stage 1 　穴埋め インタビュー・リスニング

音声変化に注意してCDでインタビューを聴きながら空欄部分を埋めてみよう。CDのナチュラル音声での聴き取りが難しいときは、次のトラックに収録されたスロー音声で聴いてみよう。

M: Movies like Cocktail or Coyote Ugly have long glamorized the job of being a bartender. Today we are ① _____ _____ bartender Katie Stevens, who ② _____ authored the book "Shaken Up — The Home Bartender Handbook." Katie is bartending all it's cracked up to be?

F: Well it certainly can be a lot of fun. It has its upsides and downsides though, just like any other job. The biggest challenge for the average bartender, just like any other restaurant server, is there can be big fluctuations in income. Some days you make a lot of money, and other days you ③ _____ _____ ④ _____ _____ nothing. We don't ⑤ _____ _____ even minimum wage, and live on tips. Another thing people often don't think ⑥ _____ _____ while our customers sit on their barstools, we are ⑦ _____ _____ feet eight to twelve hours.

M: In the movies, bartenders are often shown drinking on the job. What's your position on this?

F: Other than large corporate chains, I don't know too many bars that prohibit drinking by their bartenders. A lot of people come to the bar to spend time with their favorite bartender, and buying a drink for them is ⑧ _____ revenue for the bar. As bartenders we ⑨ _____ _____ serve drinks, we are marriage counselors, psychologists and friends to lonely customers who are ⑩ _____ _____ drown their sorrows. Of course, drinking

100

too much on the job is never a good thing, and can ⑪ _____ _____ money in the end, ⑫ _____ _____ defeating the purpose of being there.

M: Tell us a little ⑬ _____ _____ new book.

F: Basically, serving cocktails while entertaining at home is all the rage today, and I wanted to put ⑭ _____ _____ book that kind of helped people learn the basics of making mixed drinks. Most people don't know that you really only ⑮ _____ _____ few different bottles to make a wide variety of mixed drinks. This book serves as a guide on ⑯ _____ _____ buy based on your budget and the cocktails you like.

M: Lastly ... what's your favorite drink?

F: The "Duck Fart," a shot with Crown Royal, Kahlua and Baileys, layered in that order. ⑰ _____ _____!

Stage 2 インタビュー解説

日本語訳と、解説を参照しながら、インタビュー内容を確認しよう。そのあとで、Stage1の穴埋めに再チャレンジしてみよう。

M: Movies like Cocktail or Coyote Ugly have long glamorized the job of being a bartender. Today we are ① **visited by** bartender Katie Stevens, who ② **recently** authored the book "Shaken Up — The Home Bartender Handbook." Katie is bartending all it's cracked up to be?

> 『カクテル』や『コヨーテ・アグリー』のような映画が、長いことバーテンダーという仕事を美化してきました。今日は、最近『シェイクン・アップ―ザ・ホーム・バーテンダー・ハンドブック』という本を書いたバーテンダーのケイティー・スティーヴンスが来てくれました。ケイティー、バーテンダーの仕事は評判どおりにすばらしいものですか?
>
> * glamorize「美化する;魅力的にする」 be cracked up to be ...「…であるとほめそやされる」

F: Well it certainly can be a lot of fun. It has its upsides and downsides though, just like any other job. The biggest challenge for the average bartender, just like any other restaurant server, is there can be big fluctuations in income. Some days you make a lot of money, and other days you ③ **might make** ④ **next to** nothing. We don't ⑤ **get paid** even minimum wage, and live on tips. Another thing people often don't think ⑥ **about is** while our customers sit on their barstools, we are ⑦ **on our** feet eight to twelve hours.

> ええ、確かにとても楽しいところはあるわね。でも、ちょうどほかの仕事と同じで、いい面も悪い面もあるのよ。ふつうのバーテンダーにとっていちばんの問題は、ほかのレストランの給仕と同様で、収入に大きな揺れ動きがあることなの。ある日は大金が稼げて、別の日にはほぼ一文も稼ぎがないの。私たちには、最低賃金さえも支払われなくて、チップで生活しているのよ。もうひとつたいていの人がほとんど考えないのは、お客さんがバーのスツールに腰掛けている一方で、私たちは8時間から12時間、立ちっぱなしなのよね。
>
> ＊ upsides and downsides「よい面や悪い面；有利な面や不利な面」 fluctuation「変異；動揺」
>   next to nothing「非常に少ない；ほぼ皆無の」 minimum wage「最低賃金」

M: In the movies, bartenders are often shown drinking on the job. What's your position on this?

> 映画では、バーテンダーはよく仕事でお酒を飲んでいますよね。これについてあなたのご意見は？
>
> ＊ position「立ち位置；立場；見解」

F: Other than large corporate chains, I don't know too many bars that prohibit drinking by their bartenders. A lot of people come to the bar to spend time with their favorite bartender, and buying a drink for them is ⑧ **extra** revenue for the bar. As bartenders we ⑨ **not only** serve drinks, we are marriage counselors, psychologists and friends to lonely customers who are ⑩ **trying to** drown their sorrows. Of course, drinking too much on the job is never a good thing, and can ⑪ **cost you** money in the end, ⑫ **kind of** defeating the purpose of being there.

> 大きな企業のチェーン店でなければ、バーテンダーが飲むのを禁止しているバーはあまり知らないわ。多くの人がお気に入りのバーテンダーと時間を過ごすためにバーにやってくるの。そして、バーテンダーにお酒をおごることは、バーにとっては余分の収入になるわけ。バー

テンダーとして、私たちは飲み物を出すだけじゃなくて、結婚相談員や精神分析医、あるいは、悲しみを紛らそうとするさみしいお客さんたちの友人でもあるのよ。もちろん、仕事で飲み過ぎるのは、決していいことではないし、結局お金もかかってしまうわ。ある意味、働いている意味がなくなっちゃうしね。

---
* prohibit「禁止する」 revenue「収入」 drown one's sorrows「悲しみを紛らす」
defeat the purpose「目的を失う；無にする」

M: Tell us a little ⑬ **about your** new book.

あなたの新しい本について少し教えてください。

F: Basically, serving cocktails while entertaining at home is all the rage today, and I wanted to put ⑭ **out a** book that kind of helped people learn the basics of making mixed drinks. Most people don't know that you really only ⑮ **need a** few different bottles to make a wide variety of mixed drinks. This book serves as a guide on ⑯ **what to** buy based on your budget and the cocktails you like.

基本的に、家で接待しているときにカクテルを振る舞うのがいまは大流行でしょ。で、なんとなくカクテル作りの基礎を学ぶときの助けになる本を出したかったの。ホントにいくつかの違う種類のボトルさえあれば、幅広いカクテルが作れることを、ほとんどの人が知らないのよ。この本は、予算やカクテルの好みによってなにを買えばいいか、ガイドの役目をしているの。

---
* all the rage「大流行して；ブームで」 put out「出版する；発表する」 mixed drink「カクテル」

M: Lastly ... what's your favorite drink?

最後に…あなたの好きなお酒は？

F: The "Duck Fart," a shot with Crown Royal, Kahlua and Baileys, layered in that order. ⑰ **Try it**!

「ダック・ファート」ね。ウイスキーのクラウン・ロイヤル、カルア、それとベイリーズをその順に層にするの。ぜひ試してみてね！

---
* layered「層にされて；層状の」

バーテンダーのインタビュー

Stage 3　英文トランスクリプション

インタビュー全体を英文の原稿で確認しながらCDで耳慣らししよう！　その上で、インタビューを聴きながら、まだできていない部分の穴埋めに再チャレンジしよう。

M: Movies like Cocktail or Coyote Ugly have long glamorized the job of being a bartender. Today we are ① **visited by** bartender Katie Stevens, who ② **recently** authored the book "Shaken Up — The Home Bartender Handbook." Katie is bartending all it's cracked up to be?

F: Well it certainly can be a lot of fun. It has its upsides and downsides though, just like any other job. The biggest challenge for the average bartender, just like any other restaurant server, is there can be big fluctuations in income. Some days you make a lot of money, and other days you ③ **might make** ④ **next to** nothing. We don't ⑤ **get paid** even minimum wage, and live on tips. Another thing people often don't think ⑥ **about is** while our customers sit on their barstools, we are ⑦ **on our** feet eight to twelve hours.

M: In the movies, bartenders are often shown drinking on the job. What's your position on this?

F: Other than large corporate chains, I don't know too many bars that prohibit drinking by their bartenders. A lot of people come to the bar to spend time with their favorite bartender, and buying a drink for them is ⑧ **extra** revenue for the bar. As bartenders we ⑨ **not only** serve drinks, we are marriage counselors, psychologists and friends to lonely customers who are ⑩ **trying to** drown their sorrows. Of course, drinking too much on the job is never a good thing, and can ⑪ **cost you** money in the end, ⑫ **kind of** defeating the purpose of being there.

M: Tell us a little ⑬ **about your** new book.

F: Basically, serving cocktails while entertaining at home is all the rage today, and I wanted to put ⑭ **out a** book that kind of helped people learn the basics of making mixed drinks. Most people don't know that you really only ⑮ **need a** few different bottles to make a wide variety of mixed drinks. This book serves as a guide on ⑯ **what to** buy based on your budget and the cocktails you like.

M: Lastly ... what's your favorite drink?

F: The "Duck Fart," a shot with Crown Royal, Kahlua and Baileys, layered in that order. ⑰ **Try it**!

Stage 4))) 音声変化をチェック

まとめとして、穴埋め部分の音声変化の特徴を**スロー・スピード**と**ナチュラル・スピード**で確認しよう。下記に示したカタカナ表記で音声変化を確認して、もう一度インタビューを聴き直してみよう。発音変化のルールは適宜復習しよう。

❶ **visited by** ヴィジティッド・バイ ▶ ヴィジディ[リ]ッ_バイ
☞ visited で破裂音 [t] の弾音化が起こる。visited 末尾の破裂音 [d] が脱落する。

❷ **recently** リースントゥリー ▶ リースン_リー
☞ [tl] で [t] 音の脱落が生じる。

❸ **might make** マイト・メイク ▶ マイッ_メイ（ク）
☞ 破裂音 [t] が脱落する。

❹ **next to** ネクスト・トゥー ▶ ネクスッ_トゥー
☞ 破裂音の連続で片方が脱落する。

❺ **get paid** ゲット・ペイド ▶ ゲッ_ペイド
☞ 破裂音の連続で片方が脱落する。

❻ **about is** アバウト・イズ ▶ アバウディ[リ]ズ
☞ 連結部で破裂音 [t] が弾音化する。

❼ **on our** オン・アウァ ▶ オナウァ
☞ 2語が連結する。

❽ **extra** エクストゥラ ▶ エクスチュラ
☞ [tr] 部分の [t] 音が [チュ] に近い音に変化する。

❾ **not only** ナット・オウンリー ▶ ナッド[ロ]ウンリー
☞ 連結部で破裂音 [t] が弾音化する。

❿ **trying to** トゥライイング・トゥー ▶ チュライン_トゥー
☞ [tr] 部分の [t] 音が [チュ] に近い音に変化する。trying 末尾の [g] 音が脱落することもある。

⓫ **cost you** コースト・ユー ▶ コースチュー
☞ [t] + [j] の部分で音が混じり合い、[チュ] に近い音に変化する。

⓬ **kind of** カインド・アヴ ▶ カイナ（ヴ）
☞ kind の破裂音 [d] が脱落しつつ、2語が連結する。of の [v] 音も脱落しやすい。

⓭ **about your** アバウト・ユア ▶ アバウチュア
☞ [t] + [j] の部分で音が混じり合い、[チュ] に近い音に変化する。

⓮ **out a** アウト・ア ▶ アウダ[ラ]
☞ 連結部で [t] 音が弾音化する。

⓯ **need a** ニード・ア ▶ ニーダ[ラ]
☞ 2語が連結する。連結部で [d] 音が弾音化することもある。

⓰ **what to** ワット・トゥー ▶ ワッ_トゥー
☞ 破裂音 [t] の脱落が起こる。

⓱ **Try it** トゥライ・イット ▶ チュライッ_
☞ [tr] 部分の [t] 音が [チュ] に近い音に変化する。it 末尾の [t] 音も脱落しやすい。

INTERVIEW WITH A DOCTOR

Unit 17　医師のインタビュー

Stage 1　穴埋め インタビュー・リスニング

音声変化に注意してCDでインタビューを聴きながら空欄部分を埋めてみよう。CDのナチュラル音声での聴き取りが難しいときは、次のトラックに収録されたスロー音声で聴いてみよう。

F: Visiting our studio today is Dr. Tim Schindler, board member of the Center for Disease ① _____ and head pathologist at Emory Hospital in Atlanta, Georgia. Dr. Schindler was one of several doctors on the team that successfully ② _____ America's first case of the Ebola virus. Dr. Schindler, welcome.

M: Thank you for having me on your show.

F: First off, can you tell us, in layman's terms, just how infected your patient was, say ③ _____ _____ scale of one to ten?

M: I would say that number ④ _____ _____ be ten. The patient's blood was flooded with the virus. Of course, this being the first case of its kind in the US, I am basing ⑤ _____ _____ comparisons with other case data from source countries in Africa. It was really ⑥ _____ _____ _____ from the beginning, as we had never faced anything like this before.

F: What kinds of steps were taken to prevent doctors and nurses from contracting the disease?

M: The virus is highly contagious, and spreads through bodily fluids, so the patient ⑦ _____ _____ be quarantined and ⑧ _____ _____ _____ special clean room. Physicians or anyone involved in ⑨ _____ the patient had to wear several layers of protective clothing, masks etc. Even though it is a controlled environment, it is still a ⑩ _____ _____.

106

F: This virus is feared for its ⑪ _____ contagious nature, and for the fact that there is no known cure. How ⑫ _____ _____ treat the patient without any antivirus medication?

M: Unfortunately, as you mentioned, ⑬ _____ there is no known cure for Ebola. One of the primary symptoms is severe diarrhea, which causes the body to lose electrolytes and other important fluids and minerals. The only thing you can do is try to keep the patient hydrated and nourished through intravenous fluids, and by stabilizing the patient, hopefully their own immune systems stay strong enough to attack the virus and flush it ⑭ _____ _____ their system. ⑮ _____ in this case, that's ⑯ _____ _____ _____.

F: Indeed. Dr. Schindler, thank you for your continued ⑰ _____ and for your time here today.

Stage 2 インタビュー解説

日本語訳と、解説を参照しながら、インタビュー内容を確認しよう。そのあとで、Stage1の穴埋めに再チャレンジしてみよう。

F: Visiting our studio today is Dr. Tim Schindler, board member of the Center for Disease ① **Control** and head pathologist at Emory Hospital in Atlanta, Georgia. Dr. Schindler was one of several doctors on the team that successfully ② **treated** America's first case of the Ebola virus. Dr. Schindler, welcome.

> 今日スタジオにいらしていただいたのは、ティム・シンドラー医師です。彼は疾病コントロール・センターの委員であり、ジョージア州アトランタにあるエモリー病院の病理学部門の長でもあります。シンドラー先生は、アメリカ初のエボラ・ウイルスのケースの治療に成功したチームの、数人の医師ひとりでした。シンドラー先生、ようこそ。
>
> * board member「委員；役員」 disease「病気；疾病」 pathologist「病理学者」
> Ebola virus「エボラ・ウイルス」

M: Thank you for having me on your show.

> 番組にお招きいただき、ありがとうございます。

医師のインタビュー 107

F: First off, can you tell us, in layman's terms, just how infected your patient was, say ③ **on a** scale of one to ten?

> まず、素人にもわかる平易な言葉で、患者がどのように感染していたのかを教えてもらえますか？例えば、1～10の尺度で言えば？
>
> * in layman's terms「素人にもわかる言葉で」 say ...「例えば…；言ってみれば…」

M: I would say that number ④ **would definitely** be ten. The patient's blood was flooded with the virus. Of course, this being the first case of its kind in the US, I am basing ⑤ **that on** comparisons with other case data from source countries in Africa. It was really ⑥ **touch and go** from the beginning, as we had never faced anything like this before.

> その数字は、完全に10になるでしょうね。患者の血液はウイルスに満ちていました。もちろん、この種のケースではこれがアメリカで最初なので、アフリカの感染源諸国で得たほかのケースのデータとの比較に根拠を置いていますが。初っぱなから、とても危険な状態でした。これまでに、このような事態に直面したことはありませんでしたから。
>
> * definitely「明確に；絶対に」 base on ...「…に根拠を置く」 comparison「比較」
>   source countries「感染源の諸国」 touch and go「危険な（状態）」 face「直面する」

F: What kinds of steps were taken to prevent doctors and nurses from contracting the disease?

> 医師や看護師たちのエボラ出血熱への感染を防ぐために、どのようなステップが取られたのでしょう？
>
> * prevent A from -ing「Aが…するのを防ぐ；妨げる」 contract「（重病に）感染する」

M: The virus is highly contagious, and spreads through bodily fluids, so the patient ⑦ **had to** be quarantined and ⑧ **isolated in a** special clean room. Physicians or anyone involved in ⑨ **treating** the patient had to wear several layers of protective clothing, masks etc. Even though it is a controlled environment, it is still a ⑩ **bit unnerving**.

> ウイルスは非常に感染性が高く、飛沫感染によって拡散するので、患者は特別な無菌室に隔離しなければなりませんでした。医師、あるいは患者の治療に関係している人間はだれでも何層かの防護服やマスクなどを着用しなければなりませんでした。コントロールされた環境ではありますが、それでも、ちょっとおっかなびっくりなのです。
>
> * contagious「伝染性の」 bodily fluids「カラダの液体部分；飛沫」 quarantine「隔離する」

clean room「無菌室；クリーン・ルーム」 unnerving「おびえさせる；びくびくさせる」

F: This virus is feared for its ⑪ **extremely** contagious nature, and for the fact that there is no known cure. How ⑫ **did you** treat the patient without any antivirus medication?

このウイルスは、非常に感染力が高い性質や、既知の治療法がないという事実のために恐れられていますね。抗ウイルス剤なしに、どのように患者を治療なさったんですか？

* the fact that ...「…という事実」 known cure「既知の治療法」
antivirus medication「ウイルス対策の薬剤」

M: Unfortunately, as you mentioned, ⑬ **currently** there is no known cure for Ebola. One of the primary symptoms is severe diarrhea, which causes the body to lose electrolytes and other important fluids and minerals. The only thing you can do is try to keep the patient hydrated and nourished through intravenous fluids, and by stabilizing the patient, hopefully their own immune systems stay strong enough to attack the virus and flush it ⑭ **out of** their system. ⑮ **Fortunately** in this case, that's ⑯ **exactly what happened**.

残念ながら、おっしゃるとおり、現在エボラ・ウイルスに対する既知の治療法はありません。初期症状のひとつに激しい下痢がありますが、これが原因で、電解質やその他の重要な体液、ミネラル分がカラダから失われます。できることと言えば、静脈内輸液投与によって患者の水分と栄養を保つように努めることだけです。そして、患者の容態を安定させることで、うまくいけば、患者自身の免疫システムを十分に強く保ち、ウイルスを攻撃しカラダの外に流し出すことができるんです。今回のケースでは、幸運にもまさにそれが起こったわけです。

* electrolyte「電解質」 hydrate「(患者の) 体内に水分・水溶液を補給する」
through intravenous fluids「静脈内輸液投与で」 hopefully「うまくいけば」
flush out of ...「…から流し出す」 system「組織；身体」

F: Indeed. Dr. Schindler, thank you for your continued ⑰ **contributions** and for your time here today.

なるほど。シンドラー先生の引き続きの貢献と、本日お時間を割いていただいたことに感謝申し上げます。

* Indeed.「なるほど；そうだね」 continued contributions「継続的な貢献」

Stage 3 英文トランスクリプション

インタビュー全体を英文の原稿で確認しながらCDで耳慣らししよう！ その上で、インタビューを聴きながら、まだできていない部分の穴埋めに再チャレンジしよう。

F: Visiting our studio today is Dr. Tim Schindler, board member of the Center for Disease ① **Control** and head pathologist at Emory Hospital in Atlanta, Georgia. Dr. Schindler was one of several doctors on the team that successfully ② **treated** America's first case of the Ebola virus. Dr. Schindler, welcome.

M: Thank you for having me on your show.

F: First off, can you tell us, in layman's terms, just how infected your patient was, say ③ **on a** scale of one to ten?

M: I would say that number ④ **would definitely** be ten. The patient's blood was flooded with the virus. Of course, this being the first case of its kind in the US, I am basing ⑤ **that on** comparisons with other case data from source countries in Africa. It was really ⑥ **touch and go** from the beginning, as we had never faced anything like this before.

F: What kinds of steps were taken to prevent doctors and nurses from contracting the disease?

M: The virus is highly contagious, and spreads through bodily fluids, so the patient ⑦ **had to** be quarantined and ⑧ **isolated in a** special clean room. Physicians or anyone involved in ⑨ **treating** the patient had to wear several layers of protective clothing, masks etc. Even though it is a controlled environment, it is still a ⑩ **bit unnerving**.

F: This virus is feared for its ⑪ **extremely** contagious nature, and for the fact that there is no known cure. How ⑫ **did you** treat the patient without any antivirus medication?

M: Unfortunately, as you mentioned, ⑬ **currently** there is no known cure for Ebola. One of the primary symptoms is severe diarrhea, which causes the body to lose electrolytes and other important fluids and minerals. The only thing you can do is try to keep the patient hydrated and nourished through intravenous fluids, and by stabilizing the patient, hopefully their own immune systems stay strong enough to attack the virus and flush it ⑭ **out of** their system. ⑮ **Fortunately** in this case, that's ⑯ **exactly what happened**.

F: Indeed. Dr. Schindler, thank you for your continued ⑰ **contributions** and for your time here today.

Stage 4 🔊 音声変化をチェック

まとめとして、穴埋め部分の音声変化の特徴を**スロー・スピード**と**ナチュラル・スピード**で確認しよう。下記に示したカタカナ表記で音声変化を確認して、もう一度インタビューを聴き直してみよう。発音変化のルールは適宜復習しよう。

---

❶ **Control**　　　　　　　　　カントゥロウゥ　　　　　▶ カンチュロウゥ
☞ [tr] 部分の [t] 音が [チュ] に近い音に変化する。

❷ **treated**　　　　　　　　　トゥリーティッド　　　　▶ チュリーディ [リ] ッド
☞ [tr] 部分の [t] 音が [チュ] に近い音に変化する。中程の [t] 音が弾音化することもある。

❸ **on a**　　　　　　　　　　　オン・ア　　　　　　　　▶ オナ
☞ 2 語が連結する。

❹ **would definitely**　　　　　ウッド・ディファニットリー　▶ ウッ_ディファニッ_リー
☞ would 末尾の [d] 音や definitely の [t] 音が脱落する。

❺ **that on**　　　　　　　　　ザット・オン　　　　　　▶ ザッド [ロ] ン
☞ 連結部で破裂音 [t] が弾音化する。

❻ **touch and go**　　　　　　　タッチ・アンド・ゴウ　　▶ タッチアン_ゴウ
☞ and の破裂音 [d] の脱落が起こる。

❼ **had to**　　　　　　　　　　ハッド・トゥー　　　　　▶ ハッ_トゥー
☞ 破裂音の連続で、had の [d] 音の脱落が生じる。

❽ **isolated in a**　　　　　　　アイソレイティッド・イン・ア　▶ アイソレイディ [リ] ッディ [リ] ナ
☞ isolated の破裂音 [t] で弾音化が起こる。3 語が連結するが、isolated in の連結部で [d] 音が弾音化することもある。

❾ **treating**　　　　　　　　　トゥリーティング　　　　▶ チュリーティング
☞ [tr] の [t] 音は [チュ] のように変化する。

❿ **bit unnerving**　　　　　　　ビット・アンナーヴィング　▶ ビッダ [ラ] ンナーヴィン (グ)
☞ 連結部で [t] 音が弾音化する。末尾の [g] 音が脱落することもある。

⓫ **extremely**　　　　　　　　　イクストゥリームリー　　▶ イクスチュリームリー
☞ [tr] の [t] 音は [チュ] のように変化する。

⓬ **did you**　　　　　　　　　　ディッド・ユー　　　　　▶ ディッジュー
☞ [d] + [j] の部分で音が混じり合い、[ジュ] に近い音に変化する。

⓭ **currently**　　　　　　　　　カレントゥリー　　　　　▶ カレン_リー
☞ [tl] で [t] 音の脱落が生じる。

⓮ **out of**　　　　　　　　　　アウト・アヴ　　　　　　▶ アウダ [ラ] (ヴ)
☞ 連結部で [t] 音が弾音化する。末尾の [v] 音が脱落することもある。

⓯ **Fortunately**　　　　　　　　フォーチャナットゥリー　　▶ フォーチャナッ_リー
☞ [tl] で [t] 音の脱落が生じる。

⓰ **exactly what happened**　　　イグザクトゥリー・ワット・ハプンド
　　　　　　　　　　　　　　　　　　　　　　　　　　　▶ イグザク_リーワッダ [ラ] ップンド
☞ exactly から [t] 音が脱落。what happened では happened の [h] 音が脱落しながら連結。連結部で [t] 音が弾音化する。

⓱ **contributions**　　　　　　　カーントゥラビューシャンズ　▶ カーンチュラビューシャンズ
☞ [tr] の [t] 音は [チュ] のように変化する。

医師のインタビュー

INTERVIEW WITH A FARMER

Unit 18 農場経営者のインタビュー

Stage 1 穴埋め インタビュー・リスニング

音声変化に注意してCDでインタビューを聴きながら空欄部分を埋めてみよう。CDのナチュラル音声での聴き取りが難しいときは、次のトラックに収録されたスロー音声で聴いてみよう。

F: As the devastating drought ① _____ _____ plagued the American Midwest enters its fourth month, we are speaking today ② _____ _____ 5th generation farmer from Indiana, Bill Walsh. Just how tough has this year been for you Bill?

M: Well I ③ _____ tell ya, I've been farming this land for five decades now, just like my father did before me, ④ _____ _____ have never seen anything like this. ⑤ _____ _____ was forecasted to be dry, but we never thought it'd be this bad. I farm 1,500 acres and since ⑥ _____ _____ we had a bumper crop year with corn, I ⑦ _____ more corn this year than soybeans. We ⑧ _____ _____ plant late when the drought started, but by May first we had to get the seed in the ground. My corn should be five feet tall by now, and most of it is only two.

F: Is the government able to do anything for you?

M: They can't make it rain, so no. We've applied for relief through federal agencies, but the process can take many months. A few years back they ⑨ _____ paid some of us subsidies to leave our fields fallow, ⑩ _____ _____ just about broke us even for the year. I'm ⑪ _____ _____ lucky since I did so good last year, but a lot of my neighbors are struggling just to stay above

112

⑫ _____. Two of my friends have had their farms repossessed this year. Those farms were ⑬ _____ _____ family for over a century!

F: When ⑭ _____ _____ say the drop-dead date is for rain?

M: If we ⑮ _____ _____ something in the next two weeks or so, we're dead in the water. I guess that's a bad euphemism ⑯ _____ _____ the truth. We're really up against it here, and from ⑰ _____ _____ heard most of the Midwest is the same way. This is simply devastating for all of us.

Stage 2 インタビュー解説

日本語訳と、解説を参照しながら、インタビュー内容を確認しよう。そのあとで、Stage1の穴埋めに再チャレンジしてみよう。

F: As the devastating drought ① **that has** plagued the American Midwest enters its fourth month, we are speaking today ② **with a** 5th generation farmer from Indiana, Bill Walsh. Just how tough has this year been for you Bill?

> 壊滅的な干ばつがアメリカ中西部に被害を与え始めてから4カ月目になるところですが、われわれは今日、インディアナの5代続く農場経営者、ビル・ウォルシュとお話ししています。今年はあなたにとってどれくらい大変な状況でしょうか、ビル?
>
> ----
> * devastating「破壊的な;ひどい」 drought「干ばつ」 plague「損害を与える;苦しめる」
>   5th generation farmer「5代続く農場経営者」

M: Well I ③ **gotta** tell ya, I've been farming this land for five decades now, just like my father did before me, ④ **and I** have never seen anything like this. ⑤ **This year** was forecasted to be dry, but we never thought it'd be this bad. I farm 1,500 acres and since ⑥ **last year** we had a bumper crop year with corn, I ⑦ **planted** more corn this year than soybeans. We ⑧ **tried to** plant late when the drought started, but by May first we had to get the seed in the ground. My corn should be five feet tall by now, and most of it is only two.

> そうだね、私の前に父がやっていたとおりに、もうこの土地で50年農業をしているけど、こんなのは見たことがないよ。今年は乾燥すると予測されていたが、これほどひどくなるとは思ってもみなかったね。1,500エーカーの農場を経営していて、昨年はトウモロコシが豊作だったので、今年は大豆よりもトウモロコシを多く植えたんだ。干ばつが始まったので、遅くに種を蒔こうとしたんだが、5月1日までには種まきをしなければならなかったんだよ。うちのトウモロコシはいまの時期までに5フィートに育ってるはずなんだけど、ほとんどはまだ2フィートさ。
>
> * farm「農場を経営する；耕作する」　acre「エーカー」1エーカーは約4047平米。
>   bumper crop year「豊作の年」　soybean「大豆」

F: Is the government able to do anything for you?

> 政府があなたにできることは、なにかあるでしょうか？
>
> * government「政府」

M: They can't make it rain, so no. We've applied for relief through federal agencies, but the process can take many months. A few years back they ⑨ **actually** paid some of us subsidies to leave our fields fallow, ⑩ **and that** just about broke us even for the year. I'm ⑪ **kind of** lucky since I did so good last year, but a lot of my neighbors are struggling just to stay above ⑫ **water**. Two of my friends have had their farms repossessed this year. Those farms were ⑬ **in their** family for over a century!

> 政府は雨を降らせることはできないのだから、ないね。連邦機関を通じて、救済支援を申請したが、プロセスには何カ月もかかる可能性があるんだよ。数年前に政府が、われわれの耕作地を休耕地にさせるための補助金を実際に払ってくれたことがあったんだけど、それでもその年は、ちょうど損得なしくらいだったんだよ。うちは去年豊作だったから、私はある意味、運がいいよ。でも、近所の奴らの多くは、ひどく苦しんでいるよ。友達ふたりは、今年、農地を取り上げられたんだよ。ふたりの農場は、1世紀以上彼らの家族のものだったのに。

> * apply「申請する；申し込む」 relief「救済」 federal agency「連邦機関」
> subsidies「補助金」 fallow「休耕地の」 break even「とんとんになる；損得なしになる」
> struggle to stay above water「ひどく苦しむ」 repossess「担保として取り上げる」

F: When ⑭ **would you** say the drop-dead date is for rain?

> 最悪、いつまでに雨が降らなければダメだと思いますか？
>
> * drop-dead date「ぎりぎりの最終期限」

M: If we ⑮ **don't get** something in the next two weeks or so, we're dead in the water. I guess that's a bad euphemism ⑯ **but it's** the truth. We're really up against it here, and from ⑰ **what I've** heard most of the Midwest is the same way. This is simply devastating for all of us.

> もし、次の2週間かそこいらになにもなければ、おしまいだね。ひどい比喩だろうが、ほんとうのことさ。ここの私らは、ホントにその問題に直面しているんだ。それに、聞いたところでは、中西部のほとんどが同じだそうなんだ。私ら全員にとって、単純に破壊的な出来事なんだよ。
>
> * be dead in the water「おしまいだ」 up against ...「…に直面して」

農場経営者のインタビュー 115

Stage 3　英文トランスクリプション

インタビュー全体を英文の原稿で確認しながらCDで耳慣らししよう！ その上で、インタビューを聴きながら、まだできていない部分の穴埋めに再チャレンジしよう。

F: As the devastating drought ① **that has** plagued the American Midwest enters its fourth month, we are speaking today ② **with a** 5th generation farmer from Indiana, Bill Walsh. Just how tough has this year been for you Bill?

M: Well I ③ **gotta** tell ya, I've been farming this land for five decades now, just like my father did before me, ④ **and I** have never seen anything like this. ⑤ **This year** was forecasted to be dry, but we never thought it'd be this bad. I farm 1,500 acres and since ⑥ **last year** we had a bumper crop year with corn, I ⑦ **planted** more corn this year than soybeans. We ⑧ **tried to** plant late when the drought started, but by May first we had to get the seed in the ground. My corn should be five feet tall by now, and most of it is only two.

F: Is the government able to do anything for you?

M: They can't make it rain, so no. We've applied for relief through federal agencies, but the process can take many months. A few years back they ⑨ **actually** paid some of us subsidies to leave our fields fallow, ⑩ **and that** just about broke us even for the year. I'm ⑪ **kind of** lucky since I did so good last year, but a lot of my neighbors are struggling just to stay above ⑫ **water**. Two of my friends have had their farms repossessed this year. Those farms were ⑬ **in their** family for over a century!

F: When ⑭ **would you** say the drop-dead date is for rain?

M: If we ⑮ **don't get** something in the next two weeks or so, we're dead in the water. I guess that's a bad euphemism ⑯ **but it's** the truth. We're really up against it here, and from ⑰ **what I've** heard most of the Midwest is the same way. This is simply devastating for all of us.

🎧 Stage 4 🔊 音声変化をチェック

まとめとして、穴埋め部分の音声変化の特徴を**スロー・スピード**と**ナチュラル・スピード**で確認しよう。下記に示したカタカナ表記で音声変化を確認して、もう一度インタビューを聴き直してみよう。発音変化のルールは適宜復習しよう。

❶ **that has**　　　　　　　ザット・ハズ　　　　　　▶ ザッダ[ラ]ズ
　☞ 連結部で破裂音[t]の弾音化が起こる。

❷ **with a**　　　　　　　　ウィズ・ア　　　　　　　▶ ウィザ
　☞ 2語が連結する。

❸ **gotta**　　　　　　　　　ガッタ　　　　　　　　　▶ ガッダ[ラ]
　☞ 破裂音[t]が弾音化する。

❹ **and I**　　　　　　　　　アンド・アイ　　　　　　▶ アナイ
　☞ and の[d]音が脱落しつつ2語が連結する。

❺ **This year**　　　　　　　ズィス・イヤー　　　　　▶ ズィシャー
　☞ [s]+[j]の部分で音が混じり合い、[シュ]に近い音に変化する。

❻ **last year**　　　　　　　ラスト・イヤー　　　　　▶ ラスチャー
　☞ [t]+[j]の部分で音が混じり合い、[チュ]に近い音に変化する。

❼ **planted**　　　　　　　　プランティッド　　　　　▶ プラニッ(ド)
　☞ [nt]で[t]音の脱落が生じる。末尾の[d]音が脱落することもある。

❽ **tried to**　　　　　　　　トゥライド・トゥー　　　▶ チュライ＿ドゥ[ル]ー
　☞ [tr]部分の[t]音が[チュ]に近い音に変化する。tried末尾の[d]音の脱落や、to の[t]音の弾音化が生じる場合もある。

❾ **actually**　　　　　　　　アクチュアリー　　　　　▶ アクシュアリー
　☞ 破裂音[t]の脱落が起こる。

❿ **and that**　　　　　　　　アンド・ザット　　　　　▶ アナット
　☞ and の[d]音が脱落。連結部で[n]+[ð]が[n]音に変化する。

⓫ **kind of**　　　　　　　　　カインド・アヴ　　　　　▶ カイナ(ヴ)
　☞ kind の[d]音が脱落して of に連結。of 末尾の[v]音も脱落しやすい。

⓬ **water**　　　　　　　　　　ワーター　　　　　　　　▶ ワーダ[ラ]ー
　☞ 破裂音[t]の弾音化が起こる。

⓭ **in their**　　　　　　　　　イン・ゼア　　　　　　　▶ イネア
　☞ [n]+[ð]が[n]音に変化する。

⓮ **would you**　　　　　　　　ウッド・ユー　　　　　　▶ ウッジュー
　☞ [d]+[j]の部分で音が混じり合い、[ジュ]に近い音に変化する。

⓯ **don't get**　　　　　　　　ドウント・ゲット　　　　▶ ドン＿ゲッ(ト)
　☞ don't は[ドン]と弱化。don't や get の[t]音は脱落しやすい。

⓰ **but it's**　　　　　　　　　バット・イッツ　　　　　▶ バッディ[リ]ッツ
　☞ 連結部で破裂音[t]の弾音化が起こる。

⓱ **what I've**　　　　　　　　ワット・アイヴ　　　　　▶ ワッダ[ラ]イ(ヴ)
　☞ 連結部で破裂音[t]の弾音化が起こる。末尾の[v]音が脱落する場合もある。

INTERVIEW WITH AN ACTRESS

Unit 19 女優のインタビュー

Stage 1 穴埋め インタビュー・リスニング

音声変化に注意してCDでインタビューを聴きながら空欄部分を埋めてみよう。CDのナチュラル音声での聴き取りが難しいときは、次のトラックに収録されたスロー音声で聴いてみよう。

M: Today we are talking with Michelle Lewis, recently ① _____ for an Oscar for her role in the hit movie "Fairplay." Welcome Michelle. Where were you when you were ② _____ of the nomination?

F: ③ _____ it's kind of funny. My hair stylist was doing my hair when I ④ _____ _____ call from the committee to tell me I was nominated. The funny ⑤ _____ _____ that my hair stylist is named "Oscar." He was happy for me at first ⑥ _____ _____ _____ _____ what happened, but after that he was kind of irritated with me because I ⑦ _____ sit still! The first thing I did was call my parents. They have been so ⑧ _____ of me throughout my career, ⑨ _____ _____ have been with me through all of the highs and the lows.

M: Tell us a little ⑩ _____ _____ _____ was like working for director Michael Stone.

F: It was an amazing experience. He is so talented I can't even begin to ⑪ _____ _____ _____ words. What struck me the most about him is that he always knew exactly ⑫ _____ _____ _____ from us actors, and he could ⑬ _____ _____ perfectly. That being said, he also spent hours and hours on and off the set discussing different aspects of the script and getting our feedback and interpretation of certain scenes. I can honestly say he's the best I've ever worked with, and I ⑭ _____ look forward to working with him again.

M: You've recently married and have your first child on the way. What is the ⑮ _____ _____ _____ balancing your work as an actress and family life?

F: Well, it hasn't been easy, and it will only get more difficult when the baby arrives. My husband is also an actor, so we are both away from home on location a ⑯ _____ _____ the time. We are going to have to just cut back on our workload a bit. Myself first, of course, while the baby is younger. I do hope to do a bit of screenwriting myself, however, and ⑰ _____ _____ something that I can do from home.

Stage 2 インタビュー解説

日本語訳と、解説を参照しながら、インタビュー内容を確認しよう。そのあとで、Stage1の穴埋めに再チャレンジしてみよう。

M: Today we are talking with Michelle Lewis, recently ① **nominated** for an Oscar for her role in the hit movie "Fairplay." Welcome Michelle. Where were you when you were ② **notified** of the nomination?

> 今日は、ヒット映画『フェアプレー』の中の役柄で、最近オスカーにノミネートされたミシェル・ルイスとお話ししています。ミシェル、ようこそ。ノミネートを知らされたとき、どちらにいましたか？
>
> ＊ nominate「(賞や候補などに) 指名する；ノミネートする」 notify「知らせる；通知する；通告する」

F: ③ **Actually** it's kind of funny. My hair stylist was doing my hair when I ④ **got a** call from the committee to tell me I was nominated. The funny ⑤ **part is** that my hair stylist is named "Oscar." He was happy for me at first ⑥ **when I told him** what happened, but after that he was kind of irritated with me because I ⑦ **couldn't** sit still! The first thing I did was call my parents. They have been so ⑧ **supportive** of me throughout my career, ⑨ **and they** have been with me through all of the highs and the lows.

> 実はちょっとおもしろいんですよ。ノミネートされたと委員会から電話を受けたときは、ヘア・スタイリストに施術してもらっていたんです。おもしろいのは、スタイリストの名前が『オスカー』だってことなんです。なにが起こったかを伝えると、彼は、まずよろこんでくれました。でも、そのあと、私がじっと座っていられないものだから、彼はちょっと私にいらだっちゃって。私が最初にしたのは両親への電話なんです。キャリアを通して、ずっと私を応援してくれて、いい時期にも悪い時期にも、いつでもそばにいてくれたんです。
>
> ＊ funny「おもしろおかしい；滑稽な」 do one's hair「髪を整える」 committee「委員会」
>   sit still「じっと座っている」 supportive「支持する；支援する」

M: Tell us a little ⑩ **about what it** was like working for director Michael Stone.

> 監督のマイケル・ストーン氏と仕事をするのはどうだったか、ちょっと教えてください。
>
> ＊ what it was like「それがどんなふうだったか」

F: It was an amazing experience. He is so talented I can't even begin to ⑪ **put it into** words. What struck me the most about him is that he always knew exactly ⑫ **what he wanted** from us actors, and he could ⑬ **communicate it** perfectly. That being said, he also spent hours and hours on and off the set discussing different aspects of the script and getting our feedback and interpretation of certain scenes. I can honestly say he's the best I've ever worked with, and I ⑭ **certainly** look forward to working with him again.

> すばらしい経験でした。彼はものすごく才能があって、言葉にもできないほどなんです。彼に関してもっとも印象的だったことは、彼が私たち俳優に求めるものをいつも正確に知っていて、それを完璧に伝えることができたことですね。とは言え、彼はセットの中でも外でも、特定のシーンについて脚本のさまざまな側面を議論し、私たちのフィードバックや解釈を得ながら、長時間を費やしてもいましたけれども。正直に、彼はこれまでに仕事をした中で

> は最高です。そして、ほんとうに彼と再び仕事をすることを楽しみにしています。
>
> * strike「印象を与える」 That being said, ...「とは言っても…」 aspect「側面」 script「脚本」

M: You've recently married and have your first child on the way. What is the ⑮ **hardest part about** balancing your work as an actress and family life?

> あなたは最近ご結婚なさって、第一子がもうすぐ生まれますよね。女優としての仕事と家庭生活のバランスを取るのに、もっとも苦慮している点はなんですか?
>
> * have one's child on the way「子どもを身ごもっている;妊娠している」

F: Well, it hasn't been easy, and it will only get more difficult when the baby arrives. My husband is also an actor, so we are both away from home on location a ⑯ **lot of** the time. We are going to have to just cut back on our workload a bit. Myself first, of course, while the baby is younger. I do hope to do a bit of screenwriting myself, however, and ⑰ **that is** something that I can do from home.

> はい、これまでも、かんたんではありませんでしたね。赤ちゃんが生まれたら、さらに難しくなるだけでしょうね。夫も俳優ですから、私たちふたりとも、たいていはロケに出ていて家を留守にします。ふたりの仕事の量を少々減らさざるを得ないでしょう。赤ちゃんが小さいときは、まず私自身でしょうね。でも、私は、自分でもちょっと脚本を書きたいと思っているんです。それなら、私が家でできることですしね。
>
> * a lot of the time「たいてい」 cut back on ...「…を減らす;削減する」 workload「仕事量」

Stage 3 英文トランスクリプション

インタビュー全体を英文の原稿で確認しながらCDで耳慣らししよう！ その上で、インタビューを聴きながら、まだできていない部分の穴埋めに再チャレンジしよう。

M: Today we are talking with Michelle Lewis, recently ① **nominated** for an Oscar for her role in the hit movie "Fairplay." Welcome Michelle. Where were you when you were ② **notified** of the nomination?

F: ③ **Actually** it's kind of funny. My hair stylist was doing my hair when I ④ **got a** call from the committee to tell me I was nominated. The funny ⑤ **part is** that my hair stylist is named "Oscar." He was happy for me at first ⑥ **when I told him** what happened, but after that he was kind of irritated with me because I ⑦ **couldn't** sit still! The first thing I did was call my parents. They have been so ⑧ **supportive** of me throughout my career, ⑨ **and they** have been with me through all of the highs and the lows.

M: Tell us a little ⑩ **about what it** was like working for director Michael Stone.

F: It was an amazing experience. He is so talented I can't even begin to ⑪ **put it into** words. What struck me the most about him is that he always knew exactly ⑫ **what he wanted** from us actors, and he could ⑬ **communicate it** perfectly. That being said, he also spent hours and hours on and off the set discussing different aspects of the script and getting our feedback and interpretation of certain scenes. I can honestly say he's the best I've ever worked with, and I ⑭ **certainly** look forward to working with him again.

M: You've recently married and have your first child on the way. What is the ⑮ **hardest part about** balancing your work as an actress and family life?

F: Well, it hasn't been easy, and it will only get more difficult when the baby arrives. My husband is also an actor, so we are both away from home on location a ⑯ **lot of** the time. We are going to have to just cut back on our workload a bit. Myself first, of course, while the baby is younger. I do hope to do a bit of screenwriting myself, however, and ⑰ **that is** something that I can do from home.

Stage 4 ◀)) 音声変化をチェック

まとめとして、穴埋め部分の音声変化の特徴を**スロー・スピード**と**ナチュラル・スピード**で確認しよう。下記に示したカタカナ表記で音声変化を確認して、もう一度インタビューを聴き直してみよう。発音変化のルールは適宜復習しよう。

❶ nominated
ノーマネイティッド　　　　▶　ノーマネイディ［リ］ッド
☞ 破裂音［t］の弾音化が起こる。

❷ notified
ノウタファイド　　　　▶　ノウダ［ラ］ファイド
☞ 破裂音［t］の弾音化が起こる。

❸ Actually
アクチュアリー　　　　▶　アクシュアリー
☞ 破裂音［t］の脱落が起こる。

❹ got a
ガット・ア　　　　▶　ガッダ［ラ］
☞ 連結部で破裂音［t］の弾音化が起こる。

❺ part is
パート・イズ　　　　▶　パーディ［リ］ズ
☞ 連結部で破裂音［t］の弾音化が起こる。

❻ when I told him
ウェン・アイ・トウゥド・ヒム　　　　▶　ウェナイトウゥディ［リ］ム
☞ when I は連結。told him では、弱化した him［イム］に told が連結。連結部で［d］音が弾音化することもある。

❼ couldn't
クドゥント　　　　▶　クドゥン__；クんン__
☞ 末尾の破裂音［t］音の脱落が生じる。［dn］音が声門閉鎖音化し［んン］と発音されることもある。

❽ supportive
サポーティヴ　　　　▶　サポーディ［リ］ヴ
☞ 破裂音［t］の弾音化が起こる。

❾ and they
アンド・ゼイ　　　　▶　アネイ
☞ and の［d］音が脱落。連結部で［n］＋［ð］が［n］音に変化する。

❿ about what it
アバウト・ワット・イット　　　　▶　アバウッ__ワッディ［リ］ッ__
☞ about の［t］音が脱落。what it の連結部で［t］音が弾音化する。it 末尾の［t］音も脱落する。

⓫ put it into
プット・イット・イントゥー　　　　▶　プッディ［リ］ッディ［リ］ンドゥ［ル］ー
☞ 3語が連結。2カ所の連結部と into で［t］音が弾音化する。

⓬ what he wanted
ワット・ヒー・ワンティッド　　　　▶　ワッディ［リ］ーワニッ（ド）
☞ what に弱化した he［イー］が連結。連結部で［t］音の弾音化が起こる。wanted からは［t］や［d］の音が脱落しやすい。

⓭ communicate it
カミューナケイト・イット　　　　▶　カミューナケイディ［リ］ッ（ト）
☞ 連結部で破裂音［t］が弾音化する。末尾の［t］音も脱落しやすい。

⓮ certainly
スートゥンリー　　　　▶　スーんンリー
☞［tn］の部分が声門閉鎖音化する。

⓯ hardest part about
ハーデスト・パート・アバウト　　　　▶　ハーデ［レ］ス__パーダ［ラ］バウ（ト）
☞ hardest の［d］音や part about 連結部の［t］音が弾音化する。hardest と about の［t］音が脱落することもある。

⓰ lot of
ラット・アヴ　　　　▶　ラッダ［ラ］ヴ
☞ 連結部で破裂音［t］の弾音化が起こる。

⓱ that is
ザット・イズ　　　　▶　ザッディ［リ］ズ
☞ 連結部で破裂音［t］の弾音化が起こる。

🎤 女優のインタビュー

INTERVEIW WITH A LAWYER
Unit 20　法律家のインタビュー

🎤 Stage 1　穴埋め インタビュー・リスニング

音声変化に注意してCDでインタビューを聴きながら空欄部分を埋めてみよう。CDのナチュラル音声での聴き取りが難しいときは、次のトラックに収録されたスロー音声で聴いてみよう。

M: The Supreme Court is in session this week addressing the issue of cellphones and privacy, and we have ① _____ our legal consultant Michelle Walters to weigh in on the situation. Michelle, how do you see this case playing out?

F: Well I'll tell you Jim, this is really just the tip of the iceberg for this issue, which is likely to be before the courts for several years to come. At issue is the basic ② _____ _____ privacy versus technology. The basis of the current case is whether police have the right to search suspects' cell phones for potential evidence ③ _____ _____ crime. The court ④ _____ _____ whether police acted legally by searching suspect's phones without ⑤ _____ a search warrant.

M: Police do have ⑥ _____ to conduct a search upon arrest though, ⑦ _____ _____ right?

F: That is true. Police have the ⑧ _____ _____ conduct searches when an arrest is made to ensure their safety ⑨ _____ _____ collect and protect evidence. The issue here though, is that by searching a person's cell phone they are accessing a large amount of personal information. The ⑩ _____ _____ ... do they have the right to sift through that private ⑪ _____ and correspondence. ⑫ _____ _____

⑬ _____ _____ Supreme Court must establish.

M: As technology evolves even further, and more and more private information is contained "on one's person," this decision ⑭ _____ _____ to be an easy one.

F: That's ⑮ _____ right. Another spin-off to this case that has people talking is whether pictures or video taken on cell phones by private ⑯ _____ can be used as evidence. With the invention of smart phones, there is almost always someone watching and recording events as they unfold. Can this be subpoenaed? Can this information be confiscated or conversely volunteered to ⑰ _____? These are all questions the Supreme Court Justices must consider.

M: As always Michelle, thank you for your insight.

Stage 2 インタビュー解説

日本語訳と、解説を参照しながら、インタビュー内容を確認しよう。そのあとで、Stage1の穴埋めに再チャレンジしてみよう。

M: The Supreme Court is in session this week addressing the issue of cellphones and privacy, and we have ① **asked** our legal consultant Michelle Walters to weigh in on the situation. Michelle, how do you see this case playing out?

> 今週、携帯電話とプライバシーの問題を取り扱って、最高裁が開廷しています。私たちは、弊社の法律顧問であるミシェル・ウォルターに状況に関する議論に加わるようお願いしました。ミシェル、このケースはどのような展開になっていると思いますか？
>
> * Supreme Court「最高裁判所」 address「扱う；処理する」 weigh in「議論に加わる」 play out「展開する」

F: Well I'll tell you Jim, this is really just the tip of the iceberg for this issue, which is likely to be before the courts for several years to come. At issue is the basic ② **right of** privacy versus technology. The basis of the current case is whether police have the right to search suspects' cell phones for potential evidence ③ **of a** crime. The court ④ **must decide** whether police acted legally by searching suspect's phones without ⑤ **getting** a search warrant.

> えー、ジム、あのですね、これはこの問題のほんの氷山の一角なんです。それは今後数年で法廷に出てくるだろうと思いますが。ポイントになっているのは、基本的なプライバシーの権利とテクノロジーの対立なんです。今回の件のおもなポイントは、警察が犯罪の潜在的な証拠を求めて、容疑者の携帯電話を搜索する権利があるかどうかということです。法廷は、警察が搜索令状なしに、容疑者の携帯電話を搜索したことは、法に準じたものだったのかどうかを判断しなければなりません。
>
> ＊ at issue「問題になっている（こと）」 … versus …「…対…；…と…の対立」 basis「おもなポイント」 suspect「容疑者」 evidence「証拠」 crime「犯罪」 search warrant「搜索令状」

M: Police do have ⑥ **authority** to conduct a search upon arrest though, ⑦ **isn't that** right?

> しかし、警察には、逮捕にあたり、搜索を行う権限がありますよね？
>
> ＊ authority「権限；権力」

F: That is true. Police have the ⑧ **right to** conduct searches when an arrest is made to ensure their safety ⑨ **and to** collect and protect evidence. The issue here though, is that by searching a person's cell phone they are accessing a large amount of personal information. The ⑩ **question is** … do they have the right to sift through that private ⑪ **data** and correspondence. ⑫ **That is** ⑬ **what the** Supreme Court must establish.

> そのとおりです。警察には、自らの安全を確保したり、証拠を収集・保護するために、逮捕時に搜索を行う権利があります。しかし、ここで問題になっているのは、ある人物の携帯電話を搜索することによって、大量の個人情報にアクセスすることになるということです。問題は…警察に個人の情報や通信を詳しく調べる権利があるのかということです。これこそ、最高裁がはっきりさせなければならないことです。

> * ensure「確実にする」 protect「保護する」 personal information「個人情報」
>   sift through ...「…を細かく調べる」 correspondence「通信」
>   establish「はっきりさせる；立証する；証明する」

M: As technology evolves even further, and more and more private information is contained "on one's person," this decision ⑭ **doesn't seem** to be an easy one.

> テクノロジーがさらに進化し、さらに多くの個人的な情報が、「携帯」しているものに含まれるようになるのですから、今回の判決はかんたんなものには思えません。
>
> * evolve「発展する；進化する」 contain「含む」 on one's person「携帯して；携帯電話に」

F: That's ⑮ **exactly** right. Another spin-off to this case that has people talking is whether pictures or video taken on cell phones by private ⑯ **citizens** can be used as evidence. With the invention of smart phones, there is almost always someone watching and recording events as they unfold. Can this be subpoenaed? Can this information be confiscated or conversely volunteered to ⑰ **authorities**? These are all questions the Supreme Court Justices must consider.

> まさしくそのとおりです。今回の件から派生する事柄で、みんなが話題にしているものには、市民個人の携帯で撮影された写真やビデオを証拠として使えるのかどうかという点です。携帯電話の発明によって、ほぼ必ずだれかが起こっている出来事を見たり記録したりしています。これは、法廷に提出を命じることができるのでしょうか？ この情報は没収されたり、逆に自発的に当局に提供されたりしていいのでしょうか？ こういった問題のすべてを、最高裁の判事たちは考えなければならないのです。
>
> * spin-off「副産物」 unfold「(出来事などが) 展開する」 subpoena「(法廷への) 提出を命じる」
>   confiscate「没収する」 conversely「逆に」 volunteer「自発的に提供する」
>   authority「当局」 Supreme Court Justice「最高裁の判事」

M: As always Michelle, thank you for your insight.

> ミシェル、いつものように、あなたの慧眼に感謝いたします。
>
> * insight「見識；洞察」

Stage 3　英文トランスクリプション

インタビュー全体を英文の原稿で確認しながらCDで耳慣らししよう！ その上で、インタビューを聴きながら、まだできていない部分の穴埋めに再チャレンジしよう。

M: The Supreme Court is in session this week addressing the issue of cellphones and privacy, and we have ① **asked** our legal consultant Michelle Walters to weigh in on the situation. Michelle, how do you see this case playing out?

F: Well I'll tell you Jim, this is really just the tip of the iceberg for this issue, which is likely to be before the courts for several years to come. At issue is the basic ② **right of** privacy versus technology. The basis of the current case is whether police have the right to search suspects' cell phones for potential evidence ③ **of a** crime. The court ④ **must decide** whether police acted legally by searching suspect's phones without ⑤ **getting** a search warrant.

M: Police do have ⑥ **authority** to conduct a search upon arrest though, ⑦ **isn't that** right?

F: That is true. Police have the ⑧ **right to** conduct searches when an arrest is made to ensure their safety ⑨ **and to** collect and protect evidence. The issue here though, is that by searching a person's cell phone they are accessing a large amount of personal information. The ⑩ **question is** … do they have the right to sift through that private ⑪ **data** and correspondence. ⑫ **That is** ⑬ **what the** Supreme Court must establish.

M: As technology evolves even further, and more and more private information is contained "on one's person," this decision ⑭ **doesn't seem** to be an easy one.

F: That's ⑮ **exactly** right. Another spin-off to this case that has people talking is whether pictures or video taken on cell phones by private ⑯ **citizens** can be used as evidence. With the invention of smart phones, there is almost always someone watching and recording events as they unfold. Can this be subpoenaed? Can this information be confiscated or conversely volunteered to ⑰ **authorities**? These are all questions the Supreme Court Justices must consider.

M: As always Michelle, thank you for your insight.

Stage 4))) 音声変化をチェック

まとめとして、穴埋め部分の音声変化の特徴を**スロー・スピード**と**ナチュラル・スピード**で確認しよう。下記に示したカタカナ表記で音声変化を確認して、もう一度インタビューを聴き直してみよう。発音変化のルールは適宜復習しよう。

❶ **asked** アスクト ▶ アスッ＿ト
☞ 破裂音［k］の脱落が起こる。

❷ **right of** ライト・アヴ ▶ ライダ［ラ］ヴ
☞ 連結部で［t］音が弾音化する。

❸ **of a** アヴ・ア ▶ アヴァ
☞ 2語が連結する。

❹ **must decide** マスト・ディサイド ▶ マスッ＿ディサイド
☞ 破裂音の連続で片方が脱落する。

❺ **getting** ゲッティング ▶ ゲッディ［リ］ン（グ）
☞ 破裂音［t］が弾音化する。末尾の［g］音も脱落しやすい。

❻ **authority** オソーラティー ▶ オソーラディ［リ］ー
☞ 破裂音［t］が弾音化する。

❼ **isn't that** イズント・ザット ▶ イズン＿ザッ（ト）
☞ 破裂音［t］の脱落が生じる。

❽ **right to** ライト・トゥー ▶ ライッ＿トゥー
☞ 破裂音［t］の脱落が生じる。

❾ **and to** アンド・トゥー ▶ アン＿トゥー
☞ 破裂音［d］の脱落が生じる。

❿ **question is** クェスチャン・イズ ▶ クェスチャニズ
☞ 2語が連結する。

⓫ **data** デイタ ▶ デイダ［ラ］
☞ 破裂音［t］が弾音化する。

⓬ **That is** ザット・イズ ▶ ザッディ［リ］ズ
☞ 連結部で破裂音［t］の弾音化が起こる。

⓭ **what the** ワット・ザ ▶ ワッ＿ザ
☞ 破裂音［t］の脱落が生じる。

⓮ **doesn't seem** ダズント・スィーム ▶ ダズン＿スィーム
☞ 破裂音［t］の脱落が生じる。

⓯ **exactly** イグザックトゥリー ▶ イグザック＿リー
☞［tl］で［t］音の脱落が生じる。

⓰ **citizens** スィティズンズ ▶ スィディ［リ］ズンズ
☞ 破裂音［t］が弾音化する。

⓱ **authorities** オソーラティーズ ▶ オソーラディ［リ］ーズ
☞ 破裂音［t］が弾音化する。

法律家のインタビュー

INTERVIEW WITH AN ELEMENTARY SCHOOL TEACHER

Unit 21　小学校教員のインタビュー

Stage 1　穴埋めインタビュー・リスニング

音声変化に注意してCDでインタビューを聴きながら空欄部分を埋めてみよう。CDのナチュラル音声での聴き取りが難しいときは、次のトラックに収録されたスロー音声で聴いてみよう。

M: What ① _____ _____ say is the biggest challenge facing teachers today?

F: To be honest with you, it's the same problem many professionals in various other fields face — financing. While the economy is seemingly on the rebound, educational budgets are ② _____ than ever, and sadly they are some of the first to take cuts when the ③ _____ _____ tough. Public schools in particular are dependent on tax levies and other local government support financially, and it's always an uphill ④ _____.

M: America is often ⑤ _____ _____ being way behind in comparison to education levels and standardized test results from other countries. What is your take ⑥ _____ _____?

F: Well, that's tough to properly evaluate, I think. Education standards and cultures vary from country to country, so I think it is more ⑦ _____ to work towards developing a standard curriculum and evaluation method for the US that makes sense. I do believe we have lost ground ⑧ _____ _____ last few decades, as dropout rates have increased, and proficiency levels have fallen across the board. That is a big problem ⑨ _____ _____ of us as educators are working hard to change, ⑩ _____ _____ think we are making some real progress. On the other hand, it is hard to do when your hands are tied, financially speaking.

M: You teach in a very cosmopolitan urban area of Atlanta. What percentage of students ⑪ _____ _____ say you have whose native language is not English?

F: Based ⑫ _____ _____ latest data I have seen from our district it's ⑬ _____ to be about ⑭ _____ percent, which corresponds to ⑮ _____ _____ see in the classroom every day. In our school we have had an early-education ESL program, which is ⑯ _____ _____ the core curriculum and available as extra-curricular classwork. Truth be told, any language barriers don't represent a problem for the students, ⑰ _____ _____ becomes more of an issue when we have to communicate with the parents during parent-teach conferences and the like.

Stage 2 インタビュー解説

日本語訳と、解説を参照しながら、インタビュー内容を確認しよう。そのあとで、Stage1の穴埋めに再チャレンジしてみよう。

M: What ① **would you** say is the biggest challenge facing teachers today?

> 今日の教師がぶつかっている最大の壁はなんでしょうか？
> --
> ＊challenge「難問；課題」 face「直面する」

F: To be honest with you, it's the same problem many professionals in various other fields face — financing. While the economy is seemingly on the rebound, educational budgets are ② **tighter** than ever, and sadly they are some of the first to take cuts when the ③ **going gets** tough. Public schools in particular are dependent on

小学校教員のインタビュー 131

tax levies and other local government support financially, and it's always an uphill ④ **battle**.

> 正直に言いますと、ほかのさまざまな分野で多くのプロフェッショナルが直面している問題と同じく資金面です。どうやら経済が立ち直ってきている一方で、教育予算はこれまでになく引き締められています。悲しいかな、教育予算は、状況が悪化すると最初に削減を受けるもののひとつなんです。特に公立の学校は、財政的に税の徴収や地方政府からのその他のサポートに頼っていて、いつも厳しい闘いを強いられています。
>
> ＊ seemingly「どうやら；見たところ；うわべ上」　on the rebound「（経済が）立ち直って」
>   going「状況」　tough「厳しい；難しい」　tax levies「税の徴収」
>   uphill battle「厳しい戦い；苦闘」

M: America is often ⑤ **touted as** being way behind in comparison to education levels and standardized test results from other countries. What is your take ⑥ **on that**?

> アメリカは、外国の教育レベルや標準テストの結果と比較するとはるかに遅れていると、しばしば喧伝されています。この点について、あなたの見解はいかがでしょう？
>
> ＊ be touted「喧伝される」　in comparison to ...「…と比較すると」
>   standardized test「（一斉）標準テスト」

F: Well, that's tough to properly evaluate, I think. Education standards and cultures vary from country to country, so I think it is more ⑦ **important** to work towards developing a standard curriculum and evaluation method for the US that makes sense. I do believe we have lost ground ⑧ **in the** last few decades, as dropout rates have increased, and proficiency levels have fallen across the board. That is a big problem ⑨ **that all** of us as educators are working hard to change, ⑩ **and I** think we are making some real progress. On the other hand, it is hard to do when your hands are tied, financially speaking.

> ええ、的確に評価するのはとても難しいと思います。教育水準や文化は国によってさまざまですから、アメリカにとって合理的に納得できる標準的なカリキュラムと評価法の開発に向けて取り組むほうが重要だと思います。過去数十年で、私たちは後退したと思っています。ドロップアウトの率が上昇し、全般的に達成度は落ち込んでいます。これは、教育者として私たち全員が変えようと懸命に取り組んでいる大問題で、私たちはほんとうの意味でいくら

> か前進していると考えています。一方、それは両手が縛られているときに、実行するのは難しいことなのです。財政的な意味でですが。
>
> ---
>
> * evaluate「評価する」 education standards「教育水準」 vary「多様である；さまざまだ」
>   make sense「(合理的で) 納得できる」 lose ground「後退する」
>   dropout「ドロップアウト；中退；落第」 proficiency「熟達」
>   across the board「全面的に；一律に」 progress「前進；進歩」
>   financially speaking「財政的な見地から言えば」

M: You teach in a very cosmopolitan urban area of Atlanta. What percentage of students ⑪ **would you** say you have whose native language is not English?

> あなたは、アトランタの非常に国際的で都会的なエリアで教鞭を執っていますね。英語が母国語でない生徒はどのくらいの率でいると思われますか？
>
> ---
>
> * cosmopolitan「国際的な」 native language「母国語」

F: Based ⑫ **on the** latest data I have seen from our district it's ⑬ **reported** to be about ⑭ **twenty** percent, which corresponds to ⑮ **what I** see in the classroom every day. In our school we have had an early-education ESL program, which is ⑯ **part of** the core curriculum and available as extra-curricular classwork. Truth be told, any language barriers don't represent a problem for the students, ⑰ **but it** becomes more of an issue when we have to communicate with the parents during parent-teach conferences and the like.

> 私が見たわれわれの地域の直近のデータによれば、約20%という報告でした。この数字は毎日私がクラスで見かける光景と一致しています。私の学校では、早期教育のESLプログラムを実施していますが、これは、コア・カリキュラムの一部で、課外授業として提供されています。正直なところ、言葉の壁は、生徒たちにとって問題にはならないのです。しかし、むしろ父母会などで両親とコミュニケーションを取らねばならない場面で問題になるんです。
>
> ---
>
> * correspond to ...「…に一致する；合致する」 early-education「早期教育の」
>   ESL program「第二言語としての英語教育プログラム」 extra-curricular「課外の」
>   Truth be told, ...「正直なところ…」 language barrier「言葉の壁」
>   more of a/an ...「むしろ…」

Stage 3 英文トランスクリプション

インタビュー全体を英文の原稿で確認しながらCDで耳慣らししよう！ その上で、インタビューを聴きながら、まだできていない部分の穴埋めに再チャレンジしよう。

M: What ① **would you** say is the biggest challenge facing teachers today?

F: To be honest with you, it's the same problem many professionals in various other fields face — financing. While the economy is seemingly on the rebound, educational budgets are ② **tighter** than ever, and sadly they are some of the first to take cuts when the ③ **going gets** tough. Public schools in particular are dependent on tax levies and other local government support financially, and it's always an uphill ④ **battle**.

M: America is often ⑤ **touted as** being way behind in comparison to education levels and standardized test results from other countries. What is your take ⑥ **on that**?

F: Well, that's tough to properly evaluate, I think. Education standards and cultures vary from country to country, so I think it is more ⑦ **important** to work towards developing a standard curriculum and evaluation method for the US that makes sense. I do believe we have lost ground ⑧ **in the** last few decades, as dropout rates have increased, and proficiency levels have fallen across the board. That is a big problem ⑨ **that all** of us as educators are working hard to change, ⑩ **and I** think we are making some real progress. On the other hand, it is hard to do when your hands are tied, financially speaking.

M: You teach in a very cosmopolitan urban area of Atlanta. What percentage of students ⑪ **would you** say you have whose native language is not English?

F: Based ⑫ **on the** latest data I have seen from our district it's ⑬ **reported** to be about ⑭ **twenty** percent, which corresponds to ⑮ **what I** see in the classroom every day. In our school we have had an early-education ESL program, which is ⑯ **part of** the core curriculum and available as extra-curricular classwork. Truth be told, any language barriers don't represent a problem for the students, ⑰ **but it** becomes more of an issue when we have to communicate with the parents during parent-teach conferences and the like.

❄️ Stage 4 🔊 音声変化をチェック

まとめとして、穴埋め部分の音声変化の特徴を**スロー・スピード**と**ナチュラル・スピード**で確認しよう。下記に示したカタカナ表記で音声変化を確認して、もう一度インタビューを聴き直してみよう。発音変化のルールは適宜復習しよう。

---

❶ **would you** ウッド・ユー ▶ ウッジュー
☞ [d] + [j] の部分で音が混じり合い、[ジュ] に近い音に変化する。

❷ **tighter** タイター ▶ タイダ [ラ] ー
☞ 破裂音 [t] が弾音化する。

❸ **going gets** ゴウイング・ゲッツ ▶ ゴウイン_ゲッツ
☞ 破裂音の連続で片方の [g] 音が脱落する。

❹ **battle** バトゥ ▶ バドゥ [ル] ゥ
☞ 破裂音 [t] が弾音化する。

❺ **touted as** タウティッド・アズ ▶ タウディ [リ] ッダ [ラ] ズ
☞ touted の破裂音 [t] が弾音化する。2語の連結部の [d] 音も弾音化しやすい。

❻ **on that** オン・ザット ▶ オナッ (ト)
☞ [n] + [ð] が [n] 音に変化する。末尾の [t] 音も脱落しやすい。

❼ **important** イムポートゥント ▶ イムポーンン (ト)
☞ [tn] の部分が声門閉鎖音化する。末尾の [t] 音は脱落しやすい。

❽ **in the** イン・ザ ▶ イナ
☞ [n] + [ð] が [n] 音に変化する。

❾ **that all** ザット・オーゥ ▶ ザッド [ロ] ーゥ
☞ 連結部で破裂音 [t] が弾音化する。

❿ **and I** アンド・アイ ▶ アナイ
☞ and の [d] 音が脱落して、2語が連結する。

⓫ **would you** ウッド・ユー ▶ ウッジュー
☞ [d] + [j] の部分で音が混じり合い、[ジュ] に近い音に変化する。

⓬ **on the** オン・ザ ▶ オナ
☞ [n] + [ð] が [n] 音に変化する。

⓭ **reported** リポーティッド ▶ リポーディ [リ] ッ (ド)
☞ 破裂音 [t] が弾音化する。末尾の [d] 音が脱落することもある。

⓮ **twenty** トゥエンティー ▶ トゥエニー
☞ [nt] で [t] 音の脱落が生じる。

⓯ **what I** ワット・アイ ▶ ワッダ [ラ] イ
☞ 連結部で [t] 音が弾音化する。

⓰ **part of** パート・アヴ ▶ パーダ [ラ] ヴ
☞ 連結部で [t] 音が弾音化する。

⓱ **but it** バット・イット ▶ バッディ [リ] ッ (ト)
☞ 連結部で [t] 音が弾音化する。末尾の [t] 音は脱落しやすい。

INTERVIEW WITH A SOLDIER

Unit 22　兵士のインタビュー

Stage 1　穴埋め インタビュー・リスニング

音声変化に注意してCDでインタビューを聴きながら空欄部分を埋めてみよう。CDのナチュラル音声での聴き取りが難しいときは、次のトラックに収録されたスロー音声で聴いてみよう。

M: With us today is Col. Carol Edwards, one of the first female fighter pilots in the ① _____ States Air Force, and the first woman ② _____ _____ a fighter group wing commander. Col. Edwards, what ③ _____ _____ on the path to becoming an air-force pilot?

F: I was in a college program ④ _____ _____ us to "shadow" people in different fields. In my case, as I had always been interested in the Air Force, it gave me the chance to take back-seat rides in F-16 fighter jets ⑤ _____ _____ nearby air base. From that ⑥ _____ _____ I was hooked. Luckily for me, I was just ⑦ _____ the program when the Pentagon changed its position and started to allow women to fly fighter jets, even though ground combat was still "only for the boys."

M: Was there pressure on you as one of the first women to train?

F: ⑧ _____ _____ point, I didn't care anything about being first or all of the attention that later came ⑨ _____ _____. I just ⑩ _____ _____ fly, and serve my country to the best of my ability. Honestly, I didn't know I was the first until I was awarded my wings.

M: You've served in both Iraq and Afghanistan. How did your fellow pilots treat you?

F: Some were more ⑪ _____ than others ... that's for sure. But in the end, when you are in a combat situation in particular, the ⑫ _____ thing everyone wants to know is whether you can do the job. In the end that supersedes everything. Once I proved my ability and competence, ⑬ _____ towards me changed almost overnight.

M: After you pioneered the way, so to speak, many other women have since become combat aviators. Did you feel the need to reach out to them?

F: No. I think the entire ⑭ _____ _____ this whole topic is gender ⑮ _____. It doesn't make a difference whether a pilot is a woman or a man, what makes a difference is how capable they are of flying their aircraft and completing their mission. There should be equal standards, and slowly but surely, we are ⑯ _____ _____ _____ direction.

Stage 2))) インタビュー解説

日本語訳と、解説を参照しながら、インタビュー内容を確認しよう。そのあとで、Stage1の穴埋めに再チャレンジしてみよう。

M: With us today is Col. Carol Edwards, one of the first female fighter pilots in the ① **United** States Air Force, and the first woman ② **to be** a fighter group wing commander. Col. Edwards, what ③ **started you** on the path to becoming an air-force pilot?

> 今日はキャロル・エドワーズ大佐をお招きしています。アメリカ空軍初の女性戦闘機パイロットのおひとりで、女性初の戦闘航空群の航空団長でもあります。エドワーズ大佐、空軍パイロットの道に入ったきっかけは？
>
> * Col. = colonel「大佐」 path to ...「…への道」

F: I was in a college program ④ **that allowed** us to "shadow" people in different fields. In my case, as I had always been interested in the Air Force, it gave me the chance to take back-seat rides in F-16 fighter jets ⑤ **at a** nearby air base. From that ⑥ **point on** I was hooked. Luckily for me, I was just ⑦ **entering** the program when the Pentagon changed its position and started to allow women to fly fighter jets, even though ground combat was still "only for the boys."

> 私は、いろいろな分野の人たちのそばで学べる、大学のプログラムに参加していました。私の場合、ずっと空軍に興味があって、近くの空軍基地で F-16 戦闘機の後部座席に乗るチャンスをもらえたんです。そこから私はハマってしまったんですよ。私にとって幸運なことに、ペンタゴンが方針を変え、女性にも戦闘機で飛ぶことを許し始めた頃に、ちょうど私はそのプログラムに参加しようとしていたんです。でも、地上での戦闘はまだ男性だけのものでしたが。
>
> * shadow …「…のそばで学ぶ」 air base「空軍基地」 be hooked「ハマる」

M: Was there pressure on you as one of the first women to train?

> 最初に訓練を受けた女性のひとりとして、プレッシャーはありましたか?

F: ⑧ **At that** point, I didn't care anything about being first or all of the attention that later came ⑨ **with that**. I just ⑩ **wanted to** fly, and serve my country to the best of my ability. Honestly, I didn't know I was the first until I was awarded my wings.

> その時点では、最初の女性であることや、そのことであとから発生したあらゆる注目など、まったく気にしませんでした。私は単純に空を飛んで、自分にできる限りの力で自国に奉仕したかったのです。正直に言うと、パイロットの資格を与えられるまで、自分が最初だということも知りませんでしたし。
>
> * to the best of one's ability「自分の能力の最大まで」 award「与える」
>   wing「翼」ここではパイロットの資格を指す。

M: You've served in both Iraq and Afghanistan. How did your fellow pilots treat you?

> イラクとアフガニスタンの両方に従軍なさいましたね。あなたの同僚パイロットたちは、あなたをどう扱いましたか?
>
> * fellow「仲間 ; 同僚」

F: Some were more ⑪ **supportive** than others ... that's for sure. But in the end, when you are in a combat situation in particular, the ⑫ **important** thing everyone wants to know is whether you can do the job. In the end that supersedes everything. Once I proved my ability and competence, ⑬ **attitudes** towards me changed almost overnight.

> いくらかは協力的な人もいましたね…それは確かです。でも、結局、特に戦闘状態に入ったとき、みんなが知りたい重要なことは、戦えるのかどうかということなんですよ。結局ほかのことは不要なんです。いったん、私が自分の能力や資質を証明したとたん、私に対する態度は、瞬時に変わってしまいました。
>
> ＊ supersede「取って代わる；ほかの不要なものと入れ替わる」 overnight「一夜で；突然に；瞬時に」

M: After you pioneered the way, so to speak, many other women have since become combat aviators. Did you feel the need to reach out to them?

> 言わば、あなたがその道を切り開いて以来、多くのほかの女性たちが戦闘機の操縦士になりました。彼女たちに手を差し伸べる必要は感じましたか？
>
> ＊ pioneer「先駆けとなる」 combat aviator「戦闘機の操縦士」 reach out to ...「…を支援する」

F: No. I think the entire ⑭ **point of** this whole topic is gender ⑮ **neutrality**. It doesn't make a difference whether a pilot is a woman or a man, what makes a difference is how capable they are of flying their aircraft and completing their mission. There should be equal standards, and slowly but surely, we are ⑯ **heading in that** direction.

> いいえ。この問題全体のポイントは、まるまる性の中立という点にあります。パイロットは女性でも男性でもかまわないのです。問題になるのは、どれだけ航空機の操縦やミッションの完遂の能力があるかということです。（男女に）同じ基準があるべきで、ゆっくりとではありますが確実に、われわれはその方向に進んでいます。
>
> ＊ neutrality「中立（的な態度）」 capable of ...「…の能力がある」 mission「任務」
>   equal standards「同一の基準」

Stage 3 英文トランスクリプション

インタビュー全体を英文の原稿で確認しながらCDで耳慣らししよう！ その上で、インタビューを聴きながら、まだできていない部分の穴埋めに再チャレンジしよう。

M: With us today is Col. Carol Edwards, one of the first female fighter pilots in the ① **United** States Air Force, and the first woman ② **to be** a fighter group wing commander. Col. Edwards, what ③ **started you** on the path to becoming an air-force pilot?

F: I was in a college program ④ **that allowed** us to "shadow" people in different fields. In my case, as I had always been interested in the Air Force, it gave me the chance to take back-seat rides in F-16 fighter jets ⑤ **at a** nearby air base. From that ⑥ **point on** I was hooked. Luckily for me, I was just ⑦ **entering** the program when the Pentagon changed its position and started to allow women to fly fighter jets, even though ground combat was still "only for the boys."

M: Was there pressure on you as one of the first women to train?

F: ⑧ **At that** point, I didn't care anything about being first or all of the attention that later came ⑨ **with that**. I just ⑩ **wanted to** fly, and serve my country to the best of my ability. Honestly, I didn't know I was the first until I was awarded my wings.

M: You've served in both Iraq and Afghanistan. How did your fellow pilots treat you?

F: Some were more ⑪ **supportive** than others … that's for sure. But in the end, when you are in a combat situation in particular, the ⑫ **important** thing everyone wants to know is whether you can do the job. In the end that supersedes everything. Once I proved my ability and competence, ⑬ **attitudes** towards me changed almost overnight.

M: After you pioneered the way, so to speak, many other women have since become combat aviators. Did you feel the need to reach out to them?

F: No. I think the entire ⑭ **point of** this whole topic is gender ⑮ **neutrality**. It doesn't make a difference whether a pilot is a woman or a man, what makes a difference is how capable they are of flying their aircraft and completing their mission. There should be equal standards, and slowly but surely, we are ⑯ **heading in that** direction.

Stage 4))) 音声変化をチェック

まとめとして、穴埋め部分の音声変化の特徴を**スロー・スピード**と**ナチュラル・スピード**で確認しよう。下記に示したカタカナ表記で音声変化を確認して、もう一度インタビューを聴き直してみよう。発音変化のルールは適宜復習しよう。

---

❶ **United** 　　　　　　　　　ユナイティッド　　　　　　　▶ ユナイディ［リ］ッ［ド］
　☞ 破裂音［t］の弾音化が起こる。末尾の［d］音が脱落することもある。

❷ **to be** 　　　　　　　　　　トゥー・ビー　　　　　　　　▶ ドゥ［ル］ービー
　☞ to の破裂音［t］が弾音化することがある。

❸ **started you** 　　　　　　　スターティッド・ユー　　　　▶ スターディ［リ］ッジュー
　☞ started の破裂音［t］が弾音化する。［d］＋［j］の部分で音が混じり合い、[ジュ] に近い音に変化する。

❹ **that allowed** 　　　　　　　ザット・アラウド　　　　　　▶ ザッダ［ラ］ラウド
　☞ 連結部で破裂音［t］が弾音化する。

❺ **at a** 　　　　　　　　　　　アット・ア　　　　　　　　　▶ アッダ［ラ］
　☞ 連結部で破裂音［t］が弾音化する。

❻ **point on** 　　　　　　　　　ポイント・オン　　　　　　　▶ ポイノン
　☞ 破裂音［t］が脱落しながら、2語が連結する。

❼ **entering** 　　　　　　　　　エンタリング　　　　　　　　▶ エンチャリン（グ）；エナリン（グ）
　☞ [tər] 部分の［tə］音が［チャ］に近い音に変化する。［nt］で［t］音の脱落が生じる場合もある。

❽ **At that** 　　　　　　　　　アット・ザット　　　　　　　▶ アッ＿ザッ（ト）
　☞ 破裂音［t］が脱落する。末尾の［t］音も脱落することがある。

❾ **with that** 　　　　　　　　ウィズ・ザット　　　　　　　▶ ウィッ＿ザッ（ト）
　☞ [ð] の連続で片方が脱落する。末尾の［t］音も脱落することがある。

❿ **wanted to** 　　　　　　　　ワンティッド・トゥー　　　　▶ ワニッ＿トゥー
　☞ wanted から［t］音と［d］音がともに脱落する。

⓫ **supportive** 　　　　　　　　サポーティヴ　　　　　　　　▶ サポーディ［リ］ヴ
　☞ 破裂音［t］が弾音化する。

⓬ **important** 　　　　　　　　イムポートゥント　　　　　　▶ イムポーんン（ト）
　☞ [tn] の［t］音が声門閉鎖音化する場合がある。末尾の［t］音も脱落することがある。

⓭ **attitudes** 　　　　　　　　アティテューズ　　　　　　　▶ アディ［リ］デ［リ］ューズ
　☞ 破裂音［t］が弾音化する。

⓮ **point of** 　　　　　　　　　ポイント・アヴ　　　　　　　▶ ポイナヴ
　☞ 破裂音［t］が脱落しながら、2語が連結する。

⓯ **neutrality** 　　　　　　　　ニュートゥラリティー　　　　▶ ニュートゥラリディ［リ］ー
　☞ 破裂音［t］が弾音化する。

⓰ **heading in that** 　　　　　ヘッディング・イン・ザット　▶ ヘッディ［リ］ニナッ（ト）
　☞ heading の［d］音は弾音化することがある。heading の［g］が脱落して in に連結する。in that の連結部では［n］＋［ð］が［n］音に変化する。末尾の［t］も脱落する場合がある。

INTERVIEW WITH A TAXI DRIVER

Unit 23　タクシー運転手のインタビュー

Stage 1　穴埋め インタビュー・リスニング

音声変化に注意してCDでインタビューを聴きながら空欄部分を埋めてみよう。CDのナチュラル音声での聴き取りが難しいときは、次のトラックに収録されたスロー音声で聴いてみよう。

F: I'm sure as a taxi-driver you have seen a lot of crazy things. What's the most memorable experience you've had behind the wheel?

M: ① _____ _____ cabbing here in Las Vegas for over twenty years now. I'd have to say the most surprising thing was when I picked up a couple from a popular club and the man ② _____ _____ his girlfriend in the backseat of my taxi. ③ _____ _____ itself is pretty uncommon, but the best part was when she said "yes" and they told me to take them ④ _____ _____ a drive through ceremony. They got hitched ⑤ _____ _____ in my car. I guess since I was the only other person there you could say I was the "best man." ⑥ _____ _____ that, they paid me double the fare for the entire time the meter was running!

F: I think a lot of people ⑦ _____ _____ think your job is an easy one. Is that so?

M: Well ... ⑧ _____ _____. We spend a lot of time just ⑨ _____ for a customer. I have to compete with many other taxi drivers, and if I don't make more than it costs me to rent my vehicle, I'm in the hole for the day. Also, you have to remember that we are responsible for the safety of our passengers ... so there's ⑩ _____ _____ _____ _____ stress built into the job.

F: Have you ever been robbed?

M: I've had people ⑪ _____ _____ _____ the fare, not paying me and running away when we stop. As far as someone trying to steal my money or robbing me at gunpoint, no … ⑫ _____ _____ know people that have been through that. It's always in the back of our minds, especially when we are working ⑬ _____ _____ night.

F: What's the most enjoyable part of your job?

M: I ⑭ _____ _____ meet so many different people. Through our conversations, I learn a ⑮ _____ _____ many different things. Of course, there are customers who don't want to chat, or are ⑯ _____ _____ bad mood, but for the most part the ⑰ _____ with my riders is the best part.

Stage 2 インタビュー解説

日本語訳と、解説を参照しながら、インタビュー内容を確認しよう。そのあとで、Stage1の穴埋めに再チャレンジしてみよう。

F: I'm sure as a taxi-driver you have seen a lot of crazy things. What's the most memorable experience you've had behind the wheel?

> きっとタクシードライバーとして、多くのとんでもない出来事をご覧になってきたことでしょうね。運転中のもっとも記憶に残る体験はなんですか？
>
> ＊memorable「記憶に残る」 behind the wheel「運転席で；運転中に」

M: ① **I've been** cabbing here in Las Vegas for over twenty years now. I'd have to say the most surprising thing was when I picked up a couple from a popular club and the man ② **proposed to**

his girlfriend in the backseat of my taxi. ③ **That in** itself is pretty uncommon, but the best part was when she said "yes" and they told me to take them ④ **right to** a drive through ceremony. They got hitched ⑤ **right there** in my car. I guess since I was the only other person there you could say I was the "best man." ⑥ **Not only** that, they paid me double the fare for the entire time the meter was running!

> ラスベガスで、もう20年以上もタクシー運転手をしてます。もっとも驚いたのは、人気のクラブから出てきたカップルを拾ったときでしょうね。タクシーの後部座席で男性が彼女にプロポーズしたんですよ。それ自体、かなりめずらしいことなんだけど、でも最高だったのは彼女が「イエス」って言って、まっすぐにドライブスルーの式場に行ってくれって、ふたりに頼まれたときだね。ふたりは、私の車の中で結婚しちゃったんですよ。その場にいたのは私だけなんだから、私が『花婿の付添人』だったと言ってもいいのかもね。それだけじゃなくて、彼らは、メーターが回っていた全部の時間分の2倍の料金を支払ってくれたんですよ!
>
> ＊ cab「タクシーを運転する」 backseat「後部座席」 in itself「それ自体（では）」
>   get hitched「結婚する」 best man「花婿の付添人の男性」

F: I think a lot of people ⑦ **out there** think your job is an easy one. Is that so?

> 世の中の多くの人が、あなたの仕事はかんたんだと思っていると思うんですが。そのとおりですか?

M: Well … ⑧ **not really**. We spend a lot of time just ⑨ **waiting** for a customer. I have to compete with many other taxi drivers, and if I don't make more than it costs me to rent my vehicle, I'm in the hole for the day. Also, you have to remember that we are responsible for the safety of our passengers … so there's ⑩ **quite a bit of** stress built into the job.

> いや…そうでもないですよ。お客さんを待つだけで多くの時間を使うんですよ。多くのタクシー・ドライバーとの競争もあるし。自動車のレンタルにかかる費用以上に稼がないと、その日は赤字になるんですよ。それに、運転手は乗客の安全に対して責任があることも忘れてはならないんです。だから、仕事には多くのストレスがつきまとうんです。
>
> ＊ in the hole「赤字の；マイナスの」 passenger「乗客」 built into …「…に組み込まれて」

F: Have you ever been robbed?

> 強盗に遭ったことはありますか?
> --
> * rob「強盗する;盗む」

M: I've had people ⑪ **run out on** the fare, not paying me and running away when we stop. As far as someone trying to steal my money or robbing me at gunpoint, no … ⑫ **but I** know people that have been through that. It's always in the back of our minds, especially when we are working ⑬ **late at** night.

> 料金を客に踏み倒されたことはありますよ。支払いをせずに、停車したときに逃げちゃうんですよ。だれかが金を盗もうとしたり、拳銃を突きつけて私に強盗を働こうとしたりということなら、ありません。しかし、そういった経験をした人は知ってますよ。それはいつも頭の片隅にありますね。特に夜遅くに仕事をしているときにはね。
> --
> * run out on …「…を踏み倒す」　at gunpoint「拳銃を突きつけて」
>   be through …「…を経験する」　in the back of one's mind「心の隅に」

F: What's the most enjoyable part of your job?

> 仕事でいちばん楽しい部分はなんでしょう?

M: I ⑭ **get to** meet so many different people. Through our conversations, I learn a ⑮ **lot about** many different things. Of course, there are customers who don't want to chat, or are ⑯ **in a** bad mood, but for the most part the ⑰ **interaction** with my riders is the best part.

> いろいろな人と会う機会がある点ですね。会話を通して、いろいろなことが学べるんです。もちろん、おしゃべりをしたがらないお客さんもいますし、あるいは機嫌の悪い人もいますが、ほとんどの場合、乗客との触れ合いがいちばんの楽しみですね。
> --
> * get to …「…する機会がある」　in a bad mood「機嫌の悪い」
>   interaction「やりとり;触れ合い」

Stage 3 英文トランスクリプション

インタビュー全体を英文の原稿で確認しながらCDで耳慣らししよう！ その上で、インタビューを聴きながら、まだできていない部分の穴埋めに再チャレンジしよう。

F: I'm sure as a taxi-driver you have seen a lot of crazy things. What's the most memorable experience you've had behind the wheel?

M: ① **I've been** cabbing here in Las Vegas for over twenty years now. I'd have to say the most surprising thing was when I picked up a couple from a popular club and the man ② **proposed to** his girlfriend in the backseat of my taxi. ③ **That in** itself is pretty uncommon, but the best part was when she said "yes" and they told me to take them ④ **right to** a drive through ceremony. They got hitched ⑤ **right there** in my car. I guess since I was the only other person there you could say I was the "best man." ⑥ **Not only** that, they paid me double the fare for the entire time the meter was running!

F: I think a lot of people ⑦ **out there** think your job is an easy one. Is that so?

M: Well … ⑧ **not really**. We spend a lot of time just ⑨ **waiting** for a customer. I have to compete with many other taxi drivers, and if I don't make more than it costs me to rent my vehicle, I'm in the hole for the day. Also, you have to remember that we are responsible for the safety of our passengers … so there's ⑩ **quite a bit of** stress built into the job.

F: Have you ever been robbed?

M: I've had people ⑪ **run out on** the fare, not paying me and running away when we stop. As far as someone trying to steal my money or robbing me at gunpoint, no … ⑫ **but I** know people that have been through that. It's always in the back of our minds, especially when we are working ⑬ **late at** night.

F: What's the most enjoyable part of your job?

M: I ⑭ **get to** meet so many different people. Through our conversations, I learn a ⑮ **lot about** many different things. Of course, there are customers who don't want to chat, or are ⑯ **in a** bad mood, but for the most part the ⑰ **interaction** with my riders is the best part.

🎙 Stage 4 🔊 音声変化をチェック

まとめとして、穴埋め部分の音声変化の特徴を**スロー・スピード**と**ナチュラル・スピード**で確認しよう。下記に示したカタカナ表記で音声変化を確認して、もう一度インタビューを聴き直してみよう。発音変化のルールは適宜復習しよう。

❶ **I've been**　　　　　アイヴ・ビーン　　　▶ アイッ_ビン
　☞ I've の破裂音 [v] が脱落する。been は弱化して [ビン] と発音。

❷ **proposed to**　　　　プラポウズド・トゥー　▶ プラポウズッ_トゥー
　☞ 破裂音の連続で [d] 音が脱落する。

❸ **That in**　　　　　　ザット・イン　　　　　▶ ザッディ [リ] ン
　☞ 連結部で [t] 音が弾音化する。

❹ **right to**　　　　　　ライト・トゥー　　　　▶ ライッ_トゥー
　☞ right の [t] 音が脱落する。

❺ **right there**　　　　ライト・ゼア　　　　　▶ ライッ_ゼア
　☞ right の [t] 音が脱落する。

❻ **Not only**　　　　　ナット・オウンリー　　　▶ ナッド [ロ] ウンリー
　☞ 連結部で [t] 音が弾音化する。

❼ **out there**　　　　　アウト・ゼア　　　　　▶ アウッ_ゼア
　☞ out の [t] 音が脱落する。

❽ **not really**　　　　　ナット・リアリー　　　▶ ナッ_リアリー
　☞ not の [t] 音が脱落する。

❾ **waiting**　　　　　　ウェイティング　　　　▶ ウェイディ [リ] ン (グ)
　☞ 破裂音 [t] が弾音化する。末尾の [g] 音が脱落することもある。

❿ **quite a bit of**　　　クワイト・ア・ビット・アヴ　▶ クワイダ [ラ] ビッダ [ラ] (ヴ)
　☞ 2 カ所の連結部で [t] 音が弾音化する。

⓫ **run out on**　　　　ラン・アウト・オン　　　▶ ラナウド [ロ] ン
　☞ 3 語が連結。out on の連結部で [t] 音が弾音化する。

⓬ **but I**　　　　　　　バット・アイ　　　　　▶ バッダ [ラ] イ
　☞ 連結部で [t] 音が弾音化する。

⓭ **late at**　　　　　　レイト・アット　　　　　▶ レイダ [ラ] ッ (ト)
　☞ 連結部で [t] 音が弾音化する。末尾の [t] 音が脱落することもある。

⓮ **get to**　　　　　　ゲット・トゥー　　　　　▶ ゲッ_トゥー
　☞ 破裂音の連続で片方の [t] 音が脱落する。

⓯ **lot about**　　　　　ラット・アバウト　　　　▶ ラッダ [ラ] バウ (ト)
　☞ 連結部で [t] 音が弾音化する。末尾の [t] 音が脱落することもある。

⓰ **in a**　　　　　　　イン・ア　　　　　　　▶ イナ
　☞ 2 語の音が連結する。

⓱ **interaction**　　　　インタラクシャン　　　　▶ イナラクシャン
　☞ [nt] で [t] 音の脱落が生じる。

INTERVIEW WITH AN UNEMPLOYED PERSON

Unit 24　失業者のインタビュー

Stage 1　穴埋め インタビュー・リスニング

音声変化に注意してCDでインタビューを聴きながら空欄部分を埋めてみよう。CDのナチュラル音声での聴き取りが難しいときは、次のトラックに収録されたスロー音声で聴いてみよう。

M: While most media is proclaiming the economy to be recovering, ① _____ _____ _____ local temp agency I spoke today with Mary Simpson, an unemployed mother of three. She did not share the same opinion. Here's what she had to say.
Ms. Simpson, how long have you been ② _____ _____ work?

F: I was laid off in late 2011. I worked in an ③ _____ assembly factory for more than ten years. Since then, I have been looking for work constantly. I've been able to pick up some temp jobs here and there, ④ _____ _____ have yet to land a full-time position anywhere. There just ⑤ _____ _____ to be anything available in my skill set. The few jobs I see offer less than half of ⑥ _____ _____ used to make.

M: Were you able to collect welfare or unemployment benefits?

F: Initially yes. But ⑦ _____ _____ that was nowhere near enough to support three children. Heck ⑧ _____ _____ _____ pay for the groceries. I ⑨ _____ _____ year cleaning houses and working two part-time jobs waitressing ⑩ _____ _____ make ends meet. It's really frustrating, to work menial jobs like that after having the job I had, ⑪ _____ _____ was no choice. Sadly, there is still no choice.

148

M: You had an interview today, right? How ⑫ _____ _____ go?

F: I think it ⑬ _____ _____. ⑭ _____ _____ problem is they want me to move to fill an available position in Alabama. I don't see how I can do that. I would have to take my kids ⑮ _____ _____ school, and I've already spent all of my savings. I'm living hand to mouth, and the money I make working part-time I have to spend on ⑯ _____. The talking heads on TV all say the economy has recovered, ⑰ _____ I don't see it that way. To me it seems like a no-win situation.

M: That's the word on the street. This is Jim Johnson reporting for ABD local news.

Stage 2 インタビュー解説

日本語訳と、解説を参照しながら、インタビュー内容を確認しよう。そのあとで、Stage1の穴埋めに再チャレンジしてみよう。

M: While most media is proclaiming the economy to be recovering, ① **outside of a** local temp agency I spoke today with Mary Simpson, an unemployed mother of three. She did not share the same opinion. Here's what she had to say.
Ms. Simpson, how long have you been ② **out of** work?

> ほとんどのメディアが、経済は回復しつつあると公言している一方、私は今日、地方の派遣会社の外で、メアリ・シンプソンさんと話しました。彼女は3人の子どもの母親で失業中です。彼女の意見は（メディアのものとは）異なっていました。では、彼女の話をお聞きください。シンプソンさん、あなたは、どのくらい失業しているんですか？
>
> ＊proclaim「宣言する；公言する」 temp agency「派遣会社」

F: I was laid off in late 2011. I worked in an ③ **automotive** assembly factory for more than ten years. Since then, I have been looking for

失業者のインタビュー 149

work constantly. I've been able to pick up some temp jobs here and there, ④ **but I** have yet to land a full-time position anywhere. There just ⑤ **doesn't seem** to be anything available in my skill set. The few jobs I see offer less than half of ⑥ **what I** used to make.

> 私は、2011年の暮れに解雇されました。10年以上自動車の組み立て工場で働いていたんです。それ以来、ずっと仕事を探しています。あちこちで、派遣の仕事に就くことはできましたが、まだ、どこでもフルタイムの仕事は見つかりません。私のスキルで空いている仕事はひとつもなさそうに思えます。私が見かけたわずかな仕事では、以前の稼ぎの半分以下しかもらえないんです。
>
> * laid off「(一時)解雇されて」 assembly factory「組み立て工場」
>   constantly「しきりに；絶えず」 have yet to ...「まだ…していない」
>   land「(仕事を)見つける」 skill set「もっているスキル(一式)」

M: Were you able to collect welfare or unemployment benefits?

> 生活保護や失業給付金は受け取ることはできましたか？
>
> * collect「(保険金・給料などを)受け取る」 welfare「生活保護」
>   unemployment benefits「失業給付」

F: Initially yes. But ⑦ **even then** that was nowhere near enough to support three children. Heck ⑧ **that didn't even** pay for the groceries. I ⑨ **spent a** year cleaning houses and working two part-time jobs waitressing ⑩ **just to** make ends meet. It's really frustrating, to work menial jobs like that after having the job I had, ⑪ **but there** was no choice. Sadly, there is still no choice.

> 当初はもらえました。でも、そのときでさえ、3人の子どもを支えるにはまったく不十分でした。忌々しいったら、食料品の支出もまかなえなかったんです。家の掃除とふたつのウェイトレスのパートをしながら、なんとか1年間食いつなぎました。前の仕事をやったあとで、こういった熟練のいらない仕事をするのは、とても不満でしたが、ほかの選択肢はありませんでした。悲しいかな、いまでも選択肢がないのです。
>
> * be nowhere near enough to ...「…するにはまったく不十分だ」
>   make ends meet「(やり繰りして)なんとか生計を立てる」 menial「雑用の；熟練の不要な」

M: You had an interview today, right? How ⑫ **did that** go?

> 今日は面接を受けたんですよね？ いかがでしたか？
> --
> ✽ (job) interview「(就職) 面接」

F: I think it ⑬ **went okay**. ⑭ **But the** problem is they want me to move to fill an available position in Alabama. I don't see how I can do that. I would have to take my kids ⑮ **out of** school, and I've already spent all of my savings. I'm living hand to mouth, and the money I make working part-time I have to spend on ⑯ **babysitters**. The talking heads on TV all say the economy has recovered, ⑰ **but** I don't see it that way. To me it seems like a no-win situation.

> うまくいったと思います。でも、問題は、アラバマで空きのある仕事を務めるために、引っ越してほしいそうなんです。でも、そうする方法がわからないんです。子どもたちを退学させなければならないでしょうし、すでに貯金は使い果たしているんです。私はその日暮らしで、パートで稼いでいるお金はベビーシッターに使わなければならないんですよ。テレビの番組解説者はみんな、経済は回復したと言っていますが、私はそういうふうに思いません。私にとっては八方ふさがりの状態なんです。
> --
> ✽ fill「務める；役職を埋める」　position「職；勤め口」　take ... out of school「…を退学させる」
>   savings「貯金」　live hand to mouth「その日暮らしをする」
>   talking head「(ニュースなどの) 番組の解説者」　no-win situation「八方ふさがりの状態」

M: That's the word on the street. This is Jim Johnson reporting for ABD local news.

> 街の声をお聞きいただきました。ABD ローカル・ニュースのジム・ジョンソンのレポートでした。
> --
> ✽ word on the street「街の声；一般の人の声」

Stage 3 ◀)) 英文トランスクリプション

インタビュー全体を英文の原稿で確認しながらCDで耳慣らししよう！　その上で、インタビューを聴きながら、まだできていない部分の穴埋めに再チャレンジしよう。

M: While most media is proclaiming the economy to be recovering, ① **outside of a** local temp agency I spoke today with Mary Simpson, an unemployed mother of three. She did not share the same opinion. Here's what she had to say.
Ms. Simpson, how long have you been ② **out of** work?

F: I was laid off in late 2011. I worked in an ③ **automotive** assembly factory for more than ten years. Since then, I have been looking for work constantly. I've been able to pick up some temp jobs here and there, ④ **but I** have yet to land a full-time position anywhere. There just ⑤ **doesn't seem** to be anything available in my skill set. The few jobs I see offer less than half of ⑥ **what I** used to make.

M: Were you able to collect welfare or unemployment benefits?

F: Initially yes. But ⑦ **even then** that was nowhere near enough to support three children. Heck ⑧ **that didn't even** pay for the groceries. I ⑨ **spent a** year cleaning houses and working two part-time jobs waitressing ⑩ **just to** make ends meet. It's really frustrating, to work menial jobs like that after having the job I had, ⑪ **but there** was no choice. Sadly, there is still no choice.

M: You had an interview today, right? How ⑫ **did that** go?

F: I think it ⑬ **went okay**. ⑭ **But the** problem is they want me to move to fill an available position in Alabama. I don't see how I can do that. I would have to take my kids ⑮ **out of** school, and I've already spent all of my savings. I'm living hand to mouth, and the money I make working part-time I have to spend on ⑯ **babysitters**. The talking heads on TV all say the economy has recovered, ⑰ **but** I don't see it that way. To me it seems like a no-win situation.

M: That's the word on the street. This is Jim Johnson reporting for ABD local news.

🎲 Stage 4 🔊 音声変化をチェック

まとめとして、穴埋め部分の音声変化の特徴を**スロー・スピード**と**ナチュラル・スピード**で確認しよう。下記に示したカタカナ表記で音声変化を確認して、もう一度インタビューを聴き直してみよう。発音変化のルールは適宜復習しよう。

❶ **outside of a** アウトゥサイド・アヴ・ア ▶ アウトゥサイダヴァ
☞ 3語の音の連結が起こる。

❷ **out of** アウト・アヴ ▶ アウダ［ラ］ヴ
☞ 2語が連結。連結部で［t］音が弾音化する。

❸ **automotive** オータモウティヴ ▶ オーダ［ラ］モウディ［リ］ヴ
☞ 破裂音［t］が弾音化する。

❹ **but I** バット・アイ ▶ バッダ［ラ］イ
☞ 連結部で破裂音［t］が弾音化する。

❺ **doesn't seem** ダズント・スィーム ▶ ダズン＿スィーム
☞ 破裂音［t］が脱落する。

❻ **what I** ワット・アイ ▶ ワッダ［ラ］イ
☞ 連結部で破裂音［t］が弾音化する。

❼ **even then** イーヴン・ゼン ▶ イーヴネン
☞ ［n］＋［ð］が［n］音に変化する。

❽ **that didn't even** ザット・ディドゥント・イーヴン ▶ ザッ＿ディドゥ［ル］ニーヴン
☞ that末尾の破裂音［t］の脱落が起こる。didn'tの［t］音が脱落しながらevenに連結。didn't中程の［d］音は弾音化することもある。

❾ **spent a** スペント・ア ▶ スペンナ
☞ spent末尾の［t］音が脱落しながらaに連結。

❿ **just to** ジャスト・トゥー ▶ ジャスッ＿トゥー
☞ 破裂音の連続で片方が脱落する。

⓫ **but there** バット・ゼア ▶ バッ＿ゼア
☞ butの破裂音［t］が脱落する。

⓬ **did that** ディッド・ザット ▶ ディッ＿ザッ（ト）
☞ didの破裂音［d］の脱落が起こる。that末尾の［t］音も脱落する場合がある。

⓭ **went okay** ウェント・オウケイ ▶ ウェノウケイ
☞ went末尾の破裂音［t］が脱落しながらokayに連結する。

⓮ **But the** バット・ザ ▶ バッ＿ザ
☞ butの破裂音［t］が脱落する。

⓯ **out of** アウト・アヴ ▶ アウダ［ラ］ヴ
☞ 連結部で破裂音［t］が弾音化する。

⓰ **babysitters** ベイビー・スィッターズ ▶ ベイビースィッダ［ラ］ーズ
☞ -sittersの破裂音［t］が弾音化する。

⓱ **but** バット ▶ バッ＿
☞ 末尾の破裂音［t］が脱落する。

🎤 失業者のインタビュー 153

INTERVIEW WITH AN MLB BASEBALL PLAYER

Unit 25　メジャー・リーグ選手のインタビュー

Stage 1　穴埋め インタビュー・リスニング

音声変化に注意してCDでインタビューを聴きながら空欄部分を埋めてみよう。CDのナチュラル音声での聴き取りが難しいときは、次のトラックに収録されたスロー音声で聴いてみよう。

F: How does it feel to be voted MVP in your second World Series in a row?

M: It's an amazing honor. The emotions right now ... I really ① _____ _____ begin to ② _____ _____ _____ words. I just ③ _____ _____ thank all of my teammates and everyone in our organization ④ _____ _____ helped make this happen. I have to give props to my beautiful wife Jen as well, as I could never have done this ⑤ _____ _____.

F: What do you think was the key ⑥ _____ your comeback win?

M: We all gave 110% out there. Losing the first two games of the series was tough, ⑦ _____ _____ came together as a team, kept our eyes focused on the end goal, and persevered. That's easier said than done sometimes, but we just had to ⑧ _____ _____ of what already happened and stay positive. Like the saying goes ... "it's never over till it's over" ⑨ _____ _____ _____ our ⑩ _____ in the locker room.

F: The stats you posted in the post season have broken all of the previous records. Were you aware of that during the games?

M: I ⑪ _____ _____ _____ think about records and

154

statistics. I just take each game as ⑫ _____ _____ and try to go out there and deliver my stuff. As a pitcher, I have enough to think ⑬ _____ _____ _____ _____. ⑭ _____ _____ the end it's a team effort, and even individual records are still only possible because we all worked together.

F: It's safe to say that there are millions of children around the world who wish they could have your job. Does being such a role model put pressure on you?

M: As a professional athlete there is already pressure ⑮ _____ _____ _____ _____ myself, ⑯ _____ _____ comes from the desire to win. That being said, being a role model is something I take very seriously, and I try to keep that in mind both on and off the field. I'm also very ⑰ _____ _____ giving back to my community by supporting youth baseball and devoting my time to charities.

Stage 2 インタビュー解説

日本語訳と、解説を参照しながら、インタビュー内容を確認しよう。そのあとで、Stage1の穴埋めに再チャレンジしてみよう。

F: How does it feel to be voted MVP in your second World Series in a row?

> 2回連続でワールド・シリーズのMVPに選ばれた気分は？
> ------
> * vote「投票で選ぶ」　MVP = most valuable player「最優秀選手」　in a row「連続で」

M: It's an amazing honor. The emotions right now ... I really ① **can't even** begin to ② **put it into** words. I just ③ **want to** thank all of my teammates and everyone in our organization ④ **that has** helped make this happen. I have to give props to my beautiful wife Jen as well, as I could never have done this ⑤ **without her**.

メジャー・リーグ選手のインタビュー　155

すばらしい栄誉ですよ。いまの感情は…言葉にもできないほどですよ。すべてのチームメートと、こうなることを支援してくれた組織のみんなにとにかく感謝したいです。僕の美しいワイフ、ジェンにも敬意を表さねばなりません。彼女なしでは、MVPを取ることはできませんでした。

＊ honor「名誉；栄誉」　give props「(相応の) 敬意を表する」

F: What do you think was the key ⑥ **to** your comeback win?

逆転勝利へのカギとなったのはなんだったのでしょう？

＊ comeback win「逆転勝利」

M: We all gave 110% out there. Losing the first two games of the series was tough, ⑦ **but we** came together as a team, kept our eyes focused on the end goal, and persevered. That's easier said than done sometimes, but we just had to ⑧ **let go** of what already happened and stay positive. Like the saying goes … "it's never over till it's over" ⑨ **and that was** our ⑩ **motto** in the locker room.

試合では、全員が110％でプレーしました。シリーズの最初の2戦を落としたのは厳しかったのですが、チームとして団結し、最終目標に集中し、がんばり抜きました。時として、言うは易く、行うのは難しいものですが、私たちは単にすでに起こったことを捨て去り、ポジティヴであり続けなければならなかったのです。ことわざにも言うように、「最後までなにが起こるはかわからない」のです。そして、それがわれわれのロッカー・ルームでのスローガンでした。

＊ come together「一丸となる；団結する」　persevere「がんばり抜く；やり抜く」
　let go of …「…を放す；捨て去る」　motto「スローガン；モットー」

F: The stats you posted in the post season have broken all of the previous records. Were you aware of that during the games?

ポスト・シーズンに、あなたが出した成績はこれまでの記録をすべて塗り替えましたね。シーズン中、そのことに気づいていましたか？

＊ stats「(統計上の) 数字；記録」　post「記録する」
　post season「ポスト・シーズン」予選を勝ち進んだチームが、優勝や順位決定などのためにゲームを行う時期のこと。メジャー・リーグでは、地区シリーズから、ワールド・シリーズを指す。

M: I ⑪ **try not to** think about records and statistics. I just take each game as ⑫ **it comes** and try to go out there and deliver my stuff. As a pitcher, I have enough to think ⑬ **about as it is**. ⑭ **But in** the end it's a team effort, and even individual records are still only possible because we all worked together.

> 私は記録や数字については考えないようにしているんです。1ゲームごとに試合をこなし、試合では自分のやるべきことをやるんです。投手ですから、それだけで、十分考えることはありますからね。しかし、結局、チームの努力なんです。そして、個人の記録でさえ、全員がともにがんばるからこそ可能なものなんですよ。
>
> ＊ deliver one's stuff「(野球のピッチャーが) 実力どおりの投球をする」
>   individual record「個人の記録」

F: It's safe to say that there are millions of children around the world who wish they could have your job. Does being such a role model put pressure on you?

> 世界中に、あなたと同じ仕事をしたいと考えている子どもたちが何百万といると言ってもいいでしょう。そんな子どもたちのお手本になることは大きな負担でしょうか？
>
> ＊ It's safe to say ...「…と言ってもいいだろう」 role model「ロール・モデル；お手本」

M: As a professional athlete there is already pressure ⑮ **that I put on** myself, ⑯ **and that** comes from the desire to win. That being said, being a role model is something I take very seriously, and I try to keep that in mind both on and off the field. I'm also very ⑰ **committed to** giving back to my community by supporting youth baseball and devoting my time to charities.

> プロの運動選手として、いつでも自分自身に課しているプレッシャーがあります。それは、勝利への強い願望から生じるものなんです。とは言え、お手本になることについては、真剣に考えていて、グラウンドにいるときでも、そうでなくても、頭の隅に置いておくようにしています。また、私は、若者たちの野球へのサポートやチャリティーに時間を充てることで、地元のコミュニティーへの恩返しにも尽力しているんです。
>
> ＊ desire「強い願望」 on and off the field「グラウンドの中でも外でも」
>   be committed to ...「…に献身的に尽くす；尽力する」 give back to ...「…に返す」
>   devote「充てる；捧げる」

Stage 3　英文トランスクリプション

インタビュー全体を英文の原稿で確認しながらCDで耳慣らししよう！ その上で、インタビューを聴きながら、まだできていない部分の穴埋めに再チャレンジしよう。

F: How does it feel to be voted MVP in your second World Series in a row?

M: It's an amazing honor. The emotions right now ... I really ① **can't even** begin to ② **put it into** words. I just ③ **want to** thank all of my teammates and everyone in our organization ④ **that has** helped make this happen. I have to give props to my beautiful wife Jen as well, as I could never have done this ⑤ **without her**.

F: What do you think was the key ⑥ **to** your comeback win?

M: We all gave 110% out there. Losing the first two games of the series was tough, ⑦ **but we** came together as a team, kept our eyes focused on the end goal, and persevered. That's easier said than done sometimes, but we just had to ⑧ **let go** of what already happened and stay positive. Like the saying goes ... "it's never over till it's over" ⑨ **and that was** our ⑩ **motto** in the locker room.

F: The stats you posted in the post season have broken all of the previous records. Were you aware of that during the games?

M: I ⑪ **try not to** think about records and statistics. I just take each game as ⑫ **it comes** and try to go out there and deliver my stuff. As a pitcher, I have enough to think ⑬ **about as it is**. ⑭ **But in** the end it's a team effort, and even individual records are still only possible because we all worked together.

F: It's safe to say that there are millions of children around the world who wish they could have your job. Does being such a role model put pressure on you?

M: As a professional athlete there is already pressure ⑮ **that I put on** myself, ⑯ **and that** comes from the desire to win. That being said, being a role model is something I take very seriously, and I try to keep that in mind both on and off the field. I'm also very ⑰ **committed to** giving back to my community by supporting youth baseball and devoting my time to charities.

Stage 4 🔊 音声変化をチェック

まとめとして、穴埋め部分の音声変化の特徴を**スロー・スピード**と**ナチュラル・スピード**で確認しよう。下記に示したカタカナ表記で音声変化を確認して、もう一度インタビューを聴き直してみよう。発音変化のルールは適宜復習しよう。

❶ **can't even** 　　キャント・イーヴン　　▶ キャニーヴン
☞ can't の破裂音 [t] が脱落しながら、2 語が連結する。

❷ **put it into** 　　プット・イット・イントゥー　　▶ プッディ[リ]ッディ[リ]ンドゥ[ル]ー
☞ 2 カ所の連結部や into で [t] 音が弾音化する。

❸ **want to** 　　ワント・トゥー　　▶ ワナ
☞ 2 カ所で [t] 音が脱落しながら 2 語が連結する。

❹ **that has** 　　ザット・ハズ　　▶ ザッダ[ラ]ズ
☞ 連結部で [t] 音が弾音化する。

❺ **without her** 　　ウィザウト・ハー　　▶ ウィザウダ[ラ]ー
☞ without に弱化した her [アー] が連結。連結部で破裂音 [t] が弾音化する。

❻ **to** 　　トゥー　　▶ ドゥ[ル]ー
☞ 破裂音 [t] の弾音化が生じる。

❼ **but we** 　　バット・ウィ　　▶ バッ＿ウィ
☞ 破裂音 [t] の脱落が生じる。

❽ **let go** 　　レット・ゴウ　　▶ レッ＿ゴウ
☞ 破裂音 [t] の脱落が生じる。

❾ **and that was** 　　アンド・ザット・ワズ　　▶ アン＿ザッ＿ワズ
☞ and の [d] 音や that の [t] 音が脱落する。

❿ **motto** 　　モートウ　　▶ モード[ロ]ウ
☞ 破裂音 [t] が弾音化する。

⓫ **try not to** 　　トゥライ・ナット・トゥー　　▶ チュライナッ＿ドゥ[ル]ー
☞ tr の[t]音は[チュ]のように変化する。not の[t]音が脱落する。to の[t]音が弾音化することもある。

⓬ **it comes** 　　イット・カムズ　　▶ イッ＿カムズ
☞ 破裂音 [t] が脱落する。

⓭ **about as it is** 　　アバウト・アズ・イット・イズ　　▶ アバウダ[ラ]ズイッディ[リ]ズ
☞ about as の連結部、it is の連結部で、破裂音 [t] が弾音化する。

⓮ **But in** 　　バット・イン　　▶ バッディ[リ]ン
☞ 連結部で [t] 音が弾音化する。

⓯ **that I put on** 　　ザット・アイ・プット・オン　　▶ ザッダ[ラ]イプッド[ロ]ン
☞ that I の連結部、put on の連結部で、破裂音 [t] が弾音化する。

⓰ **and that** 　　アンド・ザット　　▶ アナッ(ト)
☞ and の [d] 音が脱落して、that に連結し、[n] + [ð] が [n] 音に変化する。

⓱ **committed to** 　　カミッティッド・トゥー　　▶ カミッディ[リ]ッ＿ドゥ[ル]ー
☞ committed の [t] 音が弾音化する。[d] 音は脱落。to の [t] 音が弾音化することもある。

INTERVIEW WITH A FIREFIGHTER

Unit 26　消防士のインタビュー

Stage 1　穴埋めインタビュー・リスニング

音声変化に注意してCDでインタビューを聴きながら空欄部分を埋めてみよう。CDのナチュラル音声での聴き取りが難しいときは、次のトラックに収録されたスロー音声で聴いてみよう。

F: A family of four narrowly escaped a house fire in Bell County last night, and on the phone with us now is Lieutenant Mark Lewis who was one of the firefighters who helped ① _____ the blaze. Lt. Lewis can you tell us, has the cause of the fire been determined?

M: Yes. The fire broke ② _____ _____ _____ bathroom on the second floor. A scented candle was left burning and ③ _____ a pet ④ _____ _____ _____. The family was asleep ⑤ _____ _____ time, but was awakened by their smoke alarms and fortunately they were all able to exit the house via their bedroom window.

F: We have received reports that the family was taken to a local ⑥ _____. Can you comment on their ⑦ _____? Was this a precaution or did they suffer any injuries?

M: I believe they were ⑧ _____ for smoke inhalation and were ⑨ _____ _____ the hospital overnight for observation. I can't emphasize enough that the reason this story has a happy ending is because the family had a pre-discussed and well-rehearsed emergency plan in place. We encourage all families to do this, and we have tips and ⑩ _____ asked questions listed on our website.

F: The house was completely destroyed by the fire ⑪ _____

_____ _____?

M: That's correct. Unfortunately there were a number of chemicals and accelerants in the basement that made it very difficult to extinguish the blaze. We had three crews on site for over five hours. We were able to contain the fire and ⑫ _____ _____ _____ spreading to any of the nearby homes, however.

F: That's certainly good news. I'm sure the community appreciates your efforts, and we ⑬ _____ ⑭ _____ your time and input.

M: Thank you. And ⑮ _____ _____ just take this opportunity to remind your viewers to please make sure ⑯ _____ _____ have fire alarms installed, check those batteries, and ⑰ _____ _____ emergency action plan in place.

Stage 2 インタビュー解説

日本語訳と、解説を参照しながら、インタビュー内容を確認しよう。そのあとで、Stage1の穴埋めに再チャレンジしてみよう。

F: A family of four narrowly escaped a house fire in Bell County last night, and on the phone with us now is Lieutenant Mark Lewis who was one of the firefighters who helped ① **battle** the blaze. Lt. Lewis can you tell us, has the cause of the fire been determined?

> 昨夜、ベル郡での家屋の火災で４人家族がかろうじて難を逃れました。いま電話がつながっているのは、マーク・ルイス副所長です。彼は消火活動を行った消防士たちのひとりでした。ルイス副所長、教えてください。火災の原因は判明しましたか？
>
> ＊ narrowly「かろうじて；危うく」　county「郡」　lieutenant「(消防署の) 副所長」
> 　battle the blaze「消火活動を行う」　determine「判定する；決定する」

M: Yes. The fire broke ② **out in a** bathroom on the second floor. A scented candle was left burning and ③ **apparently** a pet ④ **knocked it over**. The family was asleep ⑤ **at the** time, but was

消防士のインタビュー　161

awakened by their smoke alarms and fortunately they were all able to exit the house via their bedroom window.

> ええ。2階のバスルームから出火しました。香りつきのろうそくが燃えたまま置かれていて、それをペットがひっくり返したらしいのです。当時、家族は寝ついていましたが、火災報知器の音で目を覚まされ、幸運にも、全員がベッドルームの窓から家を出ることができました。
>
> ＊ apparently「おそらく…；…らしい」　smoke alarm「(煙を探知する)火災報知器」
>   via ...「…を通って」

F: We have received reports that the family was taken to a local ⑥ **hospital**. Can you comment on their ⑦ **status**? Was this a precaution or did they suffer any injuries?

> 家族は地元の病院に入院したという情報を受けています。彼らの状態についてコメントできますか？ 念のための入院だったのでしょうか、あるいは負傷していたのでしょうか？
>
> ＊ report「情報」　precaution「用心；予防策」　suffer「被る」

M: I believe they were ⑧ **treated** for smoke inhalation and were ⑨ **admitted to** the hospital overnight for observation. I can't emphasize enough that the reason this story has a happy ending is because the family had a pre-discussed and well-rehearsed emergency plan in place. We encourage all families to do this, and we have tips and ⑩ **frequently** asked questions listed on our website.

> 煙の吸引に対する治療を受け、経過観察のためにひと晩入院になったのだと思います。今回の件がハッピー・エンドになったのは、この家族が、前もって話し合い、十分に予行演習が行われた緊急時のプランをもっていたからだということを、いくら強調しても足りません。すべての家庭にこれを行っていただきたいと思います。ヒントとよくある質問が私たちのサイトに掲載されていますので。
>
> ＊ inhalation「吸入；吸引」　be admitted to the hospital「入院する」
>   observation「観察；看護」　pre-discussed「前もって話し合われた」
>   well-rehearsed「十分にリハーサルされた；想定がなされた」
>   have ... in place「…を導入している」　encourage「推奨する；促進する」　tips「ヒント；秘訣」

F: The house was completely destroyed by the fire ⑪ **was it not**?

> 家屋は火災で完全に崩壊したのですよね?
> ---
> * was it not「ですよね?；ということですよね?」強調。Was it not that the house was completely destroyed by the fire? から転じたもの。ただし、もとの表現は使われない。

M: That's correct. Unfortunately there were a number of chemicals and accelerants in the basement that made it very difficult to extinguish the blaze. We had three crews on site for over five hours. We were able to contain the fire and ⑫ **keep it from** spreading to any of the nearby homes, however.

> そのとおりです。残念ながら多くの化学薬品と燃焼促進剤が地下室にあって、消化が非常に困難だったのです。しかしながら、現場で5時間以上、3つのチームが消火に当たり、炎を封じ込めて、近隣の家屋へ燃え広がるのを防ぐことができました。
> ---
> * a number of ...「多くの…」 chemical「化学物質；化学薬品」
>   accelerant「燃焼促進剤；燃えやすいもの」 on site「現場で」 contain「（延焼を）防ぐ」

F: That's certainly good news. I'm sure the community appreciates your efforts, and we ⑬ **certainly** ⑭ **appreciate** your time and input.

> それは、ほんとうによい知らせですね。地域住民たちはみなさんの努力に、きっと感謝していますね。私たちも、貴重なお時間と情報をいただき強く感謝しています。
> ---
> * input「情報提供」

M: Thank you. And ⑮ **let me** just take this opportunity to remind your viewers to please make sure ⑯ **that you** have fire alarms installed, check those batteries, and ⑰ **put an** emergency action plan in place.

> ありがとうございます。それと、この機会を利用させていただき、視聴者のみなさんに思い出しておいていただきたいのです。火災報知器の設置があることと、そのバッテリーを確認してください、それと緊急時の行動計画を立ててください。
> ---
> * put in place「導入する；整備する」

Stage 3 英文トランスクリプション

インタビュー全体を英文の原稿で確認しながらCDで耳慣らししよう！ その上で、インタビューを聴きながら、まだできていない部分の穴埋めに再チャレンジしよう。

F: A family of four narrowly escaped a house fire in Bell County last night, and on the phone with us now is Lieutenant Mark Lewis who was one of the firefighters who helped ① **battle** the blaze. Lt. Lewis can you tell us, has the cause of the fire been determined?

M: Yes. The fire broke ② **out in a** bathroom on the second floor. A scented candle was left burning and ③ **apparently** a pet ④ **knocked it over**. The family was asleep ⑤ **at the** time, but was awakened by their smoke alarms and fortunately they were all able to exit the house via their bedroom window.

F: We have received reports that the family was taken to a local ⑥ **hospital**. Can you comment on their ⑦ **status**? Was this a precaution or did they suffer any injuries?

M: I believe they were ⑧ **treated** for smoke inhalation and were ⑨ **admitted to** the hospital overnight for observation. I can't emphasize enough that the reason this story has a happy ending is because the family had a pre-discussed and well-rehearsed emergency plan in place. We encourage all families to do this, and we have tips and ⑩ **frequently** asked questions listed on our website.

F: The house was completely destroyed by the fire ⑪ **was it not**?

M: That's correct. Unfortunately there were a number of chemicals and accelerants in the basement that made it very difficult to extinguish the blaze. We had three crews on site for over five hours. We were able to contain the fire and ⑫ **keep it from** spreading to any of the nearby homes, however.

F: That's certainly good news. I'm sure the community appreciates your efforts, and we ⑬ **certainly** ⑭ **appreciate** your time and input.

M: Thank you. And ⑮ **let me** just take this opportunity to remind your viewers to please make sure ⑯ **that you** have fire alarms installed, check those batteries, and ⑰ **put an** emergency action plan in place.

Stage 4))) 音声変化をチェック

まとめとして、穴埋め部分の音声変化の特徴を**スロー・スピード**と**ナチュラル・スピード**で確認しよう。下記に示したカタカナ表記で音声変化を確認して、もう一度インタビューを聴き直してみよう。発音変化のルールは適宜復習しよう。

❶ **battle** バトゥウ ▶ バドゥ［ル］ゥ
☞ 破裂音［t］の弾音化が起こる。

❷ **out in a** アウト・イン・ア ▶ アウディ［リ］ナ
☞ 3語が連結。out in の連結部で［t］音が弾音化する。

❸ **apparently** アパーラントゥリー ▶ アパーラン＿リー
☞［tl］で［t］音の脱落が生じる。

❹ **knocked it over** ノックト・イット・オウヴァー ▶ ノックティッド［ロ］ウヴァー
☞ 3語が連結。it over の連結部で破裂音［t］が弾音化する。

❺ **at the** アット・ザ ▶ アッ＿ザ
☞ 破裂音［t］が脱落する。

❻ **hospital** ハースピトゥウ ▶ ハースピドゥ［ル］ゥ
☞ 破裂音［t］が弾音化する。

❼ **status** スタータス ▶ スターダ［ラ］ス
☞ 破裂音［t］が弾音化する。

❽ **treated** トゥリーティッド ▶ チュリーディ［リ］ッド
☞［tr］部分の［t］音が［チュ］に近い音に変化する。-ted の［t］音が弾音化する。

❾ **admitted to** アドゥミッティッド・トゥー ▶ アドゥミッディ［リ］ッ＿トゥー
☞ admitted の破裂音［t］が弾音化、末尾の［d］音が脱落する。

❿ **frequently** フリークァントゥリー ▶ フリークァン＿リー
☞［tl］で［t］音の脱落が生じる。

⓫ **was it not** ワズ・イット・ナット ▶ ワズィッ＿ナッ＿
☞ was it は連結。it や not 末尾の破裂音［t］が脱落する。

⓬ **keep it from** キープ・イット・フラム ▶ キーピッ＿フラム
☞ keep it は連結。it 末尾の破裂音［t］が脱落する。

⓭ **certainly** スートゥンリー ▶ スーんンリー
☞［tn］の部分が声門閉鎖音化する。

⓮ **appreciate** アプリーシェイト ▶ アプリーシェイッ＿
☞ 末尾の破裂音［t］が脱落する。

⓯ **let me** レット・ミー ▶ レッ＿ミー
☞ let の破裂音［t］が脱落する。

⓰ **that you** ザット・ユー ▶ ザッチュー
☞［t］＋［j］の部分で音が混じり合い、［チュ］に近い音に変化する。

⓱ **put an** プット・アン ▶ プッダ［ラ］ン
☞ 連結部で［t］音が弾音化する。

INTERVIEW WITH A BEST-SELLING AUTHOR

Unit 27　ベストセラー作家のインタビュー

Stage 1　穴埋め インタビュー・リスニング

音声変化に注意してCDでインタビューを聴きながら空欄部分を埋めてみよう。CDのナチュラル音声での聴き取りが難しいときは、次のトラックに収録されたスロー音声で聴いてみよう。

M: Yesterday I had the pleasure of meeting New York Times best-selling author Sarah Grey ① _____ _____ book-signing in New York City. Here's what she had to say.
Sarah it's a real pleasure ② _____ you. Fans have been eagerly ③ _____ the release of your newest novel *The Shadow*. Without giving away the details, what's new in this book?

F: My pleasure Mick. This novel is the first of a trilogy involving a ④ _____ new cast of characters. It follows a group of college students who are traveling abroad and run into ⑤ _____ when one of their group gets kidnapped. It's bound to keep readers on the edge of their seats. I hope that my fans enjoy reading it as much as I enjoyed ⑥ _____ _____.

M: I've heard that there is already talk about Hollywood making a movie based on this. Is that ⑦ _____? If so, how involved ⑧ _____ _____ be in the production?

F: All I can say is talks are underway. I'm a ⑨ _____ hesitant to jump ⑩ _____ _____ that before the trilogy is finished. As with my previous series that was made into a movie, I would ⑪ _____ have to have a say in the screenwriting. It's an honor and a treat to have my work ⑫ _____ _____ the big screen, ⑬ _____ _____ also have to make sure that the movie stays

166

true to the story, and sometimes that can be difficult. I can tell you that the ⑭ _____ version of the audio book will be available for download when the paperback is released.

M: Some of the reviews for *The Shadow* were not all that ⑮ _____. Any comments on that?

F: Well, that's the nature of the beast. You ⑯ _____ _____ everyone. This series goes in a totally new direction. I'm confident that my fan base will ⑰ _____ _____, and hopefully the new content will attract new readers to my books.

Stage 2 インタビュー解説

日本語訳と、解説を参照しながら、インタビュー内容を確認しよう。そのあとで、Stage1の穴埋めに再チャレンジしてみよう。

M: Yesterday I had the pleasure of meeting New York Times best-selling author Sarah Grey ① **at a** book-signing in New York City. Here's what she had to say.
Sarah it's a real pleasure ② **meeting** you. Fans have been eagerly ③ **awaiting** the release of your newest novel *The Shadow*. Without giving away the details, what's new in this book?

> 昨日、私は光栄なことに、ニューヨーク・シティーの本のサイン会で、ニューヨーク・タイムズがリストに載せたベストセラー作家であるサラ・グレイに会うことができました。彼女の話をお聞きください。
> サラ、お会いできてほんとうに光栄です。ファンは、あなたの最新作である『ザ・シャドー』の発売を熱心に待ち続けてきました。詳しいネタバレはいりませんが、この本の新しい点はなんでしょう？

＊ give away「(秘密・答え・詳細などを) 明かす；漏らす」 details「詳細」

F: My pleasure Mick. This novel is the first of a trilogy involving a

④ **completely** new cast of characters. It follows a group of college students who are traveling abroad and run into ⑤ **trouble** when one of their group gets kidnapped. It's bound to keep readers on the edge of their seats. I hope that my fans enjoy reading it as much as I enjoyed ⑥ **writing it**.

> ミック、ありがとう。この本は、まったく新しい登場人物たちを配した三部作の第一作に当たります。この本は外国を旅行する大学生グループを追いかけます。彼らは、トラブルに遭遇し、グループのひとりが誘拐されてしまうのです。必ずや読者は手に汗を握り続けることでしょう。ファンのみんなには、私が執筆を楽しんだのと同じくらい、読むのを楽しんでいただきたいと思っています。
>
> ＊ trilogy「三部作」　kidnap「誘拐する；拉致する」　be bound to ...「必ず…するに違いない」
> 　on the edge of one's seat「手に汗を握って」

M: I've heard that there is already talk about Hollywood making a movie based on this. Is that ⑦ **true**? If so, how involved ⑧ **would you** be in the production?

> すでに、ハリウッドがこの作品をもとにした映画を作る話があると聞いています。それはほんとうでしょうか？ もしそうなら、あなたは制作にどのくらい深く関わるのでしょう？
>
> ＊ based on ...「…に基づいた」　involved「深く関わって；熱心な」

F: All I can say is talks are underway. I'm a ⑨ **little** hesitant to jump ⑩ **right into** that before the trilogy is finished. As with my previous series that was made into a movie, I would ⑪ **definitely** have to have a say in the screenwriting. It's an honor and a treat to have my work ⑫ **put on** the big screen, ⑬ **but I** also have to make sure that the movie stays true to the story, and sometimes that can be difficult. I can tell you that the ⑭ **electronic** version of the audio book will be available for download when the paperback is released.

> 私が言えるのは、話はまだ進行中だということだけです。三部作が完成する前に、それに飛びつくのには、ちょっと躊躇しているんですよ。映画化された私の前のシリーズと同様に、絶対に脚本に対する発言権はもらわねばならないでしょう。自分の作品が大きなスクリー

> ンで上映されるのは名誉であり、よろこびでもありますが、確実に映画がストーリーに忠実であるようにもしたいのです。時に、それは難しくもあるのですが。ペーパーバックの発売と同時に、電子版のオーディオ・ブックもダウンロード購入できるようになることは、申し上げておいてもいいでしょう。
>
> ✱ underway「進行中で；途中で」　hesitant「躊躇して」　say「発言権」　treat「楽しみ；よろこび」
> electronic version「電子版」　available「購入・入手可能で」

M: Some of the reviews for *The Shadow* were not all that ⑮ **flattering**. Any comments on that?

> 『ザ・シャドー』についての論評には、それほどうれしくないものも含まれていますが、それに関するコメントは？
>
> ✱ review「評論；論評；評判」

F: Well, that's the nature of the beast. You ⑯ **can't please** everyone. This series goes in a totally new direction. I'm confident that my fan base will ⑰ **like it**, and hopefully the new content will attract new readers to my books.

> それは仕方のないことですよ。すべての人をよろこばせることはできませんから。このシリーズは、完全に新しい方向に進んでいきます。私のファン層は気に入ってくれる自信がありますし、さらに、新しいコンテンツが、私の本の新たな読者を魅了してくれることも願っています。
>
> ✱ nature of the beast「変わりようのない性質；仕方のないこと」　attract「魅了する」

Stage 3　英文トランスクリプション

インタビュー全体を英文の原稿で確認しながらCDで耳慣らししよう！　その上で、インタビューを聴きながら、まだできていない部分の穴埋めに再チャレンジしよう。

M: Yesterday I had the pleasure of meeting New York Times best-selling author Sarah Grey ① **at a** book-signing in New York City. Here's what she had to say.
Sarah it's a real pleasure ② **meeting** you. Fans have been eagerly ③ **awaiting** the release of your newest novel *The Shadow*. Without giving away the details, what's new in this book?

F: My pleasure Mick. This novel is the first of a trilogy involving a ④ **completely** new cast of characters. It follows a group of college students who are traveling abroad and run into ⑤ **trouble** when one of their group gets kidnapped. It's bound to keep readers on the edge of their seats. I hope that my fans enjoy reading it as much as I enjoyed ⑥ **writing it**.

M: I've heard that there is already talk about Hollywood making a movie based on this. Is that ⑦ **true**? If so, how involved ⑧ **would you** be in the production?

F: All I can say is talks are underway. I'm a ⑨ **little** hesitant to jump ⑩ **right into** that before the trilogy is finished. As with my previous series that was made into a movie, I would ⑪ **definitely** have to have a say in the screenwriting. It's an honor and a treat to have my work ⑫ **put on** the big screen, ⑬ **but I** also have to make sure that the movie stays true to the story, and sometimes that can be difficult. I can tell you that the ⑭ **electronic** version of the audio book will be available for download when the paperback is released.

M: Some of the reviews for *The Shadow* were not all that ⑮ **flattering**. Any comments on that?

F: Well, that's the nature of the beast. You ⑯ **can't please** everyone. This series goes in a totally new direction. I'm confident that my fan base will ⑰ **like it**, and hopefully the new content will attract new readers to my books.

🎧 Stage 4 🔊 音声変化をチェック

まとめとして、穴埋め部分の音声変化の特徴を**スロー・スピード**と**ナチュラル・スピード**で確認しよう。下記に示したカタカナ表記で音声変化を確認して、もう一度インタビューを聴き直してみよう。発音変化のルールは適宜復習しよう。

❶ **at a**　　　　　　　　　アット・ア　　　　　　　▶ アッダ [ラ]
☞ 連結部で破裂音 [t] の弾音化が起こる。

❷ **meeting**　　　　　　　ミーティング　　　　　　▶ ミーディ [リ] ン（グ）
☞ 破裂音 [t] が弾音化する。末尾の [g] 音が脱落することもある。

❸ **awaiting**　　　　　　　アウェイティング　　　　▶ アウェイディ [リ] ン（グ）
☞ 破裂音 [t] が弾音化する。末尾の [g] 音が脱落することもある。

❹ **completely**　　　　　　カンプリートゥリー　　　▶ カンプリーッ_リー
☞ [tl] で [t] 音の脱落が生じる。

❺ **trouble**　　　　　　　　トゥラブウ　　　　　　　▶ チュラブウ
☞ tr の [t] 音は [チュ] のように変化する。

❻ **writing it**　　　　　　　ライティング・イット　　▶ ライディ [リ] ンギッ（ト）
☞ 2 語が連結する。writing の [t] 音が弾音化、it 末尾の破裂音 [t] が脱落することもある。

❼ **true**　　　　　　　　　トゥルー　　　　　　　　▶ チュルー
☞ tr の [t] 音は [チュ] のように変化する。

❽ **would you**　　　　　　ウッド・ユー　　　　　　▶ ウッジュー
☞ [d] + [j] の部分で音が混じり合い、[ジュ] に近い音に変化する。

❾ **little**　　　　　　　　　リトゥウ　　　　　　　　▶ リドゥ [ル] ウ
☞ 破裂音 [t] の弾音化が起こる。

❿ **right into**　　　　　　　ライト・イントゥー　　　▶ ライディ [リ] ントゥー
☞ 連結部で [t] 音が弾音化する。

⓫ **definitely**　　　　　　　ディファニットゥリー　　▶ ディファニッ_リー
☞ [tl] で [t] 音の脱落が生じる。

⓬ **put on**　　　　　　　　プット・オン　　　　　　▶ プッド [ロ] ン
☞ 連結部で [t] 音が弾音化する。

⓭ **but I**　　　　　　　　　バット・アイ　　　　　　▶ バッダ [ラ] イ
☞ 連結部で [t] 音が弾音化する。

⓮ **electronic**　　　　　　　イレクトゥラーニック　　▶ イレクチュラーニック
☞ tr の [t] 音は [チュ] のように変化する。

⓯ **flattering**　　　　　　　フラタリング　　　　　　▶ フラダ [ラ] リン（グ）
☞ 破裂音 [t] の弾音化が起こる。末尾の [g] 音が脱落する場合もある。

⓰ **can't please**　　　　　　キャント・プリーズ　　　▶ キャン_プリーズ
☞ 破裂音 [t] の脱落が起こる。

⓱ **like it**　　　　　　　　　ライク・イット　　　　　▶ ライキッ（ト）
☞ 2 語が連結。末尾の [t] 音が脱落することもある。

INTERVIEW WITH A PASTOR

Unit 28 牧師のインタビュー

Stage 1 　穴埋め インタビュー・リスニング

音声変化に注意してCDでインタビューを聴きながら空欄部分を埋めてみよう。CDのナチュラル音声での聴き取りが難しいときは、次のトラックに収録されたスロー音声で聴いてみよう。

F: We're speaking today with non-denominational Church of Christ pastor Anthony Edwards, who has made headlines ① _____ for his organization of demonstrations against video-game retailers here in the Southeastern United States. Pastor Edwards, ② _____ _____ is your issue with these retailers?

M: Well Sarah, first I ③ _____ _____ thank you for this ④ _____ to talk with you. ⑤ _____ _____ know, we've been marshaling our congregation and Christians everywhere to raise awareness of the growing ⑥ _____ of violence ⑦ _____ _____ country. I personally believe we are facing a huge moral crisis in America, and one of the primary reasons for this is the promotion of violence among our youth, both through so-called "action" video games and movies.

F: Many of the movies and now video games you refer to are ⑧ _____ and are not ⑨ _____ _____ be available to children. Designers, retailers and even users say you are ⑩ _____ their first amendment rights.

M: It is true that there are now rating systems in place for video games like Hollywood movies. However those ratings are for show ⑪ _____ _____ escape liability for their content. They are ⑫ _____ _____, and as soon as the product reaches the home there is no way to ensure that children do not ⑬ _____ _____ to it. That is not really the point, though. We take issue with the violent and aggressive content of those games, regardless of who the purchaser is.

F: Your movement has been ⑭ _____ for impeding the business of many big-box retailers, and even having an adverse effect on the economy.

M: That is our goal. The only way to effect change nowadays is to hit someone in their pocketbook. We will continue our boycotts and demonstrations until these products are off the market. That is our responsibility as Christians ⑮ _____ _____ our society.

F: All right. We'd like to hear our viewers input. Tell us ⑯ _____ _____ think by ⑰ _____ or facebooking us at USTODAY.

Stage 2 インタビュー解説

日本語訳と、解説を参照しながら、インタビュー内容を確認しよう。そのあとで、Stage1の穴埋めに再チャレンジしてみよう。

F: We're speaking today with non-denominational Church of Christ pastor Anthony Edwards, who has made headlines ① **recently** for his organization of demonstrations against video-game retailers here in the Southeastern United States. Pastor Edwards, ② **what exactly** is your issue with these retailers?

今日お話ししているのは、特定宗派に属さないキリスト教会のアンソニー・エドワーズ牧師です。彼は、ここアメリカ南東部で、テレビ・ゲーム販売店に反対する複数のデモを組織したことで大きく報じられました。エドワーズ牧師、この小売業者たちに関しては、なにが問題なのでしょう？

* non-denominational「特定宗派に属さない」 make headlines「大きく報道される」
 organization「組織化」 retailer「小売店；小売業」

M: Well Sarah, first I ③ **want to** thank you for this ④ **opportunity** to talk with you. ⑤ **As you** know, we've been marshaling our congregation and Christians everywhere to raise awareness of the growing ⑥ **trend** of violence ⑦ **in our** country. I personally believe we are facing a huge moral crisis in America, and one of the primary reasons for this is the promotion of violence among our youth, both through so-called "action" video games and movies.

> そうですね、サラ、まずは、あなたとお話できるこの機会に感謝申し上げます。ご存じのとおり、私たちはこの国でますます大きくなっている暴力的な傾向を知ってもらうために、われわれの教区とあらゆるキリスト教徒をまとめて動かしてきました。アメリカは巨大なモラルの危機に瀕していると、個人的には考えているのです。そして、その主要な原因のひとつこそ、いわゆるアクション・ゲームとアクション映画の両者を通しての、若者の間での暴力の助長なのです。
>
> * marshal「まとめて導く；動かす」 congregation「教区」 promotion「助長；普及促進」

F: Many of the movies and now video games you refer to are ⑧ **rated** and are not ⑨ **supposed to** be available to children. Designers, retailers and even users say you are ⑩ **violating** their first amendment rights.

> あなたが言及している多くの映画に、それにいまはテレビ・ゲームもですが、ランクづけ指定がなされていて、子どもたちには利用できないものとされています。デザイナーや小売業界、さらにはユーザーたちも、あなた方が言論の自由を侵害していると言っていますが。
>
> * rate「ランクをつけて指定する」 violate「違反する；侵害する」
> first amendment rights「米国憲法修正第一条に定められた言論の自由などの権利」

M: It is true that there are now rating systems in place for video games like Hollywood movies. However those ratings are for show ⑪ **and to** escape liability for their content. They are ⑫ **not enforced**, and as soon as the product reaches the home there is no way to ensure that children do not ⑬ **get exposed** to it. That is not really the point, though. We take issue with the violent and aggressive content of those games, regardless of who the purchaser is.

現在テレビ・ゲームに、ハリウッド映画のように、ランクづけのシステムが整っているのは事実です。しかし、これらのランクづけは見せかけであって、コンテンツに関して責任逃れをするためのものなんです。厳格には施行されておらず、製品が家庭に届くやいなや、もう子どもたちがそれらに手を触れないように保証する方法はなにもないのです。しかし、それが問題の核心ではありません。私たちは、購入者がだれであったとしても、こういったゲームの暴力的かつ攻撃的なコンテンツに異議を唱えているのです。

＊ for show「体裁上の；見せかけの」 liability「責任；義務」 be enforced「（厳格に）施行される」
ensure「確実にする」 get exposed to ...「…に曝される」 take issue with ...「…に異議を唱える」

F: Your movement has been ⑭ **criticized** for impeding the business of many big-box retailers, and even having an adverse effect on the economy.

あなた方の運動は、大手小売業者のビジネスの妨げになっていて、さらには経済に不利益な影響を与えているとの批判を受けていますね。

＊ impede「邪魔する；妨げになる；遅らせる」 big-box retailers「大手小売業者」
adverse「不利益な」

M: That is our goal. The only way to effect change nowadays is to hit someone in their pocketbook. We will continue our boycotts and demonstrations until these products are off the market. That is our responsibility as Christians ⑮ **and to** our society.

それこそ私たちの目的ですよ。いまの世の中で、変化を起こすには、財源に打撃を与えるしかないのです。こういった製品が市場からなくなるまで、私たちはボイコットやデモを続けていきます。それこそが、キリスト教徒としての私たちの、社会に対する責任なのです。

＊ effect change「影響して変化を起こさせる」 pocketbook「財源」

F: All right. We'd like to hear our viewers input. Tell us ⑯ **what you** think by ⑰ **tweeting** or facebooking us at USTODAY.

わかりました。視聴者の考えを聞いてみたいと思います。USTODAY 宛に、みなさんの考えを Twitter や Facebook で教えてください。

＊ at ...「…宛に；…で」

牧師のインタビュー

Stage 3　英文トランスクリプション

インタビュー全体を英文の原稿で確認しながらCDで耳慣らししよう！　その上で、インタビューを聴きながら、まだできていない部分の穴埋めに再チャレンジしよう。

F: We're speaking today with non-denominational Church of Christ pastor Anthony Edwards, who has made headlines ① **recently** for his organization of demonstrations against video-game retailers here in the Southeastern United States. Pastor Edwards, ② **what exactly** is your issue with these retailers?

M: Well Sarah, first I ③ **want to** thank you for this ④ **opportunity** to talk with you. ⑤ **As you** know, we've been marshaling our congregation and Christians everywhere to raise awareness of the growing ⑥ **trend** of violence ⑦ **in our** country. I personally believe we are facing a huge moral crisis in America, and one of the primary reasons for this is the promotion of violence among our youth, both through so-called "action" video games and movies.

F: Many of the movies and now video games you refer to are ⑧ **rated** and are not ⑨ **supposed to** be available to children. Designers, retailers and even users say you are ⑩ **violating** their first amendment rights.

M: It is true that there are now rating systems in place for video games like Hollywood movies. However those ratings are for show ⑪ **and to** escape liability for their content. They are ⑫ **not enforced**, and as soon as the product reaches the home there is no way to ensure that children do not ⑬ **get exposed** to it. That is not really the point, though. We take issue with the violent and aggressive content of those games, regardless of who the purchaser is.

F: Your movement has been ⑭ **criticized** for impeding the business of many big-box retailers, and even having an adverse effect on the economy.

M: That is our goal. The only way to effect change nowadays is to hit someone in their pocketbook. We will continue our boycotts and demonstrations until these products are off the market. That is our responsibility as Christians ⑮ **and to** our society.

F: All right. We'd like to hear our viewers input. Tell us ⑯ **what you** think by ⑰ **tweeting** or facebooking us at USTODAY.

🌀 Stage 4 🔊 音声変化をチェック

まとめとして、穴埋め部分の音声変化の特徴を**スロー・スピード**と**ナチュラル・スピード**で確認しよう。下記に示したカタカナ表記で音声変化を確認して、もう一度インタビューを聴き直してみよう。発音変化のルールは適宜復習しよう。

---

❶ **recently** リースントゥリー ▶ リースン__リー
☞ 破裂音[t]の脱落が起こる。

❷ **what exactly** ワット・イグザックトゥリー ▶ ワッディ[リ] グザック__リー
☞ 連結部で[t]音が弾音化する。exactly の[tl]で[t]音の脱落が生じる。

❸ **want to** ワント・トゥー ▶ ワナ
☞ want の[t]音が脱落しながら、弱化した to[ə]に連結する。

❹ **opportunity** アーパチューナティー ▶ アーパチューナディ[リ] ー
☞ 破裂音[t]が弾音化する。

❺ **As you** アズ・ユー ▶ アジュー
☞ [z]+[j]の部分で音が混じり合い、[ジュ]に近い音に変化する。

❻ **trend** トゥレンド ▶ チュレンド
☞ tr の[t]音は[チュ]のように変化する。

❼ **in our** イン・アウァ ▶ イナウァ
☞ 2語が連結する。

❽ **rated** レイティッド ▶ レイディ[リ] ッ(ド)
☞ 破裂音[t]が弾音化する。

❾ **supposed to** サポウズド・トゥー ▶ サポウッスッ__トゥー
☞ supposed の[z]音が[s]に変化する。末尾の[d]音は脱落。

❿ **violating** ヴァイアレイティング ▶ ヴァイアレイディ[リ] ン(グ)
☞ 破裂音[t]が弾音化する。末尾の[g]音が脱落することもある。

⓫ **and to** アンド・トゥー ▶ アン__ドゥ[ル] ー
☞ and の[d]音が脱落。to の破裂音[t]が弾音化する。

⓬ **not enforced** ナット・エンフォースト ▶ ナッデ[レ] ンフォースト
☞ 連結部で破裂音[t]の弾音化が起こる。

⓭ **get exposed** ゲット・エクスポウズド ▶ ゲッデ[レ] クスポウズ(ド)
☞ 連結部で破裂音[t]の弾音化が起こる。

⓮ **criticized** クリティサイズド ▶ クリディ[リ] サイズド
☞ 破裂音[t]が弾音化する。

⓯ **and to** アンド・トゥー ▶ __ン__トゥー
☞ and が弱化して[ə]や[d]の音が脱落する。

⓰ **what you** ワット・ユー ▶ ワッチュー
☞ [t]+[j]の部分で音が混じり合い、[チュ]に近い音に変化する。

⓱ **tweeting** トゥイーティング ▶ トゥイーディ[リ] ン(グ)
☞ 破裂音[t]が弾音化する。末尾の[g]音が脱落することもある。

INTERVIEW WITH A FOREIGN CORRESPONDENT

Unit 29 海外特派員のインタビュー

Stage 1 穴埋め インタビュー・リスニング

音声変化に注意してCDでインタビューを聴きながら空欄部分を埋めてみよう。CDのナチュラル音声での聴き取りが難しいときは、次のトラックに収録されたスロー音声で聴いてみよう。

F: You've been an AP foreign correspondent for more than twenty years. What's changed about reporting news abroad ① _____ _____ time?

M: The first thing that comes to mind is the speed with which we can now provide our reports. Technology today allows for live, on-camera broadcasts, whereas in the early days we would have to tape our broadcasts or phone interviews to be ② _____ _____. We can usually communicate seamlessly now, with cell phones, text messages, Skype and the like. The problem with that is now there is a ③ _____ _____ information ④ _____ _____, ⑤ _____ _____ hard for the average Joe to determine what's real and what's not. ⑥ _____, _____ think, is the ultimate reason it's important for experienced journalists to be there where the action is.

F: What is one of the more memorable stories you've reported on?

M: Gosh, there've been so many. If I ⑦ _____ _____ choose one it ⑧ _____ _____ the fall of the Berlin Wall. I was stationed in Berlin for six months prior. The feeling of exuberance in the air was tangible, and I can still remember the excitement of seeing family members ⑨ _____ _____ years of living on separate sides of the "Iron ⑩ _____."

F: What was the most dangerous assignment you've ever had?

178

M: That's easy. I was embedded with the 24th Mechanized Combat Infantry Division in Operation Desert Storm. That was ⑪ _____ _____ _____ coalition force that was responsible for securing an airfield on the outskirts of Iraq. We were involved in several skirmishes, and ⑫ _____ _____ _____ _____ _____ enemy fire. The bravery and ⑬ _____ those soldiers ⑭ _____ is something I'll never ⑮ _____ _____ long as I live.

F: What advice would you have for any aspiring journalists out there?

M: First and foremost would be to focus ⑯ _____ _____ particular region and make an effort to learn as much of the language and the culture as you can. This is invaluable in helping to not only collect accurate and additional information, ⑰ _____ _____ allows for a perspective that can make your reporting really come alive.

Stage 2 インタビュー解説

日本語訳と、解説を参照しながら、インタビュー内容を確認しよう。そのあとで、Stage 1の穴埋めに再チャレンジしてみよう。

F: You've been an AP foreign correspondent for more than twenty years. What's changed about reporting news abroad ① **in that** time?

> あなたは、20年以上APの海外特派員をしていらっしゃいますね。その間、どのようなことが海外ニュース報道で変化しましたか？
> --
> * foreign correspondent「海外在住の通信員」 reporting news「ニュースを報道すること」

M: The first thing that comes to mind is the speed with which we can now provide our reports. Technology today allows for live, on-camera broadcasts, whereas in the early days we would have to tape our broadcasts or phone interviews to be ② **reported later**. We can usually communicate seamlessly now, with cell phones, text messages, Skype and the like. The problem with that is now there is a ③ **flood of** information ④ **out there**, ⑤ **and it's** hard for the average Joe to determine what's real and what's not. ⑥ **That, I** think, is the ultimate reason it's important for experienced journalists to be there where the action is.

> まず頭に浮かぶのは、われわれがいまニュース報道を提供できるスピードです。今日のテクノロジーはライブの実況を可能にしていますが、昔は放送や電話インタビューをテープに記録し、その後に報道しなければなりませんでした。携帯電話や、SMS、Skype といったもので、いまはいつでも、シームレスにコミュニケーションが取れます。そういうことで生じる問題として、いまは世の中に情報が氾濫しているのです。そのため、ふつうの人には、なにがほんとうで、なにがそうでないのかの判断がつきにくくなっています。それこそが、経験を積んだジャーナリストが現場にいることが重要な、究極の理由だと考えています。
>
> * allow for ...「…を可能にする；…の機会を提供する」 on-camera「カメラの前での」
>   ..., whereas ...「…、一方…」 seamlessly「途切れることなく；継ぎ目なく」
>   average Joe「ふつうの人；凡人」 determine「判断する；判定する」 ultimate「究極の」
>   experienced「経験を積んだ」

F: What is one of the more memorable stories you've reported on?

> あなたの記憶に残っている報道をひとつ挙げてもらえますか？
>
> * memorable「記憶に残る」

M: Gosh, there've been so many. If I ⑦ **had to** choose one it ⑧ **would be** the fall of the Berlin Wall. I was stationed in Berlin for six months prior. The feeling of exuberance in the air was tangible, and I can still remember the excitement of seeing family members ⑨ **unite after** years of living on separate sides of the "Iron ⑩ **Curtain**."

> ああ、あまりにもたくさんあるんですよ。ひとつを選ばねばならないとしたら、ベルリンの壁の崩壊でしょうね。私は6カ月先立って、ベルリンに駐在していたんです。よろこびに満ちた空気の感覚が伝わってきました。そして、長年、「鉄のカーテン」の両側に暮らしてきた家族たちがひとつになるのを見たときの興奮を、いまだに思い出すことができます。
>
> * the fall of the Berlin Wall「ベルリンの壁の崩壊」
>   exuberance「よろこびに満ちた活気；ほとばしり」
>   tangible「知覚できる；(感覚によって) 認識できる」 unite「一体となる；一致団結する」

F: What was the most dangerous assignment you've ever had?

> あなたに割り当てられた仕事で、もっとも危険だったことはなんでしたか？

＊ assignment「割り当てられた任務・仕事」

M: That's easy. I was embedded with the 24th Mechanized Combat Infantry Division in Operation Desert Storm. That was ⑪ **part of the** coalition force that was responsible for securing an airfield on the outskirts of Iraq. We were involved in several skirmishes, and ⑫ **took on a lot of** enemy fire. The bravery and ⑬ **camaraderie** those soldiers ⑭ **exhibited** is something I'll never ⑮ **forget as** long as I live.

それはかんたんですね。砂漠の嵐作戦で、機械化戦闘歩兵師団に同伴させられたときのことです。その師団は、イラク郊外の飛行場を確保する責任を負った連合軍に属していました。私たちはいくつかの小規模な戦闘に巻き込まれ、多くの敵の砲火を浴びました。兵士たちが見せた勇敢さや友情は、生きている限り決して忘れないでしょう。

＊ be embedded with ...「（報道関係者として）…軍に同伴させられる」
Mechanized Combat Infantry Division「機械化戦闘歩兵師団」 secure「確保する」
airfield「飛行場」 skirmish「小規模な戦闘」 take on ...「…を受ける」 bravery「勇敢さ」
camaraderie「友愛；友情」 exhibit「（特徴・性質・感情などを）見せる」

F: What advice would you have for any aspiring journalists out there?

この番組を観ているジャーナリストを目指す人たちに、アドバイスするとしたら、どんなことでしょう？

＊ aspiring「意欲的な；野心に燃える」

M: First and foremost would be to focus ⑯ **on a** particular region and make an effort to learn as much of the language and the culture as you can. This is invaluable in helping to not only collect accurate and additional information, ⑰ **but also** allows for a perspective that can make your reporting really come alive.

なによりもまず大切なのは、ひとつの地域に的を絞って、できるだけ言語や文化を学ぶ努力をすることですね。これは、正確な情報や追加情報を集めるために計り知れないほど貴重な役割を果たしてくれるだけでなく、報道を生き生きとしたものにできる視点を与えてくれます。

＊ first and foremost「なによりもまず（大事なこと）」
invaluable in helping to ...「…する助けになる計り知れないほど貴重な」 accurate「正確な」
allow for ...「…の可能性を作る；…の機会を提供する」 perspective「観点；展望」

海外特派員のインタビュー 181

Stage 3 　英文トランスクリプション

インタビュー全体を英文の原稿で確認しながらCDで耳慣らししよう！ その上で、インタビューを聴きながら、まだできていない部分の穴埋めに再チャレンジしよう。

F: You've been an AP foreign correspondent for more than twenty years. What's changed about reporting news abroad ① **in that** time?

M: The first thing that comes to mind is the speed with which we can now provide our reports. Technology today allows for live, on-camera broadcasts, whereas in the early days we would have to tape our broadcasts or phone interviews to be ② **reported later**. We can usually communicate seamlessly now, with cell phones, text messages, Skype and the like. The problem with that is now there is a ③ **flood of** information ④ **out there**, ⑤ **and it's** hard for the average Joe to determine what's real and what's not. ⑥ **That, I** think, is the ultimate reason it's important for experienced journalists to be there where the action is.

F: What is one of the more memorable stories you've reported on?

M: Gosh, there've been so many. If I ⑦ **had to** choose one it ⑧ **would be** the fall of the Berlin Wall. I was stationed in Berlin for six months prior. The feeling of exuberance in the air was tangible, and I can still remember the excitement of seeing family members ⑨ **unite after** years of living on separate sides of the "Iron ⑩ **Curtain**."

F: What was the most dangerous assignment you've ever had?

M: That's easy. I was embedded with the 24th Mechanized Combat Infantry Division in Operation Desert Storm. That was ⑪ **part of the** coalition force that was responsible for securing an airfield on the outskirts of Iraq. We were involved in several skirmishes, and ⑫ **took on a lot of** enemy fire. The bravery and ⑬ **camaraderie** those soldiers ⑭ **exhibited** is something I'll never ⑮ **forget as** long as I live.

F: What advice would you have for any aspiring journalists out there?

M: First and foremost would be to focus ⑯ **on a** particular region and make an effort to learn as much of the language and the culture as you can. This is invaluable in helping to not only collect accurate and additional information, ⑰ **but also** allows for a perspective that can make your reporting really come alive.

🎯 Stage 4 🔊 音声変化をチェック

まとめとして、穴埋め部分の音声変化の特徴を**スロー・スピード**と**ナチュラル・スピード**で確認しよう。下記に示したカタカナ表記で音声変化を確認して、もう一度インタビューを聴き直してみよう。発音変化のルールは適宜復習しよう。

---

❶ **in that**　　　イン・ザット　　　▶ イナッ（ト）
☞ [n]＋[ð] が [n] 音に変化する。末尾の [t] 音も脱落することがある。

❷ **reported later**　　　リポーティッド・レイター　　　▶ リポーディ［リ］ッ＿レイダ［ラ］ー
☞ 2カ所の [t] 音が弾音化する。reported 末尾の [d] 音が脱落する。

❸ **flood of**　　　フラッド・アヴ　　　▶ フラダヴ
☞ 2語が連結する。

❹ **out there**　　　アウト・ゼア　　　▶ アウッ＿ゼア
☞ out の破裂音 [t] が脱落する。

❺ **and it's**　　　アンド・イッツ　　　▶ アニッツ
☞ and の破裂音 [d] が脱落しながら、2語が連結。

❻ **That, I**　　　ザット・アイ　　　▶ ザッダ［ラ］イ
☞ 連結部で破裂音 [t] の弾音化が起こる。

❼ **had to**　　　ハッド・トゥー　　　▶ ハッ＿ドゥ［ル］ー
☞ had の [d] 音の脱落が生じる。to の [t] 音は弾音化する。

❽ **would be**　　　ウッド・ビー　　　▶ ウッ＿ビ
☞ 破裂音 [d] の脱落が起こる。be は弱化して［ビ］と発音される。

❾ **unite after**　　　ユナイト・アフター　　　▶ ユナイダ［ラ］フター
☞ 連結部で破裂音 [t] の弾音化が起こる。

❿ **Curtain**　　　クートゥン　　　▶ クーンン
☞ [tn] の [t] 音が声門閉鎖音化する。

⓫ **part of the**　　　パート・アヴ・ザ　　　▶ パーダ［ラ］（ヴ）ザ
☞ part of の連結部で破裂音 [t] の弾音化が起こる。of の [v] 音は脱落しやすい。

⓬ **took on a lot of**　　　トゥック・オン・ア・ラット・アヴ　　　▶ トゥッコナラッダ［ラ］（ヴ）
☞ took on a、lot of がそれぞれ連結。lot of の連結部で破裂音 [t] の弾音化が生じる。of の [v] 音は脱落しやすい。

⓭ **camaraderie**　　　カームラーダリー　　　▶ カームラーダ［ラ］リー
☞ 破裂音 [d] が弾音化する。

⓮ **exhibited**　　　イグジビティッド　　　▶ イグジビディ［リ］ッド
☞ 破裂音 [t] が弾音化する。

⓯ **forget as**　　　フォーゲット・アズ　　　▶ フォーゲッダ［ラ］ズ
☞ 連結部で破裂音 [t] の弾音化が起こる。

⓰ **on a**　　　オン・ア　　　▶ オナ
☞ 2語が連結する。

⓱ **but also**　　　バット・オーゥソウ　　　▶ バッド［ロ］ーゥソウ
☞ 連結部で破裂音 [t] の弾音化が起こる。

INTERVIEW WITH AN ASTRONAUT

Unit 30 宇宙飛行士のインタビュー

Stage 1 穴埋め インタビュー・リスニング

音声変化に注意してCDでインタビューを聴きながら空欄部分を埋めてみよう。CDのナチュラル音声での聴き取りが難しいときは、次のトラックに収録されたスロー音声で聴いてみよう。

M: Today is the tenth anniversary of the completion of the International Space Station, and speaking with us tonight from Kazakhstan is American astronaut Kelly Sanders, who is ① _____ training for her upcoming six-month stint in orbit. Ms. Sanders, tell us a ② _____ _____ _____ _____ training regimen?

F: I've been here in Kazakhstan for the last four weeks, ③ _____ with two of my Russian ④ _____ for our upcoming launch. I've been preparing for this mission for more than two years, ⑤ _____ _____ last month has been primarily to familiarize myself with both the Soyuz rocket we will be going up in, and also for some of the on-board systems ⑥ _____ _____ Russian designed.

M: What will your primary mission be up there?

F: I am a science officer, and we have a myriad of scientific experiments we will be working on. One is to continue our ongoing study of how weightlessness affects bone density and the general health of the astronauts and cosmonauts. I am also ⑦ _____ _____ be using new generation software to study weather ⑧ _____ from space, particularly focusing on the development of hurricanes.

M: Six months seems like a long time to be up there. ⑨ _____ _____ _____ think you will miss most?

F: Well ... probably fresh food. We don't have refrigeration up there so almost all of our food is freeze-dried or canned. While the food preservation ⑩ _____ preparation has improved a ⑪ _____ _____ the years it is still not anywhere near good home-cooked food. ⑫ _____ we don't even have cold ⑬ _____ up there. So if you ⑭ _____ _____ cold drink you have to prepare it and place ⑮ _____ _____ _____ colder area of the station. Even then it doesn't ⑯ _____ _____ cold.

M: Well we certainly wish you the best of success and safe travels up there!

F: Thank you Curtis. I'm truly ⑰ _____ _____ grateful for the opportunity to do this. It's a dream come true.

Stage 2 インタビュー解説

日本語訳と、解説を参照しながら、インタビュー内容を確認しよう。そのあとで、Stage1の穴埋めに再チャレンジしてみよう。

M: Today is the tenth anniversary of the completion of the International Space Station, and speaking with us tonight from Kazakhstan is American astronaut Kelly Sanders, who is ① **currently** training for her upcoming six-month stint in orbit. Ms. Sanders, tell us a ② **little bit about your** training regimen?

今日は、国際宇宙ステーション完成の10周年記念日に当たり、今晩カザフスタンからお話ししてくれているのは、アメリカ人宇宙飛行士のケリー・サンダースさんです。彼女は現在、軌道上での6カ月の任期に備えて訓練中です。サンダースさん、あなたのトレーニングの詳細に関して少し教えてください。

＊ upcoming「やがてやってくる」　stint「(仕事や活動の) 期間・任期」

宇宙飛行士のインタビュー　185

regimen「決められたプラン」

F: I've been here in Kazakhstan for the last four weeks, ③ **training** with two of my Russian ④ **counterparts** for our upcoming launch. I've been preparing for this mission for more than two years, ⑤ **but the** last month has been primarily to familiarize myself with both the Soyuz rocket we will be going up in, and also for some of the on-board systems ⑥ **that are** Russian designed.

この4週間、ここカザフスタンに来ていて、近づいている打ち上げに備え、ふたりのロシアの同僚飛行士とトレーニングしています。2年以上、このミッションの準備をしてきましたが、このひと月は、主として打ち上げのために搭乗するソユーズと、いくつかのロシアで設計された船内システムに慣れる作業でした。

* counterpart「(同じような立場の) 相応する相手」　primarily「主として；まずは」
  on-board system「船内・機内システム」

M: What will your primary mission be up there?

ステーションでのあなたの主要なミッションはなんでしょう?

* primary「もっとも重要な；主要な」

F: I am a science officer, and we have a myriad of scientific experiments we will be working on. One is to continue our ongoing study of how weightlessness affects bone density and the general health of the astronauts and cosmonauts. I am also ⑦ **going to** be using new generation software to study weather ⑧ **patterns** from space, particularly focusing on the development of hurricanes.

私はサイエンス・オフィサーで、私たちには実行すべき科学実験が無数にあります。ひとつには、現在進行中の無重力が宇宙飛行士の骨密度や健康全般に与える影響に関する研究を継続することです。宇宙から気象パターンを研究するために、新世代のソフトウェアも使用する予定です。特に、ハリケーンの発達に焦点を当てたものです。

* myriad of ...「無数の…」　weightlessness「無重力 (状態)」　bone density「骨密度」
  cosmonaut「宇宙飛行士」(旧ソ連時代からの) ロシア人宇宙飛行士の呼称。

M: Six months seems like a long time to be up there. ⑨ **What do you** think you will miss most?

> 6カ月も、ステーションにいるのは長く思えますが。いちばん恋しくなるものはなんだと思いますか？
>
> * miss「(なくて) さみしく思う」

F: Well ... probably fresh food. We don't have refrigeration up there so almost all of our food is freeze-dried or canned. While the food preservation ⑩ **and** preparation has improved a ⑪ **lot over** the years it is still not anywhere near good home-cooked food.
⑫ **Actually** we don't even have cold ⑬ **water** up there. So if you ⑭ **want a** cold drink you have to prepare it and place ⑮ **it in a** colder area of the station. Even then it doesn't ⑯ **get that** cold.

> えー…おそらくは新鮮な食べ物ですね。ステーションでは、冷凍保存がありませんので、ほとんどすべての食べ物は、フリーズドライか缶詰です。長年の間に食品の保存と調理法は改善されましたが、それでもまだ家庭料理とはほど遠いものなんです。実はステーションには冷たい水もありません。だから、冷たい飲み物が欲しければ、作ったあとにステーションのより気温の低いエリアに置いておかなければならないんですよ。それでも、そんなに冷たくはなりませんけど。
>
> * refrigeration「冷凍保存」　canned「缶詰の」　preservation and preparation「保存と調理」

M: Well we certainly wish you the best of success and safe travels up there!

> ほんとうにあなたの大成功と軌道上での安全な旅を祈っています。

F: Thank you Curtis. I'm truly ⑰ **excited and** grateful for the opportunity to do this. It's a dream come true.

> カーティスさん、ありがとう。今回のステーション滞在がほんとうに楽しみで、うれしく思っています。夢がかなったんですから。
>
> * It's a dream come true.「(思ってもみなかった) 夢がかなった」

宇宙飛行士のインタビュー

Stage 3 英文トランスクリプション

インタビュー全体を英文の原稿で確認しながらCDで耳慣らししよう！ その上で、インタビューを聴きながら、まだできていない部分の穴埋めに再チャレンジしよう。

M: Today is the tenth anniversary of the completion of the International Space Station, and speaking with us tonight from Kazakhstan is American astronaut Kelly Sanders, who is ① **currently** training for her upcoming six-month stint in orbit. Ms. Sanders, tell us a ② **little bit about your** training regimen?

F: I've been here in Kazakhstan for the last four weeks, ③ **training** with two of my Russian ④ **counterparts** for our upcoming launch. I've been preparing for this mission for more than two years, ⑤ **but the** last month has been primarily to familiarize myself with both the Soyuz rocket we will be going up in, and also for some of the on-board systems ⑥ **that are** Russian designed.

M: What will your primary mission be up there?

F: I am a science officer, and we have a myriad of scientific experiments we will be working on. One is to continue our ongoing study of how weightlessness affects bone density and the general health of the astronauts and cosmonauts. I am also ⑦ **going to** be using new generation software to study weather ⑧ **patterns** from space, particularly focusing on the development of hurricanes.

M: Six months seems like a long time to be up there. ⑨ **What do you** think you will miss most?

F: Well ... probably fresh food. We don't have refrigeration up there so almost all of our food is freeze-dried or canned. While the food preservation ⑩ **and** preparation has improved a ⑪ **lot over** the years it is still not anywhere near good home-cooked food. ⑫ **Actually** we don't even have cold ⑬ **water** up there. So if you ⑭ **want a** cold drink you have to prepare it and place ⑮ **it in a** colder area of the station. Even then it doesn't ⑯ **get that** cold.

M: Well we certainly wish you the best of success and safe travels up there!

F: Thank you Curtis. I'm truly ⑰ **excited and** grateful for the opportunity to do this. It's a dream come true.

Stage 4 音声変化をチェック

まとめとして、穴埋め部分の音声変化の特徴を**スロー・スピード**と**ナチュラル・スピード**で確認しよう。下記に示したカタカナ表記で音声変化を確認して、もう一度インタビューを聴き直してみよう。発音変化のルールは適宜復習しよう。

❶ **currently** カレントゥリー ▶ カレン＿リー
☞ 破裂音 [t] の脱落が起こる。

❷ **little bit about your** リトゥゥ・ビット・アバウト・ユア
▶ リドゥ [ル] ビッダ [ラ] バウチュア
☞ little の [t] 音、bit about 連結部の [t] 音が弾音化する。about your の連結部では、[t] ＋ [j] の音が混じり合い [チュ] に近い音に変化する。

❸ **training** トゥレイニング ▶ チュレイニン（グ）
☞ [tr] 部分の [t] 音が [チュ] に近い音に変化する。末尾の [g] 音が脱落することもある。

❹ **counterparts** カウンターパーツ ▶ カウナーパーツ
☞ [nt] で [t] 音の脱落が生じる。

❺ **but the** バット・ザ ▶ バッ＿ザ
☞ 破裂音 [t] が脱落する。

❻ **that are** ザット・アー ▶ ザッダ [ラ] ー
☞ 破裂音 [t] の弾音化が起こる。

❼ **going to** ゴウイング・トゥー ▶ ゴウイン＿トゥー
☞ 破裂音 [g] が脱落する。

❽ **patterns** パターンズ ▶ パダ [ラ] ーンズ
☞ 破裂音 [t] の弾音化が起こる。

❾ **What do you** ワット・ドゥー・ユー ▶ ワッ＿ドゥユ
☞ What の破裂音 [t] が脱落。do、you は弱化して [ドゥユ] と短く発音される。

❿ **and** アンド ▶ ＿ン＿
☞ and が弱化して [n] 音だけが残る。

⓫ **lot over** ラット・オウヴァー ▶ ラッド [ロ] ウヴァー
☞ 連結部で破裂音 [t] が弾音化する。

⓬ **Actually** アクチュアリー ▶ アクシュアリー
☞ 破裂音 [t] の脱落が起こる。

⓭ **water** ワーター ▶ ワーダ [ラ] ー
☞ 破裂音 [t] の弾音化が起こる。

⓮ **want a** ワント・ア ▶ ワナ
☞ want の [t] 音が脱落しながら a に連結する。

⓯ **it in a** イット・イン・ア ▶ イッディ [リ] ナ
☞ 3 語が連結。it in の連結部では [t] 音が弾音化する。

⓰ **get that** ゲット・ザット ▶ ゲッ＿ザッ（ト）
☞ 1 カ所あるいは 2 カ所で破裂音 [t] の脱落が起こる。

⓱ **excited and** イクサイティッド・アンド ▶ イクサイディ [リ] ッダ [ラ] ン（ド）
☞ excited の [t] 音、さらに 2 語の連結部の [d] 音が弾音化することがある。and 末尾の [d] 音は脱落しやすい。

宇宙飛行士のインタビュー　189

INTERVIEW WITH A PROFESSIONAL GAMBLER

Unit 31　プロ・ギャンブラーのインタビュー

Stage 1　穴埋め インタビュー・リスニング

音声変化に注意してCDでインタビューを聴きながら空欄部分を埋めてみよう。CDのナチュラル音声での聴き取りが難しいときは、次のトラックに収録されたスロー音声で聴いてみよう。

F: Most of our audience has probably never heard of Mike Stone ... but every casino owner in the world knows his name. Calling us from his home in Los Angeles is perhaps the most famous card player in the world. Are you there Mike?

M: I am.

F: Tell us a ① _____ about how you ② _____ _____ the path to become a professional gambler.

M: Well ... ③ _____ _____ was in middle school my father, ④ _____ _____, moved our family to Las Vegas. Like many, I was ⑤ _____ enthralled by bright lights and lure of easy money the casinos symbolized. Back then casino security wasn't as strict as ⑥ _____ _____ now, and I could ⑦ _____ walk into a place when I was in my mid-teens. I ⑧ _____ _____ blackjack, and by the time I was finishing high school I'd already started working on ⑨ _____ models to analyze the game.

F: How often do you play, and how much would you say you earn in a year now?

M: I don't play as often as I used to, as several casinos have blackballed me. I play only high-stakes games, and probably play ⑩ _____ _____ dozen times a year or so. This year I've ⑪ _____ close to two million dollars in winnings so far.

F: Do the casino's "comp" you?

M: Many casinos will bend over backwards to accommodate a high-

190

stakes money player, often ⑫ _____ _____ in the business as a "whale." In many cases, they will try to one-up each other for our ⑬ _____. Most people don't know it, ⑭ _____ _____ we can even negotiate our own rules to the game, in order to ⑮ _____ _____ push the odds in our favor.

F: Do you believe in luck?

M: Hahaha. Of course there are positive and negative trends, which most people refer to as "luck." Those of us who gamble professionally ignore that and know that if we are playing mathematically ⑯ _____, the trend will eventually go our way. Money management is the key. You have to know when to bet big, and when to stop. ⑰ _____ _____ what keeps the average person from winning.

Stage 2 インタビュー解説

日本語訳と、解説を参照しながら、インタビュー内容を確認しよう。そのあとで、Stage1の穴埋めに再チャレンジしてみよう。

F: Most of our audience has probably never heard of Mike Stone … but every casino owner in the world knows his name. Calling us from his home in Los Angeles is perhaps the most famous card player in the world. Are you there Mike?

> オーディエンスのほとんどのみなさんは、おそらくマイク・ストーンについて聞いたことはないでしょう…しかし、世界中のすべてのカジノ経営者たちは彼の名前を知っています。ロスの彼の自宅から電話をかけてきてくれているのは、おそらくは世界でもっとも有名なカード・プレーヤーなのです。マイク、聞こえますか？
>
> ✽ casino owner「カジノの経営者；オーナー」

M: I am.

> ええ。

F: Tell us a ① **little** about how you ② **started down** the path to become a professional gambler.

> あなたが、どのようにプロ・ギャンブラーへの道を進み始めたのか、少し話してもらえますか？
>
> * start down the path「その道に進み始める；始める」

M: Well … ③ **when I** was in middle school my father, ④ **an architect**, moved our family to Las Vegas. Like many, I was ⑤ **immediately** enthralled by bright lights and lure of easy money the casinos symbolized. Back then casino security wasn't as strict as ⑥ **it is** now, and I could ⑦ **actually** walk into a place when I was in my mid-teens. I ⑧ **started playing** blackjack, and by the time I was finishing high school I'd already started working on ⑨ **computer** models to analyze the game.

> ええ、私が中学生の頃、建築家だった父が、家をラスベガスに移したのです。多くの人と同様、私はすぐにカジノが象徴する歓楽的な生活やあぶく銭の魅力の虜になりました。当時は、カジノのセキュリティーはいまほど厳しくなかったので、10代の半ばだった私も、文字どおり歩いて入っていけたんですよ。ブラックジャックをやるようになりましたが、高校を卒業する頃には、すでに（ブラック・ジャックの）ゲームを分析するコンピューター・モデルに取り組み始めていました。
>
> * enthralled「魅了されて；夢中になって」　bright lights「都会の歓楽（的な生活）」
>   lure「魅惑；魅力」

F: How often do you play, and how much would you say you earn in a year now?

> あなたは、どのくらいの頻度でプレーしているんですか？　また、いまは年間、どのくらい稼いでいると思われますか？
>
> * earn「稼ぐ」

M: I don't play as often as I used to, as several casinos have blackballed me. I play only high-stakes games, and probably play ⑩ **about a** dozen times a year or so. This year I've ⑪ **netted** close to two million dollars in winnings so far.

> 昔ほどはやっていません。複数のカジノに追放されていますのでね。賭け金の高いゲームのみでプレーしていますが、年間十数回といったところでしょう。今年はこれまでに、ゲームに勝った金で2百万ドル近く稼ぎましたよ。
>
> * blackball「排斥する；排除する；追放する」　high-stakes game「賭け金の高いゲーム」
>   net「純益を上げる」　in winnings「賞金で；勝利した金で」

F: Do the casino's "comp" you?

> カジノはあなたを無料で招待するのですか？
>
> ＊comp「無料で招待する」

M: Many casinos will bend over backwards to accommodate a high-stakes money player, often ⑫ **referred to** in the business as a "whale." In many cases, they will try to one-up each other for our ⑬ **patronage**. Most people don't know it, ⑭ **but often** we can even negotiate our own rules to the game, in order to ⑮ **try to** push the odds in our favor.

> 多くのカジノが、業界で「クジラ」と呼ばれている、高額な金を賭けるプレーヤーに宿泊してもらおうと、懸命に努力するのです。多くの場合、カジノは、われわれのひいきを得るために、互いを出し抜こうとします。ほとんどの人は知らないでしょうが、われわれは、交渉してゲームに自分のルールを採用させることもできるんですよ。自分の側に有利な条件にするためにね。
>
> ＊bend over backwards「（人をよろこばせるために）懸命に努力する」 refer to A as B「AをBと呼ぶ」
> in the business「その業界で」 one-up「出し抜く」 odds「確率」

F: Do you believe in luck?

> あなたは運を信じますか？
>
> ＊luck「運」

M: Hahaha. Of course there are positive and negative trends, which most people refer to as "luck." Those of us who gamble professionally ignore that and know that if we are playing mathematically ⑯ **correctly**, the trend will eventually go our way. Money management is the key. You have to know when to bet big, and when to stop. ⑰ **That is** what keeps the average person from winning.

> ハハハ、もちろんいい流れと悪い流れはあります。ほとんどの人はそれを「運」と呼んでいますが。プロとしてギャンブルをする私たちは、そんなものは無視するんです。で、数学的に正しくプレーしていさえすれば、いつかは流れが自分のものになると、われわれにはわかっているんです。お金のマネジメントがカギになるのです。いつ大きな賭に出るのか、そしていつやめるのかを知っておかねばなりません。それこそ、ふつうの人が勝ちを逃し続ける原因なのです。
>
> ＊eventually「いつかは；結局は」

Stage 3 　英文トランスクリプション

インタビュー全体を英文の原稿で確認しながらCDで耳慣らししよう！ その上で、インタビューを聴きながら、まだできていない部分の穴埋めに再チャレンジしよう。

F: Most of our audience has probably never heard of Mike Stone ... but every casino owner in the world knows his name. Calling us from his home in Los Angeles is perhaps the most famous card player in the world. Are you there Mike?

M: I am.

F: Tell us a ① **little** about how you ② **started down** the path to become a professional gambler.

M: Well ... ③ **when I** was in middle school my father, ④ **an architect**, moved our family to Las Vegas. Like many, I was ⑤ **immediately** enthralled by bright lights and lure of easy money the casinos symbolized. Back then casino security wasn't as strict as ⑥ **it is** now, and I could ⑦ **actually** walk into a place when I was in my mid-teens. I ⑧ **started playing** blackjack, and by the time I was finishing high school I'd already started working on ⑨ **computer** models to analyze the game.

F: How often do you play, and how much would you say you earn in a year now?

M: I don't play as often as I used to, as several casinos have blackballed me. I play only high-stakes games, and probably play ⑩ **about a** dozen times a year or so. This year I've ⑪ **netted** close to two million dollars in winnings so far.

F: 'Do the casino's "comp" you?

M: Many casinos will bend over backwards to accommodate a high-stakes money player, often ⑫ **referred to** in the business as a "whale." In many cases, they will try to one-up each other for our ⑬ **patronage**. Most people don't know it, ⑭ **but often** we can even negotiate our own rules to the game, in order to ⑮ **try to** push the odds in our favor.

F: Do you believe in luck?

M: Hahaha. Of course there are positive and negative trends, which most people refer to as "luck." Those of us who gamble professionally ignore that and know that if we are playing mathematically ⑯ **correctly**, the trend will eventually go our way. Money management is the key. You have to know when to bet big, and when to stop. ⑰ **That is** what keeps the average person from winning.

Stage 4))) 音声変化をチェック

まとめとして、穴埋め部分の音声変化の特徴を**スロー・スピード**と**ナチュラル・スピード**で確認しよう。下記に示したカタカナ表記で音声変化を確認して、もう一度インタビューを聴き直してみよう。発音変化のルールは適宜復習しよう。

❶ little リトゥゥ ▶ リドゥ［ル］ゥ
☞ 破裂音［t］の弾音化が起こる。

❷ started down スターティッド・ダウン ▶ スターディ［リ］ッ＿ダウン
☞ started の［t］音が弾音化する。started 末尾の［d］音が脱落。

❸ when I ウェン・アイ ▶ ウェナイ
☞ 2 語が連結する。

❹ an architect アン・アーキテクト ▶ アナーキテクト
☞ 2 語が連結する。

❺ immediately イミーディアトゥリー ▶ イミーディアッ＿リー
☞［tl］で［t］音の脱落が生じる。

❻ it is イット・イズ ▶ イッディ［リ］ズ
☞ 連結部で破裂音［t］が弾音化する。

❼ actually アクチュアリー ▶ アクシュアリー
☞ 破裂音［t］の脱落が起こる。

❽ started playing スターティッド・プレイイング ▶ スターディ［リ］ッ＿プレイン（グ）
☞ 破裂音［t］の弾音化が起こる。started 末尾の［d］音が脱落。playing 末尾の［g］音も脱落しやすい。

❾ computer カムピューター ▶ カムピューダ［ラ］ー
☞ 破裂音［t］の弾音化が起こる。

❿ about a アバウト・ア ▶ アバウダ［ラ］
☞ 連結部で［t］音が弾音化する。

⓫ netted ネッティッド ▶ ネッディ［リ］ッ（ド）
☞ 破裂音［t］の弾音化が起こる。末尾の［d］音が脱落することもある。

⓬ referred to リファード・トゥー ▶ リファー＿ドゥ［ル］ー
☞ referred 末尾の［d］音が脱落。to の［t］音が弾音化する場合もある。

⓭ patronage ペイトゥラニージ ▶ ペイチュラニージ
☞［tr］部分の［t］音が［チュ］に近い音に変化する。

⓮ but often バット・オーフン ▶ バッド［ロ］ーフン
☞ 連結部で破裂音［t］が弾音化する。

⓯ try to トゥライ・トゥー ▶ チュライドゥ［ル］ー
☞［tr］部分の［t］音が［チュ］に近い音に変化する。to の［t］音が弾音化する。

⓰ correctly カレクトゥリー ▶ カレック＿リー
☞［tl］で［t］音の脱落が生じる。

⓱ That is ザット・イズ ▶ ザッディ［リ］ズ
☞ 連結部で［t］音が弾音化する。

プロ・ギャンブラーのインタビュー 195

INTERVIEW WITH A BREWERY OWNER

Unit 32 醸造所の経営者のインタビュー

Stage 1 穴埋め インタビュー・リスニング

音声変化に注意してCDでインタビューを聴きながら空欄部分を埋めてみよう。CDのナチュラル音声での聴き取りが難しいときは、次のトラックに収録されたスロー音声で聴いてみよう。

M: We're here today ① _____ _____ newly opened Full Circle Brewery, and our guide is president and CEO Jamie Sparks. Jamie, tell us a ② _____ _____ _____ _____ beers you are making?

F: Our beers are carefully crafted to not miss the mark ③ _____ _____ _____ to the tasting experience. Each ④ _____ _____ our beer will work together to provide a great aroma, front taste, mouthfeel, middle taste and then ending. All of these ⑤ _____ _____ have to complement each other, and this is something that is ⑥ _____ _____ master. We love hops so our flagship beer will be a Red IPA. We plan to go slow though, as each product we create deserves special attention throughout its development.

M: Describe your brand a ⑦ _____ more and what sets you apart. Why Full Circle?

F: Beyond ⑧ _____ _____ already been mentioned with regard to our beer designs, one thing that absolutely sets us apart is our ⑨ _____. Our ⑩ _____ will recycle our waste to create energy. We are ⑪ _____ _____ share waste with another specialty company that will in turn satisfy our power needs. Doing this will allow us to eliminate waste and decrease our cost of production. Our brand is designed to ⑫ _____ all drinkers, not just beer. We are going after not just beer lovers but also those that may not have experienced craft beer yet.

M: The craft beer industry seems to be exploding right now. Where do you see Full Circle Brewery ⑬ _____ _____ long term?

F: Our goal isn't just to ⑭ "_____ _____" ⑮ _____ _____ be unique. We also want to set new standards for not only the creation of craft brews, but for the promotion as well. My personal long-term goal is to have my granddaughter printing the 100 year anniversary sign on our product. That ⑯ _____ _____ great to see ⑰ _____ _____!?

Stage 2 インタビュー解説

日本語訳と、解説を参照しながら、インタビュー内容を確認しよう。そのあとで、Stage1の穴埋めに再チャレンジしてみよう。

M: We're here today ① **at the** newly opened Full Circle Brewery, and our guide is president and CEO Jamie Sparks. Jamie, tell us a ② **little bit about the** beers you are making?

> 今日、私たちは、新しくオープンしたフル・サークル醸造所に来ています。ガイドを務めてくださるのは、社長でCEOのジェイミー・スパークスさんです。ジェイミー、おたくで作っているビールについて少し教えていただけますか?
>
> * brewery「(ビールの) 醸造所」

F: Our beers are carefully crafted to not miss the mark ③ **when it comes** to the tasting experience. Each ④ **ingredient of** our beer will work together to provide a great aroma, front taste, mouthfeel, middle taste and then ending. All of these ⑤ **different experiences** have to complement each other, and this is something that is

⑥ **difficult to** master. We love hops so our flagship beer will be a Red IPA. We plan to go slow though, as each product we create deserves special attention throughout its development.

> うちのビールは、いざ、味わい体験の場面で的外れなものにならないように、念入りに作られているんです。われわれのビールのそれぞれの素材は互いに作用し合って、すばらしい香りと、最初の味わい、口当たり、飲み込んだときの味わい、そしてあと味を作り出します。このすべてのひとつひとつの経験が互いを補い合わねばなりません。そして、これは、たやすく達成できるものではないのです。私たちはホップを愛していますので、うちの旗艦商品のビールはレッド IPA になるでしょう。しかし、私たちはゆっくりと進むつもりです。うちが作るそれぞれの商品はその進化に連れて特別な注目を得るに値するものだからです。
>
> * craft「念入りに作る」　miss the mark「失敗する；的を外す」
> tasting experience「味わいの体験」　aroma「（飲む前の）香り」
> front taste「最初の一瞬の味」　mouthfeel「口当たり」　middle taste「飲み込んだときの味」
> ending「あと味」　complement「補完する；補って完全にする」　IPA = India Pale Ale

M: Describe your brand a ⑦ **little** more and what sets you apart. Why Full Circle?

> おたくのブランドことや、よそとの違いについて、もう少し教えてください。なぜフル・サークルなんでしょう？
>
> * set ... apart「…を（ほかのものと比べて優れたものとして）区別する」

F: Beyond ⑧ **what has** already been mentioned with regard to our beer designs, one thing that absolutely sets us apart is our ⑨ **sustainability**. Our ⑩ **facility** will recycle our waste to create energy. We are ⑪ **going to** share waste with another specialty company that will in turn satisfy our power needs. Doing this will allow us to eliminate waste and decrease our cost of production. Our brand is designed to ⑫ **attract** all drinkers, not just beer. We are going after not just beer lovers but also those that may not have experienced craft beer yet.

> うちのビールの設計についてすでにお話ししたこと以外に、われわれをよそと完璧に区別するものがサステイナビリティーです。うちの設備は（生産過程の）廃棄物をリサイクルして

エネルギーを作ります。私たちはほかの専門企業に廃棄物を分け与え、その会社は、代わりにわれわれの電力需要を満たします。これによって、われわれは、廃棄物をなくし、生産コストを削減できます。われわれのブランドは、ビールだけではなく、すべての愛飲家をひきつけるように考えられています。ビールを愛する人だけではなく、まだ地ビールを飲んだことがないかもしれない人をも捕まえたいのです。

* with regard to ...「…に関して」 sustainability「(環境などの) 持続可能性」
  specialty company「専門企業」 go after ...「…を追いかけていく；求める」

M: The craft beer industry seems to be exploding right now. Where do you see Full Circle Brewery ⑬ **fitting in** long term?

地ビール業界はいま、すごい勢いで拡大しているようです。長期的には、フル・サークル醸造所はどこに適合していくのでしょうか？

* fit in「合う；はまる」 long term「長期的に見て」

F: Our goal isn't just to ⑭ **"fit in"** ⑮ **but to** be unique. We also want to set new standards for not only the creation of craft brews, but for the promotion as well. My personal long-term goal is to have my granddaughter printing the 100 year anniversary sign on our product. That ⑯ **would be** great to see ⑰ **wouldn't it**!?

われわれのゴールは単に適合することではなく、ユニークであることです。また、私たちは、地ビールの創造だけではなく、プロモーションでも、新しいスタンダードを打ち立てたいのです。私の個人的な長期目標は、孫娘に、100周年記念の署名を商品に印刷させることなんです。それが見られたらすばらしいでしょ！

* standards「スタンダード；標準」

醸造所の経営者のインタビュー

Stage 3 英文トランスクリプション

インタビュー全体を英文の原稿で確認しながらCDで耳慣らししよう！ その上で、インタビューを聴きながら、まだできていない部分の穴埋めに再チャレンジしよう。

M: We're here today ① **at the** newly opened Full Circle Brewery, and our guide is president and CEO Jamie Sparks. Jamie, tell us a ② **little bit about the** beers you are making?

F: Our beers are carefully crafted to not miss the mark ③ **when it comes** to the tasting experience. Each ④ **ingredient of** our beer will work together to provide a great aroma, front taste, mouthfeel, middle taste and then ending. All of these ⑤ **different experiences** have to complement each other, and this is something that is ⑥ **difficult to** master. We love hops so our flagship beer will be a Red IPA. We plan to go slow though, as each product we create deserves special attention throughout its development.

M: Describe your brand a ⑦ **little** more and what sets you apart. Why Full Circle?

F: Beyond ⑧ **what has** already been mentioned with regard to our beer designs, one thing that absolutely sets us apart is our ⑨ **sustainability**. Our ⑩ **facility** will recycle our waste to create energy. We are ⑪ **going to** share waste with another specialty company that will in turn satisfy our power needs. Doing this will allow us to eliminate waste and decrease our cost of production. Our brand is designed to ⑫ **attract** all drinkers, not just beer. We are going after not just beer lovers but also those that may not have experienced craft beer yet.

M: The craft beer industry seems to be exploding right now. Where do you see Full Circle Brewery ⑬ **fitting in** long term?

F: Our goal isn't just to ⑭ **"fit in"** ⑮ **but to** be unique. We also want to set new standards for not only the creation of craft brews, but for the promotion as well. My personal long-term goal is to have my granddaughter printing the 100 year anniversary sign on our product. That ⑯ **would be** great to see ⑰ **wouldn't it**!?

Stage 4))) 音声変化をチェック

まとめとして、穴埋め部分の音声変化の特徴を**スロー・スピード**と**ナチュラル・スピード**で確認しよう。下記に示したカタカナ表記で音声変化を確認して、もう一度インタビューを聴き直してみよう。発音変化のルールは適宜復習しよう。

---

❶ **at the**　　　　　　　　　アット・ザ　　　　　　　　▶ アッ__ザ
　☞ 破裂音 [t] の脱落が起こる。

❷ **little bit about the**　　リトゥゥ・ビット・アバウト・ザ
　　　　　　　　　　　　　　　　　　　　　　　　　▶ リドゥ [ル] ゥビッダ [ラ] バウッ__ザ
　☞ little の [t] 音、bit about 連結部の [t] 音が弾音化する。about 末尾の [t] 音は脱落。

❸ **when it comes**　　　　ウェン・イット・カムズ　　　▶ ウェニッ__カムズ
　☞ when it は連結。it 末尾の破裂音 [t] は脱落する。

❹ **ingredient of**　　　　　イングリーディエント・アヴ　▶ イングリーディエナヴ
　☞ ingredient の [t] 音が脱落しながら of に連結する。

❺ **different experiences**　ディファラント・イクスピアリアンスィズ
　　　　　　　　　　　　　　　　　　　　　　　　　▶ ディファラニクスピアリアンスィズ
　☞ different の [t] 音が脱落しながら experiences に連結する。

❻ **difficult to**　　　　　　ディフィカウト・トゥー　　　▶ ディフィカウッ__トゥー
　☞ difficult の破裂音 [t] の脱落が起こる。

❼ **little**　　　　　　　　　リトゥゥ　　　　　　　　　　▶ リドゥ [ル] ゥ
　☞ 破裂音 [t] の弾音化が起こる。

❽ **what has**　　　　　　　ワット・ハズ　　　　　　　　▶ ワッダ [ラ] ズ
　☞ what 弱化した has [アズ] に連結する。連結部で破裂音 [t] の弾音化が起こる。

❾ **sustainability**　　　　サステイナビラティー　　　　▶ サステイナビラディ [リ] ー
　☞ 破裂音 [t] の弾音化が起こる。

❿ **facility**　　　　　　　　ファスィラティー　　　　　　▶ ファスィラディ [リ] ー
　☞ 破裂音 [t] の弾音化が起こる。

⓫ **going to**　　　　　　　ゴウイング・トゥー　　　　　▶ ゴウイン__トゥー
　☞ 破裂音 [g] が脱落する。

⓬ **attract**　　　　　　　　アトゥラクト　　　　　　　　▶ アチュラクト
　☞ tr の [t] 音は [チュ] のように変化する。

⓭ **fitting in**　　　　　　　フィッティング・イン　　　　▶ フィッディ [リ] ンギン
　☞ fitting の破裂音 [t] が弾音化する。2 語が連結。

⓮ **"fit in"**　　　　　　　　フィット・イン　　　　　　　▶ フィッディ [リ] ン
　☞ 連結部で [t] 音が弾音化する。

⓯ **but to**　　　　　　　　バット・トゥー　　　　　　　▶ バッ__トゥー
　☞ 破裂音 [t] が脱落する。

⓰ **would be**　　　　　　　ウッド・ビー　　　　　　　　▶ ウッ__ビー
　☞ 破裂音 [d] が脱落する。

⓱ **wouldn't it**　　　　　　ウドゥント・イット　　　　　▶ ウドゥニッ__
　☞ wouldn't 末尾の [t] 音が脱落しながら it に連結する。it 末尾の [t] 音も脱落。

醸造所の経営者のインタビュー

INTERVIEW WITH A COMPANY CEO

Unit 33 企業のCEOのインタビュー

Stage 1 穴埋め インタビュー・リスニング

音声変化に注意してCDでインタビューを聴きながら空欄部分を埋めてみよう。CDのナチュラル音声での聴き取りが難しいときは、次のトラックに収録されたスロー音声で聴いてみよう。

F: Joining us by phone today from his office in Silicon Valley is Jim Vanzant, Chief ① _____ Officer of Stratos Inc., an IT firm ② _____ _____ taking the industry by storm. Jim, tell us a little about ③ _____ your company is doing.

M: Sure. Well, for ④ _____, we are first and foremost an IT solutions provider. We partner with large corporations to customize and develop a wide ⑤ _____ of services to fit each client's particular needs. In this day and age, with so much information being analyzed, transmitted and stored, there are a myriad of challenges ... ⑥ _____ _____ least of which is security. Stratos strives to develop and help maintain IT ⑦ _____ to overcome those hurdles.

F: Your IPO last month was one of the largest in the history of the stock market. Was that something that you saw ⑧ _____?

M: To be honest with you, when we planned our public offering, we were forecasting about fifty dollars a share. Never ⑨ _____ _____ wildest dreams did we imagine the interest we received, not to mention the ⑩ _____-_____ scale of investment. Our company was founded on the principle of providing much needed services, and I am ⑪ _____ confident we can continue to adapt and exceed both the expectations of our customers and now our investor base as well.

F: Rumor has it ⑫ _____ _____ are about to unveil a
⑬ _____ new way to store ⑭ _____. Can you tell us a
⑮ _____ _____ _____ _____?

M: As you can imagine, I'm not really at liberty to disclose anything on that yet ... but I can assure you that Stratos will be leading the way on many new innovations that will truly revolutionize the way data is transmitted, shared and stored. Suffice ⑯ _____ _____ say that there are big changes coming for the IT field, and we will be the primary shakers and movers — ⑰ _____ _____ speak — for a long time to come.

Stage 2 インタビュー解説

日本語訳と、解説を参照しながら、インタビュー内容を確認しよう。そのあとで、Stage1の穴埋めに再チャレンジしてみよう。

F: Joining us by phone today from his office in Silicon Valley is Jim Vanzant, Chief ① **Executive** Officer of Stratos Inc., an IT firm ② **that is** taking the industry by storm. Jim, tell us a little about ③ **what** your company is doing.

> 今日、シリコンバレーの自分のオフィスから電話で参加してくれているのは、ジム・バンザントです。彼は、業界に激震を起こしているIT企業であるストラトス・インクのCEOです。ジム、あなたの会社がやっていることについて、少しお話ししてもらえますか？
>
> * take by storm「急襲して瞬時に大きな影響を与える」

M: Sure. Well, for ④ **starters**, we are first and foremost an IT solutions provider. We partner with large corporations to customize and develop a wide ⑤ **variety** of services to fit each client's particular needs. In this day and age, with so much information being analyzed, transmitted and stored, there are a myriad of challenges ... ⑥ **not the** least of which is security. Stratos strives to develop and help maintain IT ⑦ **infrastructure** to overcome those hurdles.

> もちろんです。はじめに、なによりもまずわが社はITソリューションを提供している企業です。大企業と提携して、それぞれの顧客の特定のニーズに適合するよう、広範なサービスをカスタマイズしたり開発したりしています。多くの情報が分析、送信、蓄積されている今日、無数の難問が存在していますが、セキュリティーの問題はその最たるものです。ストラトス社では、これらのハードルを乗り越えるために、ITインフラの開発とその管理の手助けに骨を折っているのです。
>
> ----------
>
> * partner with ...「…と提携する；組む」 customize「カスタマイズする」
>   particular「特有の；特定の」 myriad of ...「無数の…」
>   not the least of which「その中で最大のもの」 strive to ...「…しようと努力する；骨を折る」
>   maintain「維持・管理する；整備する」 overcome「打ち勝つ；克服する」

F: Your IPO last month was one of the largest in the history of the stock market. Was that something that you saw ⑧ **coming**?

> 先月の御社の株式上場は、株式市場の歴史上、最大のもののひとつになりましたね。それは予測していたことでしょうか？
>
> ----------
>
> * IPO = initial public offering「未上場企業株の新規公開」

M: To be honest with you, when we planned our public offering, we were forecasting about fifty dollars a share. Never ⑨ **in our** wildest dreams did we imagine the interest we received, not to mention the ⑩ **record-setting** scale of investment. Our company was founded on the principle of providing much needed services, and I am ⑪ **extremely** confident we can continue to adapt and exceed both the expectations of our customers and now our investor base as well.

> 正直に申し上げると、上場を計画したときには、ひと株につき約50ドルを予測していました。われわれの会社が受ける関心を、夢にも想像できませんでしたし、記録破りの投資規模についても言うまでもありません。弊社は、もっとも必要とされるサービスの提供を信条として創業されました。弊社の顧客の期待と、さらにいまは投資家層の期待にも同様に適応し、

その期待を上回り続けることができると、非常に強い自信をもっています。

---

* Never in one's wildest dreams ...「夢にも…ない」
  record-setting「記録を打ち立てる；記録破りの」 be founded「創設される」
  principle「原則；信条」 adapt and exceed「適応し超える」
  investor base「投資家基盤；投資家層」

F: Rumor has it ⑫ **that you** are about to unveil a ⑬ **completely** new way to store ⑭ **data**. Can you tell us a ⑮ **little bit about that**?

御社は、データ蓄積のまったく新しい方法を公開しようとしているという、うわさがあります。その点についてちょっとお話しいただくことはできますか？

---

* store data「データを蓄積する」

M: As you can imagine, I'm not really at liberty to disclose anything on that yet ... but I can assure you that Stratos will be leading the way on many new innovations that will truly revolutionize the way data is transmitted, shared and stored. Suffice ⑯ **it to** say that there are big changes coming for the IT field, and we will be the primary shakers and movers ― ⑰ **so to** speak ― for a long time to come.

ご想像に難くないでしょうが、それに関しては、まだ私はなにも自由に発表できません…しかしデータの送信やシェア、保存などの方法をほんとうに革命的に変える多くの新しいイノベーションに関して、ストラトス社が先頭に立って進んでいくであろうことは、はっきり申し上げることができます。IT分野にとって大きな変化が訪れつつあって、われわれは今後長らく、いわゆる「もっとも重要な影響を業界に与える存在」になるだろうと申し上げれば、それで十分でしょう。

---

* be at liberty to ...「自由に…できる」 disclose「公開する；発表する；暴露する」
  lead the way「先頭に立って進む；先導する」 innovation「革新」
  revolutionize「革命を起こす；大改革する」 Suffice it to say that ...「…と言えば十分だ」
  the primary「もっとも重要な；第一の」 shakers and movers「(政財界などの)有力者・企業」

Stage 3　英文トランスクリプション

インタビュー全体を英文の原稿で確認しながらCDで耳慣らししよう！ その上で、インタビューを聴きながら、まだできていない部分の穴埋めに再チャレンジしよう。

F: Joining us by phone today from his office in Silicon Valley is Jim Vanzant, Chief ① **Executive** Officer of Stratos Inc., an IT firm ② **that is** taking the industry by storm. Jim, tell us a little about ③ **what** your company is doing.

M: Sure. Well, for ④ **starters**, we are first and foremost an IT solutions provider. We partner with large corporations to customize and develop a wide ⑤ **variety** of services to fit each client's particular needs. In this day and age, with so much information being analyzed, transmitted and stored, there are a myriad of challenges ... ⑥ **not the** least of which is security. Stratos strives to develop and help maintain IT ⑦ **infrastructure** to overcome those hurdles.

F: Your IPO last month was one of the largest in the history of the stock market. Was that something that you saw ⑧ **coming**?

M: To be honest with you, when we planned our public offering, we were forecasting about fifty dollars a share. Never ⑨ **in our** wildest dreams did we imagine the interest we received, not to mention the ⑩ **record-setting** scale of investment. Our company was founded on the principle of providing much needed services, and I am ⑪ **extremely** confident we can continue to adapt and exceed both the expectations of our customers and now our investor base as well.

F: Rumor has it ⑫ **that you** are about to unveil a ⑬ **completely** new way to store ⑭ **data**. Can you tell us a ⑮ **little bit about that**?

M: As you can imagine, I'm not really at liberty to disclose anything on that yet ... but I can assure you that Stratos will be leading the way on many new innovations that will truly revolutionize the way data is transmitted, shared and stored. Suffice ⑯ **it to** say that there are big changes coming for the IT field, and we will be the primary shakers and movers — ⑰ **so to** speak — for a long time to come.

Stage 4))) 音声変化をチェック

まとめとして、穴埋め部分の音声変化の特徴を**スロー・スピード**と**ナチュラル・スピード**で確認しよう。下記に示したカタカナ表記で音声変化を確認して、もう一度インタビューを聴き直してみよう。発音変化のルールは適宜復習しよう。

❶ **Executive** エグゼキュティヴ ▶ エグゼキュディ［リ］ヴ
☞ 破裂音［t］の弾音化が起こる。

❷ **that is** ザット・イズ ▶ ザッディ［リ］ズ
☞ 連結部で［t］音が弾音化する。

❸ **what** ワット ▶ ワッ＿
☞ 末尾の破裂音［t］が脱落する。

❹ **starters** スターターズ ▶ スターダ［ラ］ーズ
☞ 破裂音［t］の弾音化が起こる。

❺ **variety** ヴァライアティー ▶ ヴァライアディ［リ］ー
☞ 破裂音［t］の弾音化が起こる。

❻ **not the** ナット・ザ ▶ ナッ＿ザ
☞ 破裂音［t］の脱落が起こる。

❼ **infrastructure** インフラストラクチャー ▶ インフラストラクシャー
☞ 破裂音［t］の脱落が起こる。

❽ **coming** カミング ▶ カミン＿
☞ 末尾の破裂音［g］が脱落する。

❾ **in our** イン・アウァ ▶ イナウァ
☞ 2語が連結する。

❿ **record-setting** レコード・セッティング ▶ レコードセッディ［リ］ン（グ）
☞ setting の［t］音が弾音化する。末尾の破裂音［g］も脱落することがある。

⓫ **extremely** エクストゥリームリー ▶ エクスチュリームリー
☞ tr の［t］音は［チュ］のように変化する。

⓬ **that you** ザット・ユー ▶ ザッチュー；ザッ＿ユー
☞［t］＋［j］の部分で音が混じり合い、［チュ］に近い音に変化する。［t］音が脱落する場合もある。

⓭ **completely** カムプリートゥリー ▶ カムプリーツ＿リー
☞［tl］で［t］音の脱落が生じる。

⓮ **data** データ ▶ デーダ［ラ］
☞ 破裂音［t］が弾音化する。

⓯ **little bit about that** リトゥゥ・ビット・アバウト・ザット
▶ リドゥ［ル］ゥビッダ［ラ］バウッ＿ザッ（ト）
☞ little や bit about の連結部で［t］音が弾音化する。about と that 末尾の［t］音は脱落しやすい。

⓰ **it to** イット・トゥー ▶ イッ＿トゥー
☞ 破裂音［t］の脱落が起こる。

⓱ **so to** ソウ・トゥー ▶ ソウドゥ［ル］ー
☞ to の破裂音［t］が弾音化する。

企業のCEOのインタビュー

INTERVIEW WITH A UN INTERPRETER

Unit 34 通訳者のインタビュー

Stage 1 穴埋め インタビュー・リスニング

音声変化に注意してCDでインタビューを聴きながら空欄部分を埋めてみよう。CDのナチュラル音声での聴き取りが難しいときは、次のトラックに収録されたスロー音声で聴いてみよう。

M: We're speaking today with Missy Vogle, an interpreter for the United Nations here in New York. Missy, how many languages do you speak?

F: Well, I'm fluent in four languages, ① _____. I was born in the US but spent my teen years in Switzerland, where I picked up both French and German. My father was in the banking ② _____ so we traveled ③ _____ _____ _____ and I was fortunate to be ④ _____ _____ a wide variety of cultures and languages in my formative years. I went to college in Spain, where I majored in International Studies and minored in Spanish.

M: That's amazing. Like most Americans, I took two years of Spanish in high school, but don't remember any ⑤ _____ _____. What is the hardest thing about being an interpreter?

F: Well Jim, the rule to learning a foreign language is ⑥ "_____ _____ or lose it." The hard thing about interpretation is that you have to do ⑦ _____ _____ real time. Unlike a translator, we don't get to edit ⑧ _____ _____ do. There's no time to look things up in a dictionary or what have you, you only get one shot. That puts a lot of pressure on you to ⑨ _____ _____ right. It gets even more difficult when you are ⑩ _____ dignitaries or ambassadors from different countries.

M: Do you get time to prepare?

F: Well, preparation for me is to keep current on news, ⑪ _____ developments and topics that are likely to come up during our meetings or be ⑫ _____ to each of the people involved. That's a ⑬ _____ tall order. I do usually ⑭ _____ _____ _____ of the talking points in advance ⑮ _____ _____ me to bone up on the topic of discussion if I ⑯ _____ _____.

M: What's been one of your proudest moments?

F: About two years ago I helped negotiate a financial arrangement that allowed Germany and the European Union to provide bailout funds to support the Spanish Economy. That and occasionally ⑰ _____ to interpret for the president of the US, of course.

Stage 2 インタビュー解説

日本語訳と、解説を参照しながら、インタビュー内容を確認しよう。そのあとで、Stage1の穴埋めに再チャレンジしてみよう。

M: We're speaking today with Missy Vogle, an interpreter for the United Nations here in New York. Missy, how many languages do you speak?

> 本日は、ここニューヨークで国連の通訳をしているミッシー・ボウグルさんとお話ししています。ミッシー、あなたは何カ国語が話せるんですか？
>
> ＊ United Nations「国際連合」

F: Well, I'm fluent in four languages, ① **actually**. I was born in the US but spent my teen years in Switzerland, where I picked up both French and German. My father was in the banking ② **industry** so we traveled ③ **quite a lot** and I was fortunate to be ④ **exposed to** a wide variety of cultures and languages in my formative years.

I went to college in Spain, where I majored in International Studies and minored in Spanish.

> えー、実は4カ国語に堪能なんですよ。アメリカ生まれですが、10代の頃をスイスで過ごし、そこでフランス語とドイツ語を覚えました。父が銀行業界にいたので転勤が多く、人格形成期に多様な文化や言語に触れることができたのは幸運でした。スペインの大学に進み、そこで国際学を専攻し、スペイン語を副専攻にしました。
>
> * pick up「(努力せずに)知識や情報を得る」 be exposed to ...「…に触れる」
>   formative years「人格形成期」 major in ...「…を専攻する」 minor in ...「…を副専攻にする」

M: That's amazing. Like most Americans, I took two years of Spanish in high school, but don't remember any ⑤ **of it**. What is the hardest thing about being an interpreter?

> それは驚きですね。多くのアメリカ人がそうですが、私は2年間、高校でスペイン語の授業を取りましたが、なにも覚えていませんよ。通訳であることでもっとも難しいことはなんでしょうか？
>
> * interpreter「通訳」

F: Well Jim, the rule to learning a foreign language is ⑥ "**use it** or lose it." The hard thing about interpretation is that you have to do ⑦ **it in** real time. Unlike a translator, we don't get to edit ⑧ **what we** do. There's no time to look things up in a dictionary or what have you, you only get one shot. That puts a lot of pressure on you to ⑨ **get it** right. It gets even more difficult when you are ⑩ **representing** dignitaries or ambassadors from different countries.

> あのですね、ジム、外国語を学ぶときの大事なカギは「使わなければ忘れる」ということです。通訳の難しい点は、それをリアル・タイムでやらねばならないことです。翻訳家と違って、私たちには、自分のやることを編集する機会がありません。辞書で調べたりする時間はなくて、一発勝負なのです。きちんとやるためには、多くのプレッシャーがかかります。よその国の高官や駐在大使などの代わりに話すときには、さらに難しくなるのです。
>
> * rule to ...「…の重要なカギ」 edit「編集する」 ... or what have you = ... and so on
>   shot「試み」 get it right「きちんとやる；間違いなくやる」 represent「代弁する」
>   dignitary「(政府などの)高官；有力者」 ambassador「駐在大使」

M: Do you get time to prepare?

> 準備の時間は取っていますか？

F: Well, preparation for me is to keep current on news, ⑪ **political** developments and topics that are likely to come up during our meetings or be ⑫ **important** to each of the people involved. That's a ⑬ **pretty** tall order. I do usually ⑭ **get an outline** of the talking points in advance ⑮ **that allows** me to bone up on the topic of discussion if I ⑯ **need to**.

> えー、私にとっての準備は、ニュースや政治の動向、あるいはミーティングで出てきそうな話題や、関わる両者にとって重要になりそうな話題についての情報を常に更新しておくことです。これはかなり困難な仕事なんです。私は、たいてい会話のポイントの概略も前もってもらうんですが、必要な場合、それによってディスカッションのテーマに関する情報を詰め込むことができるんです。
>
> ＊ keep current on ...「…に関して更新しておく」　tall order「困難な仕事；無理な注文」
> 　bone up「(前もって) 知識を詰め込む」

M: What's been one of your proudest moments?

> あなたのもっとも誇るべき瞬間はいつでしたか？
>
> ＊ proudest「もっとも誇れる」

F: About two years ago I helped negotiate a financial arrangement that allowed Germany and the European Union to provide bailout funds to support the Spanish Economy. That and occasionally ⑰ **getting** to interpret for the president of the US, of course.

> 約2年前、財政協定の交渉を手伝いました。それによってドイツとEUは、スペイン経済をサポートする緊急援助を提供できたのです。それと、もちろんですが、時折アメリカ大統領の通訳をする機会があることもですね。
>
> ＊ bailout「(経済・財政的な) 緊急援助；救済措置」　occasionally「時折」

通訳者のインタビュー　211

Stage 3 　英文トランスクリプション

インタビュー全体を英文の原稿で確認しながらCDで耳慣らししよう！　その上で、インタビューを聴きながら、まだできていない部分の穴埋めに再チャレンジしよう。

M: We're speaking today with Missy Vogle, an interpreter for the United Nations here in New York. Missy, how many languages do you speak?

F: Well, I'm fluent in four languages, ① **actually**. I was born in the US but spent my teen years in Switzerland, where I picked up both French and German. My father was in the banking ② **industry** so we traveled ③ **quite a lot** and I was fortunate to be ④ **exposed to** a wide variety of cultures and languages in my formative years. I went to college in Spain, where I majored in International Studies and minored in Spanish.

M: That's amazing. Like most Americans, I took two years of Spanish in high school, but don't remember any ⑤ **of it**. What is the hardest thing about being an interpreter?

F: Well Jim, the rule to learning a foreign language is ⑥ "**use it** or lose it." The hard thing about interpretation is that you have to do ⑦ **it in** real time. Unlike a translator, we don't get to edit ⑧ **what we** do. There's no time to look things up in a dictionary or what have you, you only get one shot. That puts a lot of pressure on you to ⑨ **get it** right. It gets even more difficult when you are ⑩ **representing** dignitaries or ambassadors from different countries.

M: Do you get time to prepare?

F: Well, preparation for me is to keep current on news, ⑪ **political** developments and topics that are likely to come up during our meetings or be ⑫ **important** to each of the people involved. That's a ⑬ **pretty** tall order. I do usually ⑭ **get an outline** of the talking points in advance ⑮ **that allows** me to bone up on the topic of discussion if I ⑯ **need to**.

M: What's been one of your proudest moments?

F: About two years ago I helped negotiate a financial arrangement that allowed Germany and the European Union to provide bailout funds to support the Spanish Economy. That and occasionally ⑰ **getting** to interpret for the president of the US, of course.

Stage 4))) 音声変化をチェック

まとめとして、穴埋め部分の音声変化の特徴を**スロー・スピード**と**ナチュラル・スピード**で確認しよう。下記に示したカタカナ表記で音声変化を確認して、もう一度インタビューを聴き直してみよう。発音変化のルールは適宜復習しよう。

---

❶ **actually**　　　　　　　　アクチュァリー　　　　　▶ アクシュァリー
☞ 破裂音 [t] の脱落が起こる。

❷ **industry**　　　　　　　　インダストゥリー　　　　▶ インダスチュリー
☞ [tr] 部分の [t] 音が [チュ] に近い音に変化する。

❸ **quite a lot**　　　　　　　クゥァイト・ア・ラット　　▶ クゥァイダ [ラ] ラッ (ト)
☞ quite a の連結部で [t] 音が弾音化する。lot 末尾の [t] 音は脱落することもある。

❹ **exposed to**　　　　　　　イクスポウズド・トゥー　　▶ イクスポウズッ__トゥー
☞ 破裂音 [d] が脱落する。

❺ **of it**　　　　　　　　　　アヴ・イット　　　　　　　▶ アヴィッ (ト)
☞ 2 語が連結。末尾の破裂音 [t] は脱落することがある。

❻ **use it**　　　　　　　　　ユーズ・イット　　　　　　▶ ユーズィッ (ト)
☞ 2 語が連結。末尾の破裂音 [t] は脱落することがある。

❼ **it in**　　　　　　　　　　イット・イン　　　　　　　▶ イッディ [リ] ン
☞ 連結部で破裂音 [t] の弾音化が起こる。

❽ **what we**　　　　　　　　ワット・ウィ　　　　　　　▶ ワッ__ウィ
☞ 破裂音 [t] の脱落が起こる。

❾ **get it**　　　　　　　　　ゲット・イット　　　　　　▶ ゲッディ [リ] ッ__
☞ 連結部で破裂音 [t] の弾音化が起こる。末尾の [t] 音が脱落。

❿ **representing**　　　　　　レプリゼンティング　　　　▶ レプリゼニング
☞ [nt] で [t] 音の脱落が生じる。

⓫ **political**　　　　　　　　パリティカゥ　　　　　　　▶ パリディ [リ] カゥ
☞ 破裂音 [t] の弾音化が起こる。

⓬ **important**　　　　　　　イムポートゥント　　　　　▶ イムポーンン (ト)
☞ [tn] の [t] 音が声門閉鎖音化する。末尾の [t] 音は脱落することがある。

⓭ **pretty**　　　　　　　　　プリティー　　　　　　　　▶ プリディ [リ] ー
☞ 破裂音 [t] の弾音化が起こる。

⓮ **get an outline**　　　　　ゲット・アン・アウトライン　▶ ゲッダ [ラ] ナウッ__ライン
☞ 3 語が連結。get an の連結部で [t] 音が弾音化。outline の [t] 音が脱落する場合もある。

⓯ **that allows**　　　　　　　ザット・アラウズ　　　　　▶ ザッダ [ラ] ラウズ
☞ 連結部で破裂音 [t] の弾音化が起こる。

⓰ **need to**　　　　　　　　ニード・トゥー　　　　　　▶ ニーッ__トゥー
☞ 破裂音 [d] の脱落が起こる。

⓱ **getting**　　　　　　　　ゲッティング　　　　　　　▶ ゲッディ [リ] ン (グ)
☞ 破裂音 [t] の弾音化が起こる。末尾の [g] 音が脱落することもある。

INTERVIEW WITH A LEGENDARY MUSICIAN

Unit 35 伝説のミュージシャンのインタビュー

🎧 Stage 1 　穴埋め インタビュー・リスニング

音声変化に注意してCDでインタビューを聴きながら空欄部分を埋めてみよう。CDのナチュラル音声での聴き取りが難しいときは、次のトラックに収録されたスロー音声で聴いてみよう。

F: With us today in our studio is Johnny Ringold, lead singer for the Dark Side, a rock band that shot to stardom in the ① _____, and recently announced the release of a new album and world tour. Johhny, ② _____ _____ _____ all to ③ _____ _____ together after all these years?

M: Well, you know Tina, the interest was always there. ④ _____ _____ tough ya know, after spending ⑤ _____ _____ decade on the road and touring around the world, it wears on you. We ⑥ _____ _____ and life kind of gets in the way. Our band ⑦ _____ _____ in the mid 1980's, but the love of music never ⑧ _____ _____. ⑨ _____ we started kicking around the idea for a new album, ⑩ _____ _____ kind of got the creative juices flowing again. We were approached by a major music label for a comeback tour, and things just started to fall into place from there.

F: ⑪ _____ _____ some of the differences you see in the business now as opposed to back in the day?

M: Hahaha. Well for one we're not spring chickens anymore. Spending hours on end ⑫ _____ _____ recording studio and grueling months on tour ⑬ _____ _____ easy as it used to be. Recording and touring, however is somethin' we can apply our past

214

experience to. With the ⑭ _____, smartphones and portable music devices ... the marketing and music sales aspect is a ⑮ _____ different animal though.

F: Word is that your first four concert venues were sold out in a ⑯ _____ of minutes. Sounds like your fan base is ⑰ _____ glad you're back.

M: That was a pleasant surprise. We are thrilled at the prospect of performing live after all these years, and providing our fans around the world with a new experience. We are also hoping the new cuts we've recorded will resonate with the younger generation of music fans out there as well.

Stage 2 インタビュー解説

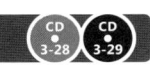

日本語訳と、解説を参照しながら、インタビュー内容を確認しよう。そのあとで、Stage1の穴埋めに再チャレンジしてみよう。

F: With us today in our studio is Johnny Ringold, lead singer for the Dark Side, a rock band that shot to stardom in the ① **70's**, and recently announced the release of a new album and world tour. Johhny, ② **what motivated you** all to ③ **get back** together after all these years?

今日、私たちといっしょにスタジオにいるのは、ジョニー・リンゴウルドです。彼は、70年代にスターダムに駆け上り、最近ニュー・アルバムの発売とワールド・ツアーを発表したロック・バンド、ダーク・サイドのリード・ボーカルです。ジョニー、長い年月を超えて、みなさんが再結成した動機はなんでしょう？

＊ shoot to stardom「スターダムに駆け上る；のし上がる」 release「発売」
motivate「動機づける」 get back together「再結成する」

M: Well, you know Tina, the interest was always there. ④ **But it's** tough ya know, after spending ⑤ **about a** decade on the road and touring around the world, it wears on you. We ⑥ **get older** and life kind of gets in the way. Our band ⑦ **split up** in the mid 1980's, but the love of music never ⑧ **went away**. ⑨ **Recently** we started kicking around the idea for a new album, ⑩ **and that** kind of got the creative juices flowing again. We were approached by a major music label for a comeback tour, and things just started to fall into place from there.

> えー、あのね、ティナ、そういう気持ちはいつもそこにあったんだよ。でも、それって、大変なことなんだよね。約十年もの間、世界中をツアーで巡ると、もううんざりになるんだよ。年を重ねると、生活がある種、支障になったりしてね。僕らのバンドは80年代の中頃に解散したけど、音楽への愛は決してなくなりはしなかったね。最近、あれこれニュー・アルバムのアイデアを検討し始めたんだ。で、それで、また、なんだか創造意欲がわき出てきたんだよ。メジャー・レーベルにカムバック・ツアーをやろうとアプローチを受けてね、そこから、いろいろと話がまとまり始めたんだよ。
>
> * on the road「旅行して；巡業して；放浪して」　wear on ...「…を疲れさせる；うんざりさせる」
> get in the way「妨げになる」　kick around「あれこれ検討する」　creative juices「創造意欲」
> fall into place「納まるべきところに納まる；軌道に乗る」

F: ⑪ **What are** some of the differences you see in the business now as opposed to back in the day?

> 当時と比べて、業界で異なっている点はどんなことでしょう？
>
> * as opposed to ...「…と対照的に」　back in the day「当時」

M: Hahaha. Well for one we're not spring chickens anymore. Spending hours on end ⑫ **in the** recording studio and grueling months on tour ⑬ **isn't as** easy as it used to be. Recording and touring, however is somethin' we can apply our past experience to. With the ⑭ **internet**, smartphones and portable music devices ... the marketing and music sales aspect is a ⑮ **totally** different animal though.

> ハハハ。あー、まずは、僕らがもう若造じゃないってことだね。何時間も連続でレコーディング・スタジオで過ごしたり、ヘトヘトになるツアーを何カ月もやるのは、昔のようにかん

たんじゃないね。しかし、レコーディングやツアーは、僕らの過去の経験を活かせるものなんだよ。でも、インターネットやスマホ、携帯音楽機器があるから…マーケティングや音楽のセールス面は、(昔とは) まったくの別物だね。

＊ spring chicken「若者；若造；うぶな女；小娘」 on end「立て続けに」
grueling「ヘトヘトにさせる；厳しい」 experience「経験」 aspect「側面」
totally different animal「まったくの別物」

F: Word is that your first four concert venues were sold out in a ⑯ **matter** of minutes. Sounds like your fan base is ⑰ **certainly** glad you're back.

最初の４カ所のコンサート会場は、一瞬で売り切れたといううわさですね。ファン層はみなさんの復帰を確実によろこんでいるみたいですね。

＊ Word is that ...「…といううわさだ」 concert venue「コンサート会場」
in a matter of minutes「一瞬で」

M: That was a pleasant surprise. We are thrilled at the prospect of performing live after all these years, and providing our fans around the world with a new experience. We are also hoping the new cuts we've recorded will resonate with the younger generation of music fans out there as well.

それは、うれしいよろこびだったね。僕らは、久々のライブ・パフォーマンスを控えてわくわくしているんだよ。世界中のファンに新しい体験を提供できることもね。それから、世界中の若い世代の音楽ファンたちも、僕らが吹き込んだ新曲に、共鳴してくれることを願っているよ。

＊ be thrilled at ...「…にわくわくする」 at the prospect of ...「…を控えて；…の可能性に」
new cut「新曲」 resonate with ...「…と共鳴する」

Stage 3 　英文トランスクリプション

インタビュー全体を英文の原稿で確認しながらCDで耳慣らししよう！ その上で、インタビューを聴きながら、まだできていない部分の穴埋めに再チャレンジしよう。

F: With us today in our studio is Johnny Ringold, lead singer for the Dark Side, a rock band that shot to stardom in the ① **70's**, and recently announced the release of a new album and world tour. Johhny, ② **what motivated you** all to ③ **get back** together after all these years?

M: Well, you know Tina, the interest was always there. ④ **But it's** tough ya know, after spending ⑤ **about a** decade on the road and touring around the world, it wears on you. We ⑥ **get older** and life kind of gets in the way. Our band ⑦ **split up** in the mid 1980's, but the love of music never ⑧ **went away**. ⑨ **Recently** we started kicking around the idea for a new album, ⑩ **and that** kind of got the creative juices flowing again. We were approached by a major music label for a comeback tour, and things just started to fall into place from there.

F: ⑪ **What are** some of the differences you see in the business now as opposed to back in the day?

M: Hahaha. Well for one we're not spring chickens anymore. Spending hours on end ⑫ **in the** recording studio and grueling months on tour ⑬ **isn't as** easy as it used to be. Recording and touring, however is somethin' we can apply our past experience to. With the ⑭ **internet**, smartphones and portable music devices … the marketing and music sales aspect is a ⑮ **totally** different animal though.

F: Word is that your first four concert venues were sold out in a ⑯ **matter** of minutes. Sounds like your fan base is ⑰ **certainly** glad you're back.

M: That was a pleasant surprise. We are thrilled at the prospect of performing live after all these years, and providing our fans around the world with a new experience. We are also hoping the new cuts we've recorded will resonate with the younger generation of music fans out there as well.

Stage 4 ◀)) 音声変化をチェック

まとめとして、穴埋め部分の音声変化の特徴を**スロー・スピード**と**ナチュラル・スピード**で確認しよう。下記に示したカタカナ表記で音声変化を確認して、もう一度インタビューを聴き直してみよう。発音変化のルールは適宜復習しよう。

❶ **70's**　　　　　　　　　　セヴンティーズ　　　　　▶ セヴンディ [リ] ーズ
　☞ 破裂音 [t] の弾音化が起こる。

❷ **what motivated you**　　　ワット・モウティヴェイティッド・ユウ
　　　　　　　　　　　　　　　　　　　　　　　　　　　▶ ワッ_モウディ [リ] ヴェイディ [リ] ッジュウ
　☞ what の破裂音 [t] が脱落。motivated の2カ所の [t] 音が弾音化。motivated you の連結部では、[d] + [j] の音が混じり合い、[ジュ] に近い音に変化する。

❸ **get back**　　　　　　　　ゲット・バック　　　　　▶ ゲッ_バッ（ク）
　☞ get の破裂音 [t] が脱落する。back 末尾の [k] 音も脱落することがある。

❹ **But it's**　　　　　　　　バット・イッツ　　　　　▶ バッディ [リ] ッツ
　☞ 連結部で [t] 音が弾音化する。

❺ **about a**　　　　　　　　アバウト・ア　　　　　　▶ アバウダ [ラ]
　☞ 連結部で [t] 音が弾音化する。

❻ **get older**　　　　　　　ゲット・オウダー　　　　▶ ゲッド [ロ] ウゥダー
　☞ 連結部で [t] 音が弾音化する。

❼ **split up**　　　　　　　　スプリット・アップ　　　▶ スプリッダ [ラ] ップ
　☞ 連結部で [t] 音が弾音化する。

❽ **went away**　　　　　　　ウェント・アウェイ　　　▶ ウェナウェイ
　☞ went の破裂音 [t] が脱落しながら2語が連結。

❾ **Recently**　　　　　　　　リースントゥリー　　　　▶ リースン_リー
　☞ [tl] で [t] 音の脱落が生じる。

❿ **and that**　　　　　　　　アンド・ザット　　　　　▶ アナッ（ト）
　☞ and の [d] 音が脱落。[n] + [ð] が [n] 音に変化する。末尾の [t] 音も脱落しやすい。

⓫ **What are**　　　　　　　　ワット・アー　　　　　　▶ ワッダ [ラ] ー
　☞ 連結部で [t] 音が弾音化する。

⓬ **in the**　　　　　　　　　イン・ザ　　　　　　　　▶ イナ
　☞ [n] + [ð] が [n] 音に変化する。

⓭ **isn't as**　　　　　　　　イズント・アズ　　　　　▶ イズンダ [ラ] ズ；イズナズ
　☞ 連結部で [t] 音が弾音化する。[t] 音が脱落しながら連結する場合もある。

⓮ **internet**　　　　　　　　インターネット　　　　　▶ イナーネット
　☞ [nt] で [t] 音の脱落が生じる。

⓯ **totally**　　　　　　　　　トウタリー　　　　　　　▶ トウダ [ラ] リー
　☞ [t] 音が弾音化する。

⓰ **matter**　　　　　　　　　マター　　　　　　　　　▶ マダ [ラ] ー
　☞ [t] 音が弾音化する。

⓱ **certainly**　　　　　　　スートゥンリー　　　　　▶ スーんンリー
　☞ [tn] の部分が声門閉鎖音化する。

INTERVIEW WITH A STUNTMAN

Unit 36　スタントマンのインタビュー

Stage 1　穴埋め インタビュー・リスニング

音声変化に注意してCDでインタビューを聴きながら空欄部分を埋めてみよう。CDのナチュラル音声での聴き取りが難しいときは、次のトラックに収録されたスロー音声で聴いてみよう。

F: The faces and names of Hollywood actors and actresses are known around the world. With us in our studio tonight, however, is ① _____ _____ _____ "unknown" heroes that helps make those actors larger than life ... ② _____ stuntman John Keller. What's a day in the life of a stuntman John?

M: Basically we have several different jobs. We work closely with the special effects people to design action scenes ③ _____ _____ exciting but safe ④ _____ _____ same time. Some actors like to do most of their own stunts, in which case stand-ins will do a sequence a few times until the director likes ⑤ _____ _____ sees and then the stars will do it for the final cut. Other times, we stand-in for the actors for the entire scene. It's ⑥ _____ _____ them you see falling from that tall building or driving that burning car!

F: Have you ever been injured?

M: Of course. I've been ⑦ _____ movie stunts for more than fifteen years, and in that time I have broken ⑧ _____ bones and been ⑨ _____ dozens of times. Modern technology like blue-screens and ⑩ _____ graphics have done a ⑪ _____ _____ make it safer, but there is still no real substitute for an accomplished stunt performer. All action sequences are

220

meticulously planned and rehearsed with an emphasis on safety though.

F: Do you ever get jealous that you ⑫ _____ _____ _____ ⑬ _____ the stars do?

M: Nah. ⑭ _____ _____ part of the job. I love my job ⑮ _____ _____ _____ do. When a movie wraps or is shown on the big screen I am just as proud as the actors are of the final product. A movie is the result of effort by thousands of individuals, from sound guys to painters.

F: Who was one of your favorite stars to work with?

M: Clint Eastwood, by far. ⑯ _____ _____ did he have a director's intuition and a ton of experience, he was just a ⑰ _____ _____ to boot!

Stage 2 インタビュー解説

日本語訳と、解説を参照しながら、インタビュー内容を確認しよう。そのあとで、Stage1の穴埋めに再チャレンジしてみよう。

F: The faces and names of Hollywood actors and actresses are known around the world. With us in our studio tonight, however, is ① **one of the** "unknown" heroes that helps make those actors larger than life … ② **veteran** stuntman John Keller. What's a day in the life of a stuntman John?

ハリウッドの男優や女優の顔や名前は世界中に知れ渡っています。しかし、今夜スタジオでごいっしょさせてもらっているのは、その俳優たちを実際よりも大きく見せることに一役買っている「名もなき」ヒーローのおひとり、ベテラン・スタントマンのジョン・ケラーです。ジョン、スタントマンの一日とはどんなものでしょう？

* unknown「知られていない；無名の」 life「実物；実際」 veteran「経験豊富な；エキスパートの」

M: Basically we have several different jobs. We work closely with the special effects people to design action scenes ③ **that are** exciting but safe ④ **at the** same time. Some actors like to do most of their own stunts, in which case stand-ins will do a sequence a few times until the director likes ⑤ **what he** sees and then the stars will do it for the final cut. Other times, we stand-in for the actors for the entire scene. It's ⑥ **not always** them you see falling from that tall building or driving that burning car!

基本的に僕らはいくつかの異なる仕事をこなしているんだ。僕らは、エキサイティングだけど同時に安全なアクション・シーンを考案するために、特撮チームの人たちと密接に関わって仕事をするんだよ。俳優にはほとんどのスタントをやりたがる人もいるけど、その場合、代役は、監督が見たものを気に入るまで1シーンを何度かやるんだよ。それから、最終カット用にスターたちがそれをやるんだ。ほかの場合は、僕らが俳優の代わりを全シーンでやる。みんなが見ている、あの高いビルから飛び降りているのや、あの燃えさかる車を運転しているのは、いつも俳優であるとは限らないんだよ。

* special effects「特撮」 stand-in「代役」 sequence「一連の場面」 final cut「最終カット」

F: Have you ever been injured?

これまでにケガをしたことはありますか？

M: Of course. I've been ⑦ **doing** movie stunts for more than fifteen years, and in that time I have broken ⑧ **27** bones and been ⑨ **hospitalized** dozens of times. Modern technology like blue-screens and ⑩ **computer** graphics have done a ⑪ **lot to** make it safer, but there is still no real substitute for an accomplished stunt performer. All action sequences are meticulously planned and rehearsed with an emphasis on safety though.

もちろん。もう15年以上も映画のスタントをやっていて、その間に27本の骨を折ったし、何十回も入院したよ。ブルー・スクリーンやCGなどの最新のテクノロジーは安全に大いに

> 役立ってきたけど、熟練したスタントマンのほんとうの代わりになるものはまだないんだよ。すべてのアクション・シーンは、細心の注意を払って計画され、リハーサルされているんだ。ただし、安全性を重視してね。
>
> * substitute「代用」 accomplished「熟達した」 meticulously「非常に注意深く；細心の注意で」

F: Do you ever get jealous that you ⑫ **don't get the** ⑬ **notoriety** the stars do?

> スターのように名を馳せることがない点でジェラシーを感じたことは？
>
> * notoriety「名を馳せること」

M: Nah. ⑭ **That's just** part of the job. I love my job ⑮ **and what I** do. When a movie wraps or is shown on the big screen I am just as proud as the actors are of the final product. A movie is the result of effort by thousands of individuals, from sound guys to painters.

> いいや、ないよ。それも仕事の一部だしね。僕は自分の仕事とやっていることが大好きなんだ。映画が仕上がったときや大スクリーンに映し出されたときには、俳優たちと同じように映画に誇りを感じるんだ。映画っていうのは、音響スタッフから絵描きまで、何千人もの個人の努力の結果なんだよ。
>
> * wrap「（撮影が）終わる」 final product「完成品」ここでは封切りになった映画を指す。

F: Who was one of your favorite stars to work with?

> いっしょに仕事をしていて気に入ったスターはだれでした？

M: Clint Eastwood, by far. ⑯ **Not only** did he have a director's intuition and a ton of experience, he was just a ⑰ **great guy** to boot!

> 断然、クリント・イーストウッドだね。ディレクターの洞察力や数え切れない経験をもっているだけじゃなくて、おまけにホントにいい人だったんだよ！
>
> * intuition「洞察力」 to boot「おまけに」

Stage 3 英文トランスクリプション

インタビュー全体を英文の原稿で確認しながらCDで耳慣らししよう！　その上で、インタビューを聴きながら、まだできていない部分の穴埋めに再チャレンジしよう。

F: The faces and names of Hollywood actors and actresses are known around the world. With us in our studio tonight, however, is ① **one of the** "unknown" heroes that helps make those actors larger than life … ② **veteran** stuntman John Keller. What's a day in the life of a stuntman John?

M: Basically we have several different jobs. We work closely with the special effects people to design action scenes ③ **that are** exciting but safe ④ **at the** same time. Some actors like to do most of their own stunts, in which case stand-ins will do a sequence a few times until the director likes ⑤ **what he** sees and then the stars will do it for the final cut. Other times, we stand-in for the actors for the entire scene. It's ⑥ **not always** them you see falling from that tall building or driving that burning car!

F: Have you ever been injured?

M: Of course. I've been ⑦ **doing** movie stunts for more than fifteen years, and in that time I have broken ⑧ **27** bones and been ⑨ **hospitalized** dozens of times. Modern technology like blue-screens and ⑩ **computer** graphics have done a ⑪ **lot to** make it safer, but there is still no real substitute for an accomplished stunt performer. All action sequences are meticulously planned and rehearsed with an emphasis on safety though.

F: Do you ever get jealous that you ⑫ **don't get the** ⑬ **notoriety** the stars do?

M: Nah. ⑭ **That's just** part of the job. I love my job ⑮ **and what I** do. When a movie wraps or is shown on the big screen I am just as proud as the actors are of the final product. A movie is the result of effort by thousands of individuals, from sound guys to painters.

F: Who was one of your favorite stars to work with?

M: Clint Eastwood, by far. ⑯ **Not only** did he have a director's intuition and a ton of experience, he was just a ⑰ **great guy** to boot!

Stage 4 ◆)) 音声変化をチェック

まとめとして、穴埋め部分の音声変化の特徴を**スロー・スピード**と**ナチュラル・スピード**で確認しよう。下記に示したカタカナ表記で音声変化を確認して、もう一度インタビューを聴き直してみよう。発音変化のルールは適宜復習しよう。

---

❶ one of the　　　　　　　　　　ワン・アヴ・ズィ　　　　▶ ワナ（ヴ）ズィ
☞ one of の音が連結する。of の [v] 音が脱落することもある。

❷ veteran　　　　　　　　　　　　ヴェテラン　　　　　　　▶ ヴェデ [レ] ラン
☞ 破裂音 [t] が弾音化する。

❸ that are　　　　　　　　　　　　ザット・アー　　　　　　▶ ザッダ [ラ] ー
☞ 連結部で [t] 音が弾音化する。

❹ at the　　　　　　　　　　　　　アット・ザ　　　　　　　▶ アッ_ザ
☞ 破裂音 [t] 音が脱落する。

❺ what he　　　　　　　　　　　　ワット・ヒー　　　　　　▶ ワッディ [リ] ー
☞ what が弱化した he [イー] に連結。連結部で破裂音 [t] が弾音化する。

❻ not always　　　　　　　　　　　ノット・オーウェイズ　　▶ ノッド [ロ] ーウェイズ
☞ 連結部で [t] 音が弾音化する。

❼ doing　　　　　　　　　　　　　ドゥーイング　　　　　　▶ ドゥーイン_
☞ 末尾の破裂音 [g] の脱落が生じる。

❽ 27　　　　　　　　　　　　　　トゥエンティーセヴン　　▶ トゥエニーセヴン
☞ [nt] で破裂音 [t] の脱落が起こる。

❾ hospitalized　　　　　　　　　　ハスピタライズド　　　　▶ ハスピダ [ラ] ライズド
☞ 破裂音 [t] が弾音化する。

❿ computer　　　　　　　　　　　カムピューター　　　　　▶ カムピューダ [ラ] ー
☞ 破裂音 [t] が弾音化する。

⓫ lot to　　　　　　　　　　　　　ラット・トゥー　　　　　▶ ラッ_トゥー
☞ 破裂音 [t] の脱落が起こる。

⓬ don't get the　　　　　　　　　　ドウント・ゲット・ザ　　▶ ドン_ゲッ_ザ
☞ don't は弱化する。don't と get 末尾の破裂音 [t] が脱落する。

⓭ notoriety　　　　　　　　　　　ノウタライアティー　　　▶ ノウダ [ラ] ライアディ [リ] ー
☞ 1カ所あるいは2カ所の破裂音 [t] が弾音化する。

⓮ That's just　　　　　　　　　　　ザッツ・ジャスト　　　　▶ ザッスジャス_
☞ 両方の単語から破裂音 [t] が脱落する。

⓯ and what I　　　　　　　　　　　アンド・ワット・アイ　　▶ アン_ワッダ [ラ] イ
☞ and 末尾の破裂音 [d] が脱落。what I の連結部で破裂音 [t] が弾音化する。

⓰ Not only　　　　　　　　　　　　ノット・オウンリー　　　▶ ノッド [ロ] ウンリー
☞ 連結部で破裂音 [t] が弾音化する。

⓱ great guy　　　　　　　　　　　グレイト・ガイ　　　　　▶ グレイッ_ガイ
☞ great 末尾で破裂音 [t] の脱落が起こる。

INTERVIEW WITH AN AWARD-WINNING PHOTOGRAPHER

Unit 37　受賞写真家のインタビュー

Stage 1　穴埋め インタビュー・リスニング

音声変化に注意してCDでインタビューを聴きながら空欄部分を埋めてみよう。CDのナチュラル音声での聴き取りが難しいときは、次のトラックに収録されたスロー音声で聴いてみよう。

F: By now most of our viewers are all familiar with the ① _____ of Jim Gallagher, particularly those that have recently graced the cover of the likes of Time Magazine and Newsweek. I had a chance to speak with him at his studio in New York last week. Here's what he had to say.
Jim … you were ② _____ awarded the Pulitzer Prize for your photo coverage during the revolution in Egypt. ③ _____ _____ _____ like being there?

M: Ya know Jill, the key to ④ _____ a good shot with a camera is all about being ⑤ _____ _____ right place and the right time. I've ⑥ _____ tell you, it was ⑦ _____ hairy over there for a while. We really didn't know what was going to happen. There was so much tension in the streets, and government soldiers were really being aggressive towards journalists, both foreign and domestic. I was about to call ⑧ _____ _____ day, when I happened to see that young girl standing there clutching that loaf of bread. I took the shot and ⑨ _____ _____ _____. The next thing I knew it was on the cover of Time.

F: How did you get started as a photographer?

M: I'm a bit embarrassed to say that I dropped ⑩ _____ _____ high school at 17. I had always loved photography and had a

226

touch of wanderlust as well. I cut my teeth selling photos to local newspapers, but things really took off for me ⑪ _____ _____ _____ _____ gig with National Geographic. I ⑫ _____ all over the world taking nature photos in some of the most ⑬ _____ locations there are. Back then ⑭ _____ _____ all about preparation. Sometimes we'd spend days ⑮ _____ _____ get the right lighting, or for a particular animal to show up. I wouldn't trade that experience for anything, though.

F: ⑯ _____ _____ your next assignment?

M: I'm off next week for Antarctica, to do a feature on iceberg calving, and how global warming is affecting the environment and wildlife ⑰ _____ _____.

Stage 2 インタビュー解説

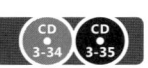

日本語訳と、解説を参照しながら、インタビュー内容を確認しよう。そのあとで、Stage1の穴埋めに再チャレンジしてみよう。

F: By now most of our viewers are all familiar with the ① **photos** of Jim Gallagher, particularly those that have recently graced the cover of the likes of Time Magazine and Newsweek. I had a chance to speak with him at his studio in New York last week. Here's what he had to say.
Jim … you were ② **recently** awarded the Pulitzer Prize for your photo coverage during the revolution in Egypt. ③ **What was it** like being there?

もう、ほとんどの視聴者のみなさんは、ジム・ギャラガーの写真をよくご存じでしょう。特に最近タイム・マガジンやニューズウィークといった雑誌のカバーを優美に飾った写真は見覚えがあるでしょう。私は、先週ニューヨークの彼のスタジオで、彼と話をする機会を得ま

> した。彼の話をお聞きください。
> ジム、あなたは最近、エジプト革命の間の写真報道でピューリッツァー賞を受賞しましたね。エジプトの現場にいたのは、どんなものだったのでしょう？
>
> * grace「優美に飾る」　the likes of ...「…といったもの・人」　photo coverage「写真報道」
>   revolution「革命」

M: Ya know Jill, the key to ④ **getting** a good shot with a camera is all about being ⑤ **at the** right place and the right time. I've ⑥ **gotta** tell you, it was ⑦ **pretty** hairy over there for a while. We really didn't know what was going to happen. There was so much tension in the streets, and government soldiers were really being aggressive towards journalists, both foreign and domestic. I was about to call ⑧ **it a** day, when I happened to see that young girl standing there clutching that loaf of bread. I took the shot and ⑨ **sent it in**. The next thing I knew it was on the cover of Time.

> あのですね、ジル、カメラでいい写真を撮るカギは適切な場所に適切な時間にいることに尽きるのです。実際、しばらくの間、エジプトはかなり危険な状態でした。なにがどうなるのかも、実はよくわからなかったんですよ。街中はかなり緊迫していて、政府の兵士たちは、国の内外を問わず、ジャーナリストに対してひどく攻撃的でした。その日の撮影を終えようとしていたときでした。そのとき、小さな女の子がパンを1斤抱きしめてそこに立っているのがたまたま目に入ったんです。その写真を撮影して、送ったんです。で、気づくと、それがタイム誌のカバーに載っていたんです。
>
> * be all about ...「…に尽きる；…がすべてだ」　hairy「危険な」　tension「緊張」
>   aggressive「攻撃的な」　both foreign and domestic「外国人も自国の人もどちらも」
>   clutch「(胸などに) 抱きしめる」　loaf of bread「パン1斤」
>   send in「(当局などに) 送る；提出する」　The next thing I knew, ...「気づいてみると…だった」

F: How did you get started as a photographer?

> あなたはどうやって写真家の仕事を始めたんですか？
>
> * get started as ...「…としてスタートを切る」

M: I'm a bit embarrassed to say that I dropped ⑩ **out of** high school at

17. I had always loved photography and had a touch of wanderlust as well. I cut my teeth selling photos to local newspapers, but things really took off for me ⑪ **when I got a** gig with National Geographic. I ⑫ **traveled** all over the world taking nature photos in some of the most ⑬ **exotic** locations there are. Back then ⑭ **it was** all about preparation. Sometimes we'd spend days ⑮ **waiting to** get the right lighting, or for a particular animal to show up. I wouldn't trade that experience for anything, though.

> ちょっと恥ずかしいのですが、17歳で高校を中退したんです。写真はずっと大好きで、ちょっと放浪癖もありました。最初は地元の新聞に写真を売ることで経験を積みましたが、いろいろとうまくいき始めたのは、ナショナル・ジオグラフィック社の仕事をもらったときでした。私は、世界中を旅して回りました。世の中でも、もっともめずらしいロケ地のいくつかで自然の写真を撮りながら。その頃は、準備がすべてでした。ときには、ぴったりな明かりや特定の動物が姿を現すのを待って何日も費やしたりしました。でも、その経験は何物にも代えがたい貴重なものでした。
>
> ＊ drop out of ...「…を中退する」 wanderlust「放浪癖」
>   cut one's teeth「始める；初期の経験を積む」 take off「うまく進みだす」 gig「仕事」

F: ⑯ **What is** your next assignment?

> あなたの次の仕事はなんでしょう？

M: I'm off next week for Antarctica, to do a feature on iceberg calving, and how global warming is affecting the environment and wildlife ⑰ **down there**.

> 私は、来週、南極大陸に旅立ちます。氷山分離の特集の仕事のためです。そして、地球温暖化がどのように環境やそこに暮らす野生生物に影響を与えているかの特集でもあります。
>
> ＊ Antarctica「南極大陸」

Stage 3 英文トランスクリプション

インタビュー全体を英文の原稿で確認しながらCDで耳慣らししよう！ その上で、インタビューを聴きながら、まだできていない部分の穴埋めに再チャレンジしよう。

F: By now most of our viewers are all familiar with the ① **photos** of Jim Gallagher, particularly those that have recently graced the cover of the likes of Time Magazine and Newsweek. I had a chance to speak with him at his studio in New York last week. Here's what he had to say. Jim ... you were ② **recently** awarded the Pulitzer Prize for your photo coverage during the revolution in Egypt. ③ **What was it** like being there?

M: Ya know Jill, the key to ④ **getting** a good shot with a camera is all about being ⑤ **at the** right place and the right time. I've ⑥ **gotta** tell you, it was ⑦ **pretty** hairy over there for a while. We really didn't know what was going to happen. There was so much tension in the streets, and government soldiers were really being aggressive towards journalists, both foreign and domestic. I was about to call ⑧ **it a** day, when I happened to see that young girl standing there clutching that loaf of bread. I took the shot and ⑨ **sent it in**. The next thing I knew it was on the cover of Time.

F: How did you get started as a photographer?

M: I'm a bit embarrassed to say that I dropped ⑩ **out of** high school at 17. I had always loved photography and had a touch of wanderlust as well. I cut my teeth selling photos to local newspapers, but things really took off for me ⑪ **when I got a** gig with National Geographic. I ⑫ **traveled** all over the world taking nature photos in some of the most ⑬ **exotic** locations there are. Back then ⑭ **it was** all about preparation. Sometimes we'd spend days ⑮ **waiting to** get the right lighting, or for a particular animal to show up. I wouldn't trade that experience for anything, though.

F: ⑯ **What is** your next assignment?

M: I'm off next week for Antarctica, to do a feature on iceberg calving, and how global warming is affecting the environment and wildlife ⑰ **down there**.

🎧 Stage 4 🔊 音声変化をチェック

まとめとして、穴埋め部分の音声変化の特徴を**スロー・スピード**と**ナチュラル・スピード**で確認しよう。下記に示したカタカナ表記で音声変化を確認して、もう一度インタビューを聴き直してみよう。発音変化のルールは適宜復習しよう。

❶ **photos** フォウトウズ ▶ フォウド［ロ］ウズ
☞ 破裂音［t］の弾音化が起こる。

❷ **recently** リースントゥリー ▶ リースン＿リー
☞［tl］で［t］音の脱落が生じる。

❸ **What was it** ワット・ワズ・イット ▶ ワッ＿ワズィッ（ト）
☞ What の破裂音［t］が脱落する。was it は連結。it 末尾の［t］音も脱落しやすい。

❹ **getting** ゲッティング ▶ ゲッディ［リ］ン（グ）
☞ 破裂音［t］の弾音化が起こる。末尾の［g］音も脱落しやすい。

❺ **at the** アット・ザ ▶ アッ＿ザ
☞ 破裂音［t］が脱落する。

❻ **gotta** ガッタ ▶ ガッダ［ラ］
☞ 破裂音［t］の弾音化が起こる。

❼ **pretty** プリティー ▶ プリディ［リ］ー
☞ 破裂音［t］の弾音化が起こる。

❽ **it a** イット・ア ▶ イッダ［ラ］
☞ 連結部で破裂音［t］の弾音化が起こる。

❾ **sent it in** セント・イット・イン ▶ センティッティン
☞ 3語が連結。連結部で［t］音が弾音化する場合もある。

❿ **out of** アウト・アヴ ▶ アウダ［ラ］ヴ
☞ 連結部で破裂音［t］の弾音化が起こる。

⓫ **when I got a** ウェン・アイ・ガット・ア ▶ ウェナイガッダ［ラ］
☞ when I は連結。got a は連結部で破裂音［t］の弾音化が起こる。

⓬ **traveled** トゥラヴゥド ▶ チュラヴゥ（ド）
☞［tr］部分の［t］音が［チュ］に近い音に変化する。末尾の［d］音が脱落することもある。

⓭ **exotic** イグゾーティック ▶ イグゾーディ［リ］ック
☞ 破裂音［t］の弾音化が起こる。

⓮ **it was** イット・ワズ ▶ イッ＿ワズ
☞ 破裂音［t］が脱落する。

⓯ **waiting to** ウェイティング・トゥー ▶ ウェイディ［リ］ン（グ）トゥー
☞ waiting では、破裂音［t］の弾音化が起こる。末尾の［g］音が脱落することもある。

⓰ **What is** ワット・イズ ▶ ワッディ［リ］ズ
☞ 連結部で破裂音［t］の弾音化が起こる。

⓱ **down there** ダウン・ゼア ▶ ダウネア
☞［n］+［ð］が［n］音に変化する。

受賞写真家のインタビュー

■ 著者略歴

長尾 和夫（Kazuo Nagao）
福岡県出身。南雲堂出版、アスク講談社、NOVA などで、大学英語教科書や語学系書籍・CD-ROM・Web サイトなどの編集・制作・執筆に携わる。現在、語学書籍の出版プロデュース・執筆・編集・翻訳などを行うアルファ・プラス・カフェ（www.alphapluscafe.com）を主宰。『絶対「英語の耳」になる！』シリーズ全14点（三修社）、『日常生活を英語でドンドン説明してみよう』（アスク出版）、『英会話 見たまま練習帳』（DHC）、『ビジネス英会話 高速変換トレーニング』（アルク）、『英語で自分をアピールできますか？』『英語でケンカができますか？』（角川グループパブリッシング）、『書き込み式・英語で自分を説明できる本』（日本経済新聞出版社）、『ネイティブ英語がこう聞こえたら、この英語だ！』（主婦の友社）ほか、著訳書・編書は250点を超える。『English Journal』（アルク）、『CNN English Express』（朝日出版社）など、雑誌媒体への寄稿も行っている。

トーマス・マーティン（Thomas Martin）
米国在住、米国オハイオ州出身。南山大学卒業。日本語・日本史専攻。株式会社 NOVA での豊富な英語指導経験を活かし、同社出版局に移籍。雑誌『NOVA Station（ノヴァ・ステーション）』、語学書籍シリーズ『NOVA Books』をはじめ、数多くの英語・異文化交流関連出版物の編集・執筆・翻訳等に携わる。98年に独立後も、語学書籍の執筆・編集や知的財産関連の翻訳、ビリヤード専門誌『CUE'S』の連載などを手がけマルチに活躍中。著書に『目で見て英語でパッと質問できる瞬間 Q&A ドリル』『つぶやき英語 ビジネス編』（アスク出版）、『絶対「英語の耳」になる！ ビジネス英語 難関トレーニング50』（三修社）、『説明するためのビジネス英語表現練習帳』（DHC）、『イラスト会話ブック・アメリカ』（JTB パブリッシング）、『新方式対応 TOEIC テスト厳選トータル問題集』（すばる舎）などがある。

絶対『英語の耳』になる！
37のインタビューで鍛える！
ネイティヴ英語リスニング

2015年2月10日 第1刷発行

著 者	長尾和夫　トーマス・マーティン
発行者	前田俊秀
発行所	株式会社三修社
	〒150-0001　東京都渋谷区神宮前 2-2-22
	TEL 03-3405-4511　FAX 03-3405-4522
	振替 00190-9-72758
	http://www.sanshusha.co.jp/
	編集担当　北村英治
印刷・製本	壮光舎印刷株式会社

©2015 A+Café　Printed in Japan
ISBN978-4-384-04633-5 C2082

®〈日本複製権センター委託出版物〉
本書を無断で複写複製（コピー）することは、著作権法上の例外を除き、禁じられています。
本書をコピーされる場合は、事前に日本複製権センター（JRRC）の許諾を受けてください。
JRRC 〈http://www.jrrc.or.jp　e-mail：info@jrrc.or.jp　電話：03-3401-2382〉